Margareta Yost

Family Circle

Family Circle

CORNELIA OTIS SKINNER

ILLUSTRATED WITH PHOTOGRAPHS

HOUGHTON MIFFLIN COMPANY BOSTON
The Riverside Press Cambridge
1948

Part of this book has appeared in the *Ladies' Home Journal.*

The Riverside Press
CAMBRIDGE · MASSACHUSETTS
PRINTED IN THE U.S.A.

To A. S. B.

Contents

Illustrations

CHAPTER ONE

Maud

THE TRACKS of the Northern Missouri sprawl across the sunbaked surface of that midmost of midwestern states, reaching out like vine tendrils in one direction for the more undulant borders of Iowa and, in the other, venturing onto the parched prairies of Kansas. Some fifty miles north of Jefferson City, the roadbed branches apart at a junction in the heart of Daniel Boone's old territory and just west of the country of Mark Twain's boyhood. And at this junction, there has grown up a town named Moberly. During the seventies and eighties it was little more than an overgrown railroad settlement whose chief activities centered about roundhouses and clanging repair shops. The leading citizens and many who were not leading were railroad employees. Life was regulated by whistles and people set their watches by the thundering passage of the St. Louis express or the Chicago fast freight.

In 1876, a very young couple stood inspecting with pride and not a little awe the excavation and rough superstructure of a frame house which was being erected on one of the town's choice sites. It was choice because it bordered on the tracks, an elegant advantage. The back yard was walled at one end by the cinder bank of the roadbed and a path led directly into the side door of the station. All this was to be of considerable convenience for the young man, who was station master and chief train dispatcher for Moberly and the vicinity. His were also the duties of division superintendent of the telegraph, and all communications for the town were received or sent by him over one noisily busy instrument in the ticket office.

The day the young couple went to inspect the excavations was a Sunday. They looked very proud and formal as they walked along the wooden sidewalk. Trotting beside them was two-year-old Maud, in her best plaid frock trimmed with rows of white rickrack, her legs in red wool stockings bulging out over the patent-leather tops of high button shoes recently arrived from a mail-order house in Kansas City. She was pleased with her finery and passers-by paused to look at her, for, even as a tiny creature, she had the quality of loveliness. Her bright eyes were flecked with so many pigments, one had to be at a fair distance to realize they were lightish brown. Her skin was clear and fair, the sort in which color came and went easily. She was sensitive to a palpitating degree and her throat throbbed visibly in response to her quick emotions. Her hair was chestnut-colored. At this period, the back portion had been pulled painfully off her small shell-like ears in two stiff pigtails, while the front had been home-clipped in a fashionable "fringe" across a brow which was in time to become something Bellini might have painted.

While her parents were inspecting the construction work, Maudie, always self-sufficient, puttered about, busying herself with stray objects of entertainment in the way of shining nails and sweet-smelling wood shavings. The parents, busy with building problems, left her to her own devices. Suddenly something drew the mother's glance in a particular direction, and with an inarticulate gasp of terror she grabbed her husband's arm.

"Look!" she managed to say, and pointed. The tiny child, in some spirit of high adventure, had crawled out onto a narrow wooden girder which spanned the gaping hole of the newly dug cellar. Already halfway across, she was balancing dizzily above a drop of some fifteen feet, at the bottom of which lay piles of brick, rough débris, and jagged building tools. William tossed aside his cane and, in spite of the fact that he had a wooden leg, managed in a flash to make his way out onto the beam, grabbed the small girl at the moment in which she seemed about to topple over, carried her back, and setting her down on firm ground gave her a scolding which, whetted by fright, was extremely severe. Maud received her reproof solemnly and without protest. She was not yet old enough for speech. She then waited until her parents had again focused their attention on some new detail of construction, then once more she crawled forth over the horrid drop. Again her mother cried out and again the father rushed to snatch her back, this time adding emphasis to his reprimand by a smart slap. Maud's wee face puckered up and a tear spilled from her deep-set eye, but still she made no sound. A third time she repeated her action, and it was with an air no longer of childish exploration but of outraged determination. Once more she was snatched back and this time her father spanked her. She cried, of course, but not profusely, waited for a bit, and then for the fourth time, like a small crusader, she attempted the forbidden journey. By now William Durbin's temper, which, like all his emotions, he took no pains to control, had passed its endurance. He grabbed up this small bit of protoplasm which had dared to defy his law and, turning it over his knee, administered the mother and father of a beating; a beating so vicious and protracted that his wife turned white and tore at his sleeve to stop him. Maud clenched what few little teeth she had and bore the flogging with desperate stoicism, managing in some way to stifle the shrieks of rage and pain which arose in her throat. The blows finally let up, and for a time she lay limp and inert, face down on the ground. Then, with great effort, she dragged herself onto her knees and racked with sobs, once more started for the girder. This was more than the mother could endure. She it was who now, in defiance of a husband whom she respected and feared, picked up the child and, without further word, started for home. This child was my mother.

On her mother's gentle shoulder, Maud's sobbing subsided. But all the way home she watched her father, with a curious, steady gaze. No one spoke. My grandfather walked behind, his cane slashing the heads off weeds, his eyes fixed broodingly on the ground, unable to meet the strange, penetrating stare of his daughter. It was as if the little girl had turned on her father a sudden clear light, showing him up to the family and, worst of all, to himself . . . which was not to be borne. He was a vain man. And perhaps, subconsciously, he never forgave her. For this was only the first of many clashes between my grandfather and my mother, clashes in which my mother always came out victorious.

And yet William Durbin was a lovable and, in many ways, an admirable person. He was kindly and intelligent. His manners were faultless and he had that indefinable quality known, for lack of a better word, as breeding. He had charm and he was expansively genial.

He was tall, handsome, and of a definite distinction, accentuated by the fact that he walked with a cane. Very few people, for a long time not even his children (of whom he eventually had eight), knew that William Durbin had a wooden leg. Instinctive poise made his slight limp appear to be so much a part of him that if it was noticed at all, it was dismissed as an aristocratic affectation. He was a native son, a Missourian as genuine as was to be found in that yet frontier state, his grandfather having been one of the early pioneers to set forth from Maryland and settle in the wilderness which lay between the Mississippi and the roiling brown Missouri. William Durbin was a smart young man, witty, charming, and clever. He had started earning a livelihood at a tender age and had given every indication of being destined for a brilliant future. When he was nineteen, he got a job with the railroad and was sent to Moberly where his popularity was instantaneous. In no time at all he was elected mayor. It is quite possible that his is the distinction of having been the youngest mayor in American history, for he went into office at the astonishing age of twenty-one.

With him to Moberly had come my grandmother, barely sixteen when he married her, not quite seventeen when my mother was born. She was a gentle person, shy, plump, and pretty, blessed with a quiet sense of humor and the great gift of wisdom. She came from the small town of Montgomery and her maiden name was Missouri Ann Pew. Born on the eve of the Civil War when regional feelings were running high, there was nothing out of the way in naming children after states. Missouri, however, sounded a little overwhelming for the endearing creature she proved to be, and she was known always as "Zou." Her attitude toward her husband was one of pride, love, and understanding, restrained by the quaint connubial formality of that mohair upholstered era which even in frontier America was colored by the shadow of the fat little widow who sat on the throne of England. She always called my grandfather Mr. Durbin, not Will, or even William, and certainly never anything so shameless as "dear." It was only in later years, when the birth of eight children had given her ample excuse for such audacity, that she made so bold as to call him "Dad."

The frame house beside the railroad tracks was finally completed and was regarded by the community as a triumph of taste. The front door, made distinguished by a panel of ground glass, led into a vestibule from which one emerged into a hallway tiled with black and white linoleum squares meant to be a dead ringer for marble. The parlor was so elegant it was used only for gala events—Christmas, New Year's, or funerals. Its walls were dazzling with white-and-gold embossed paper. The wooden trim had been finished with seven coats of enamel and admiring neighbors said it looked for all the world like ivory. A black walnut and horse-hair "suite" stood stiffly about on the cream and pink roses of a body Brussels. Hand-painted vases resting on carved deerhead wall brackets held winter bouquets of cat-tails and dried grasses, and on a marble-topped table in the bay window was a fascinating red glass arrangement "imported clear from Germany," part lamp, part bowl, in which goldfish (when they were to be had) swam serenely about in what appeared to be kerosene. The rest of the house was about like every other house in Moberly—in other words, plain and hideous.

The family moved in and began the business of filling the homestead at the rate of a new baby almost every twelve months. For the first few years, my grandmother did all the household work herself. Then after the arrival of the third child, a son, my grandfather decided that they had reached a position of sufficient importance, if not of affluence, for a servant or two. So the family dignity was enhanced by the presence of an elderly Negro couple who went by the comfortable names of Aunt Charity and Uncle Humphrey. Uncle Humphrey did the heavy chores and tended the chickens while Aunt Charity helped in the kitchen. She also served as the children's Mammy, mothering and sleeping with the newest born, scolding and keeping track of the older ones. Moberly was in the heart of a district of Missouri known as "Little Dixie" and the Durbins were Southern in their ways. In addition to the Mammy, there was also the characteristic Topsy . . . the sad-eyed, gangly colored child who hung about the back yard for the privilege of playing the goat in the white children's games, running errands for the lady of the house, and watching over a sweet-smelling pink baby napping in its go-cart.

If the frame house abutted the railroad tracks, it was definitely on the right side of that symbol of demarcation, and the Durbins belonged to Moberly's élite. Social life was simple and social functions reached their zenith in the activities of "The St. Louis, Kansas City and Northern Railway Employees' Club," known more tersely as "The Railroad Literary Club." This was a purposeful organization whose aim it was (I quote from a faded copy of its charter) "to improve morally, socially, and intellectually its members at regular meetings to be held, one each week, membership being open to all citizens of Moberly of suitable moral character." The meetings took place out in the shops in an office building directly back of the roundhouse. In a large room on the second floor, a small but adequate stage had been erected, and here "each member," again I quote the charter, "might discharge such literary and musical duties to which he might be assigned by the executive committee, furnish a substitute or pay a fine of no less than 25¢." The variety of entertainment was considerable. There were theatrical performances with scenery created by the local railway-coach painters, temperance lectures with instrumental accompaniment, evenings of dramatic recitation when members obliged with such selections as "Lochiel's Warning" or "Over the Hill to the Poor-House," and musical soirées made memorable by "Dash Along Galop" or "Gems from Grand Opera" as interpreted by the Railroad Mechanics' Band. In the annals of the society are accounts of "Longfellow Night," "Irish Night," and "Mrs. Jarley's Waxworks Night," also an extravaganza entitled "Statuary" presenting "Scenes from a Sculptor's Studio, with living tableaux of groups representing Hope, Grief, Devotion, and Rest to be enacted by the Misses Harriet Hosner, Nellie Brinkerhoff, Ollie Chamier, and Bessie Rubey." At one meeting was staged a "Young Ladies' Broom Brigade Drill," on which occasion a brigade of seventeen belles in military jackets and bustles and carrying "woman's weapon, the broom," executed a drill under the command of Captain Mix, G.A.R., at the finish of which the brooms were autographed, tied with ribbons and nosegays, and auctioned off to admiring swains, the proceeds to go to the yellow-fever sufferers of the South. The season always wound up with the Annual Conductors' Ball, when the pink lemonade flowed like water and an orchestra was imported all the way from St. Louis.

The means of transportation to and from these meetings furnished a considerable portion of their charm. At an appointed hour, members assembled at the station where they boarded a special Literary Society train, made up of coaches and cabooses. A little switch engine bustled them off to the shops, chugged patiently below the auditorium windows during the entertainment, and at the finish, returned the membership to the station. An enthusiastic citizen, one Doctor Clarkson, has expressed the flavor of these galas in the following eulogy:

> Club Night! Club Night! Oh, what sweet memories cluster about thy name! We gathered at the station. The eye had a new lustre, a new glow crimsoned on the cheek. The lip curled with a sweeter smile, the face shone with a diviner fire. As groups or single couples came filing in, glad senti-

ments of welcome went careering through the heart. The beaming light of love shone on every countenance and the joy of anticipation breathed itself in every form. When the sound of the coaches backing in was heard, there was a rush for the cars. There is hilarity in a crowd. Sayings that at other times would not produce a ripple on the surface now raise peals of joyous laughter and the very air is filled with bliss. For this short ride, the coaches, if lighted at all, were supplied with but few lamps that dimly shone o'er the fair women and brave men, and, if mistakes were made, who could tell? But we have reached the shops, the locomotive has ceased to move and there is a rush for the rooms to get the most eligible seats.

And yet for all such cultural amenities, Moberly had not outgrown its frontier character. The surrounding countryside was still a sea of grass as high as the stirrup of a man on horseback and the town itself was a jumble of crude stores and squatter shanties, with only a few private residences of modern birdcage elegance. Not far down the mud street from the Durbin house was "Whiskey Row," a ramshackle block made up of a saloon, a fly-infested butcher shop, another saloon, Miller's Grocery where the proprietor's big tortoise-shell cat dozed peacefully in the open cracker barrel, another saloon, a ragpicker's establishment with Negro workers who sang and shuffled as they baled the filthy tatters and who, after closing time, swept the floor clean and held a dance which they called "a rag," then again another saloon. And at either end of this line-up were the cautiously shuttered establishments of Moberly's demi-monde. Miss Fanny Dusenberry and Miss Mattie Larkin, deadly rivals, each conducted a discreet and thriving business in "fancy ladies." One seldom saw the daughters of joy except at County Fair time when one or two, elaborately dressed and carefully duennaed by their respectable madams, occupied grandstand seats and cast demure eyes at the flashier traveling men.

There were periods of strikes at the shops when lawlessness

ran riot and every wise person, including the sheriff, stayed behind locked doors. Saturday nights in the shanty district were rough and not infrequently a saloon brawl ended in a shooting.

There was also the local "bad man," a disciple of the James brothers (Frank James was still to be seen at Fair time, but had become a disappointingly reformed character). The Moberly desperado had a romantic appearance and a distinguished number of notches in his gun. Justice in the form of a vigilance committee finally caught up with him. The hanging took place in an open field some five miles out of town and the entire population turned out in wagon, buggy, or on foot to see the spectacle, while for the convenience of prominent citizens the ever-accommodating Wabash furnished the same little train of coaches and switch engine which bore the members of the Railroad Literary Club to festivities of a more refining nature.

There was a small theatre, called of course the "Opera House," where on rare occasions a touring company would stop for a one-night stand on the way to St. Louis. The only other sort of public entertainment was the Baptist and Methodist revivals to which people flocked chiefly for the simple pleasure of seeing who of their acquaintances would get religion and go over to the mourner's bench. One of my mother's earliest recollections was of a frightening occasion when, after her mother had taken her to a meeting, the preacher asked them to come forward as penitents. Grabbing her small child's hand, my grandmother rose and made a bolt for the nearest exit. As they scuttled out through the sawdust, the man's awful threat rang through the tent after them: "So you're taking the child to Hell along with you!"

Eight children were born to the Durbins. The only one never to reach maturity was a little girl named Lily who died at the age of two. She was the child born after William, Junior. Then had come Nell and then Dick. Two more came along later . . . Dot, whose real name was Zouella (a flight of inventive fancy of her mother's who had pieced it out of her own sobriquet and the name of her sister Ella). And lastly had come Dowell, whose late arrival amazed and charmed the entire family.

Maud from her earliest school days was a leader . . . although that word is misleading because it implies aggressiveness, and she never at any time had that unlovely quality. For she led, she conquered, and she ruled through charm. She simply and completely enchanted her companions so that they were only too pleased to submit to whatever she might suggest. Moreover, she could make up all manner of original and lovely games. The flair for acting was in her veins and she got up private theatricals: sketches she wrote herself based on historical incidents out of *McGuffey's Reader*, or dramatizations of "Marmion" and "Excelsior," which she and her playmates acted out—she doing the acting, the playmates gawkily but happily following along—before an audience of foreign children from the other side of the tracks and a sprinkling of enraptured pickaninnies. Performances took place in the Durbin barn. The hayloft was the undisputed Lodge House for the leading grammar-school set, and Maud was undisputed Grand Master.

Wonderful things happened in that hayloft. Tragic things, too. For here her brother Dick met with the accident which crippled him for life. During the course of a rough-and-tumble game, the village bully pushed him out of the high hay door, and he fell into the stable yard, fracturing his hip, an injury which turned into tuberculosis.

The most memorable occurrence in the annals of the hayloft was the affair of the circus. One Saturday morning the regular juvenile group had gathered in the upper reaches of the barn and were in the full swing of some game, when Maud suddenly held up her hand and called out a melodramatic "Hush!" Unusual sounds were coming from the railroad yards, and the children, hearing them, stopped their game and floundered through the hay to peer out of the open loft door. A wonder had come to pass. Not only had the circus come to Moberly, the show cars themselves had been shunted onto the siding within an easy stone's-throw of the goggle-eyed spectators. The sudden appearance of Noah's Ark could not have been more satisfying. Right there practically in the back yard were flatcars gaudy as festival barges, with gay cargoes of vans, cages, chariots, and calliopes, and, on one, the heroic canvas folds of the "big top." Hands and performers all in blue dungarees, bright handkerchiefs about their sweating necks, were busily unloading under the shouted commands of an overseer who wore a magenta shirt and a jeweled Stetson. Suddenly the breathless young audience crowded in the loft doorway caught the man's eye. He paused, looked them over, then deliberately strolled down from the embankment, opened the yard gate, and, advancing to within a few feet of the barn, looked up, grinned, and said "Howdy." The children, too overcome for speech, merely grinned back sheepishly; a few, in embarrassment, somersaulted backward into the hay. Maud, however, bestowed on the stranger the smile which had already won her enough adorers to insure her against ever having to carry home her own schoolbooks, and answered in a clear "Howdy."

"Any o' you folks know where I kin water my animals?" came the delicious inquiry.

The small girl didn't hesitate for a moment. She leaped to her feet, flung forth her arms in a gesture that might have done credit to Mary Anderson, and called out, "Bring them in here, my good man! The well's over there behind the chicken coop."

Then began a procession worth ten box seats for the actual show. Horses . . . slim nervous creatures of the high-schooling acts and stolid traditionals with rumps fattened out for the feet of bareback riders, work mules, trick donkeys, and a camel or two. Canvasmen hurried down with water buckets for the carnivora, and at the end of the line, with swaying heads and rhythmically flapping ears, loomed the elephants. The spectacle was short-lived. All at once, as if springing up from an avenging inferno, there appeared at the end of the path the irate figure of my grandfather, brandishing his cane and demanding in a voice of thunder what the dickens was going on and who in hell had given permission for these mountebanks to drain his well. The circus men stopped in their tracks, the overseer mumbled an incoherent explanation and shuffled away, even the animals seemed subdued as they trotted out through the gate. This time all of the children somersaulted backwards and cowered in the hay. All, that is, except Maud. Pale and shaking, she came down from the loft, faced her father, and admitted it was she who had invited in the menagerie. She was sorry. She had thought only of the thirsty animals. The father glared at her, motionless, unable to speak. His temper, always his master, seemed more uncontrollable when dealing with this baffling child. In a gesture of fury he raised his cane. Maud stood immovable, watching him with the eyes of a deer that has suddenly dared defiance. There was something of pity, too, in her expression. The father hesitated, then he lowered his cane and walked silently away.

As a child, Maud, too, had a temper. She was also the victim of quick attacks of jealousy, and the person of whom she was most jealous was her sister Laura. The fact that Laura was a beauty with blue eyes and golden hair was not the reason for her resentment. It was because Laura was her father's favorite child. He idolized and pampered her, taking no pains to conceal the fact that he loved her above all the others. On one occasion, after he had lavished some special attention on Laura, Maud in a burst of fury picked up a heavy china ornament and hurled it at her sister. The missile hit its mark, Laura crumpled to the floor, and blood streamed from an ugly gash on her pretty brow. Maud's anger turned to horror and remorse. She rushed to the parlor where her parents were receiving a caller, flung herself on her knees before her startled father, and shrieked, "Kill me, Dad! Kill me! I've just murdered Laura!"

Laura made an uneventful recovery, but the incident did not make for a better relationship between my mother and her father. Neither did that which took place the night of the St. Charles bridge wreck on the Wabash. William Durbin, as before mentioned, in addition to being chief train dispatcher, was also division superintendent of the telegraph. To be a town's "ham telegraphist" in those days was an exacting job which never let up even during hours of repose, for beside his bed at odd moments of the night an extension instrument ticked a nervous staccato. It was this instrument which one night had wakened William with the familiar dot-dash that alerted his station. Sleepily he fumbled for the matches, lit the lamp, and tapped back the receiving signal. The machine clicked out its message. Suddenly with a cry of horror he shouted, "My God, Zou! The St. Charles Bridge has just gone down with twenty-six cars of stock!" The sound awakened Maud. She had not heard his words, only the strange cry. Her instinctively dramatic reaction was to think that something dreadful had happened. Possibly Dad was at grips with a bandit, and the fact that Mama was silent could only mean that she was already lying in a welter of blood. Maud jumped out of bed, tore down to her parents' room, and —a thing she had never before done—flung open the door without knocking. What she saw made her stand frozen with blank amazement. The lamplight shone on the figure of her father, imposing even under the disadvantage of being encased in an old-fashioned nightshirt. He was standing half supporting himself against the telegraph table, and for some curious reason he was standing on one leg. For a moment she stared at him, then her eye traveled to the other side of the room, and with a little moan of fright and compassion she gasped, "Oh, Dad, why didn't anyone ever tell us?" Leaning against the wall was an artificial leg. For the first time she understood the limp, the cane he was never without, the periods when his handsome face would be drawn with unspoken pain. She wanted to rush over to her father, to sink down and lay her head against his knee, to protest the love that at times became so strained and tortured. But William Durbin's vanity had suffered a blow, and he checked her impulsive movement with a cold look. The small girl pulled her little flannel nightgown about her, turned on her bare feet into the dark hallway, and thoughtfully pattered back to her room.

In the long run, Maud's discovery was perhaps a good thing. For, once the father had become reconciled to his children's knowing about his handicap, the strained secrecy in regard to his lameness was cleared away. Moreover, it gave him the chance to add to his excellent repertory of exciting family stories the dramatic one of how the disaster had occurred . . . how, when he was a little boy of ten, while sliding down a haystack he had cut his foot on a jagged cornstalk, how some months later "white swelling" had developed and the country doctor had had to perform a hip-high amputation right there on the kitchen table, how he had come out of chloroform in the middle of the operation, but had never cried out, had never whimpered, had merely reached for his father's hand and said, through clenched teeth, "Are they through yet, Pop?" That was the great, heroic gesture of William Durbin's life. It was as if all his grit, his moral stamina, had been concentrated into that hour. As if, having proved to what heights his strength of character could soar, he found it unnecessary to make any further demands upon it. He loved his family, loved to be gay and companionable with them. But domestic responsibilities irked him, and serious problems he found it impossible to face. When the children came down with the inevitable contagions, distressed but helpless he would flee the house. The death of little Lily, the accident which permanently crippled small Dick, were tragedies he met with confusion, bitterness, and resentment.

William Durbin was an attractive man who liked flattery; there were plenty of people ready to flatter him . . . railroad employees, the gang at Murphy's Bar, and a few of those shadowy persons referred to with raised eyebrows as "other women." More and more often it would happen that the mother and children would sit down in uneasy silence to a dinner grown cold while waiting for Dad, who would come in after midnight with a cautious and unsteady tread.

His bosses in the railroad warned him, gave him a few last chances, then came to the end of their indulgence and he lost his job. For a time he searched fruitlessly for a new one, masking the wound to his pride with false gaiety fortified by innumerable ponies of bourbon. Then one day he disappeared, leaving a note with the vague explanation that he was "going somewhere to look for something." After a month he came back, having found nothing. Someone in Moberly gave him a position of sorts and for a time he kept to a path at first straight and narrow, then broader and broader and with frequent agreeable sidetracks. Again he found himself unemployed, and by now considerably in debt.

There followed hard, uneasy times. Times full of mystery and suspense when the unhappy father would be gone for weeks, even months, no one knew where. The little brood at home were merely told that Dad was away. The mother went about her daily chores, gallantly keeping up appearances, patching and eking out ends that refused to meet. Not one of the children suspected what was happening. Not one, that is, except my mother. After all, she was only seventeen years younger than her mother and their relationship had long since become one of confidence like that of an older and younger sister. Together they shared the same terror, the same humiliation, the same bitter uncertainties during the ghastly periods when the father would vanish without a word, leaving the family without funds or protection to face the tradesmen and the whispered comments of the neighbors. Mother and daughter shared also the dark terrors of such times as when the father, back home and sick of his own weaknesses, sought to escape his furies by drinking himself into blind rages or sodden insensibility.

And yet the Durbin household was not one of gloom and unhappiness. Voluble, easygoing Southerners, they were essentially amiable and cheerful. The children at an early age learned to take hardships, if not as a matter of course, at least as an inevitable evil which their optimism led them to believe would never get them down—and it never did. When living was pleasant, they made the most of it, and they made the most of it when it was desperately hard. All of them had a zest for enjoyment and all were blessed with keen humor. They had, perhaps, an exaggerated sense of clan, but it was a warm and tender clannishness, one that held them together with bonds of mutual affection and the ability to share each other's courage.

Next to her mother, the person whom Maud loved best was her crippled brother. His fall from the hayloft (and it was characteristic of Dick's almost saintlike nature that he would never divulge the name of the boy who had shoved him out) had dislocated his hip. A faulty resetting had resulted in tuberculosis of the bone, and his life was one of protracted torment. Maud loved him with passionate devotion. She would sit beside his wheel chair reading to him, talking about poetry, books, and music. Dick had a gift for music. Maud managed somehow to get him a second-hand fiddle on which he first developed his talent. Some years later, a cousin bought him a 'cello and Dick in time became a skilled performer.

There came one happy interlude for my mother. Her talent for acting and recitation was beginning to be recognized by more mature admirers than the audiences of the hayloft. One of the first to appreciate her qualities was her cousin May Franklin. She it was who paid for Maud to go to St. Louis for a number of months, live with relatives, and study "elocution, deportment, and oratory" with a certain Professor McDowell. I don't doubt he had her reciting "Mazeppa" and "The Death of Little Nell" with refined gestures and lip-pursed diction, but stilted as the method was, the girl owed a great deal to this early training.

She was now a girl of seventeen, slim to a degree that shamed her in that era of Grecian curves. Her skin was a delicate pink and white . . . a definite "complexion" . . . her olive-brown eyes were glowingly animated and her mouth was at once charmingly tender and irresistibly gay. As she walked down the street, men turned to stare after her. But the girl was candidly simple and went her way quite unaware of the little stirs she created. She was too busy making the most of those precious short months in a big city. She was full of youthful and earnest ambition, not for personal success but for the acquiring of a general education. Avid to know all she could about literature, history, and drama, she haunted museums and libraries. She went to occasional concerts and studied the program notes. And of course she bought gallery seats for every show that came during those weeks to St. Louis, for by now she knew beyond the shadow of a doubt that she wanted to go on the stage. How she would ever manage it, she didn't bother to figure out.

Those intoxicating days came to a close and Maud returned to Moberly and the family situation which was as critical as ever. William Durbin continued the tenor of his hand-to-mouth existence, going from place to place, from job to job, none of which ever lasted for more than a few months. At one time he found work in Vicksburg, Mississippi, and for a year the family lived comfortably in a white-pillared house on a hill overlooking the town—a charming place that had once served as Grant's headquarters. Just as things were going smoothly, William lost his position and again wandered off, no one knew where. Nor did anyone know how the next meal was going to be served in the elegant white house. What was worse, the child, Dick, was ailing and there was no money for a doctor. Then my grandfather wrote that something unusually promising had turned up in LeGrand, Oregon, and out they journeyed, bag and baggage, in a cluttered day coach, to a bleak land where they knew no living soul. This was the worst year of all. The father again lost his job and money was practically non-existent. The winter was one of the coldest on record for the Northwest. There were days when the family had little fuel and no food. Dick's illness was at its most critical. Large abscesses formed on the twisted joint, the pain was excruciating, and nobody expected the child to live. Maud and her mother clung to one another. There were long hours, after the other children had gone to bed, when together they sat up with the tortured little boy, facing what they assumed must be inevitable. And there was even a dreadful midnight when, unknown to the rest of the family, they went out into the back yard with a lantern to examine the frozen ground, speculating on how a grave, no matter how small, could possibly be dug.

One evening Dickie's screams were more than the mother could stand. She filled the bottom of a kitchen dipper with straight laudanum, and saying, "If it kills him, it's better than having him suffer like that," gave it to the child. It proved to be the wisest thing she could have done. Dick fell into a deep coma during which the abscess burst, and for a time at least his pain was alleviated.

It was during this winter in Oregon that Maud started taking matters into her own young hands. The father had again disappeared, leaving them stranded, and something had to be done. Maud was shy to a degree, but she was also desperate. She became a sort of professional social organizer. For modest remittances, she arranged parties, dances, and charity benefits, and whenever she could, hired herself out as professional entertainer to oblige with an evening of recitation in the plush homes of wealthy lumber folk. Out of the pittances she made, the family was able to eke out a year's existence.

In the spring, William Durbin sent word that he had found work in Denver, where his sister lived. The position was excellent, he wrote, and he furthermore hinted that he had become a partner in a newly claimed silver mine. (Nobody, needless to say, ever set eyes on the mine.) Once again the family packed up their dwindling belongings and made another long and miserably uncomfortable trip to settle in an unfamiliar locale. This time, at least, their stay was of longer duration and in agreeable surroundings.

In the early nineties, "The Queen City of the Plains" was a town of elegance which retained much of the color of the days of the bonanza kings. Italian villas and brownstone mansions rose beside ramshackle casino cribs and gaudy saloons with silver dollars embedded in tiled floors. Drabs from the bagnios of Leadville came to spend their faro earnings in the fine shops patronized by Denver's society matrons, and bearded prospectors from Central City, wandering the sunny streets, stopped open-jawed to watch the passage of Mrs. Tabor's black and pale blue enamel carriage, drawn by four black horses and driven by two black coachmen in scarlet livery. Tabor was still at his dazzling zenith. The family box at the Tabor Grand was lined with white brocaded satin and little Silver Dollar in rosepoint baby dresses costing three hundred apiece took the air in a pram whose metal fittings were fourteen-karat gold.

Life for the Durbins was pleasantly exciting. Their father's moderately well-to-do and highly respectable sister, Aunt Mag, saw to it that they met the right people, and the right people were warmly quick to accept them. Maud, through winning a number of scholarships, was able to attend Wolf Hall, a fashionable establishment which specialized in "finishing" young ladies. She and her sister Laura were popular with the younger set, and their string of beaux was the envy of every girl in town. Maud still dreamed of going on the stage, and in her spare time worked up a repertory of recitations. Word of her talent got around and the local papers began to take notice of her. A faded item from the *Rocky Mountain News* speaks of "Miss Maud Durbin, daughter of W. L. Durbin of the Colorado Honestone Company, who has for some years been gaining laurels in this city as a charming and gifted elocutionist," and another cutting says:

> All of Denver's social four hundred and a great many others were at the Broadway yesterday afternoon to witness the old favorite "Esmeralda" as played by a number of amateurs for the benefit of the Lend-a-Hand Club. In all probability a

finer audience was never assembled in the theatre. Beautiful women and handsome men were the rule, not the exception, and the play was worthy of the splendid audience. Miss Maud Durbin as Esmeralda was naturally the leading feature. Her sweet ways were peculiarly adapted to the character and her acting was most artistic while her voice was sheer music.

CHAPTER TWO

Madame Modjeska

IN 1893, HELENA MODJESKA brought her repertory company to the Tabor Grand. Maud scrimped enough to pay for a gallery seat for *As You Like It,* and absorbed with breathless eagerness every word and gesture of the lovely Pole's joyous and poetic Rosalind. She also managed to pay for standing room for a matinée of *Camille,* although she kept quiet about that. The Dumas classic was still looked upon as extremely daring, if not wicked, and Modjeska had received considerable criticism for portraying that alluring creature of frail lungs and even frailer virtue. In England the play had passed the censor only with the proviso that the title be changed to *Heartsease,* and in God-fearing America, Middlewestern mothers tried their best to boycott the performance on the grounds that this actress with her dignified grace and sensuously caressing voice made out a career of sin to be not only attractive but tenderly appealing. Even so established an intellectual as the critic William Winter publicly deplored the fact that this exquisite artist (and a countess too, mind you!) should debase her art by playing a fallen woman. Modjeska herself defended her delicate interpretation, claiming that she had gone by Arsène Houssaye's description of Marie Duplessis, the model for the Lady of the Camellias, who was, it seems, so "refined and cultivated and spoke of art with such good judgment that Franz Liszt, meeting her in the foyer of a theatre, took her for a princess." Years later, Otis Skinner was to write, "The best description of Modjeska's *Camille* is that it had fragrance." Gentle, intense, and almost unbearably touching, it was one of the great tear-jerkers of theatrical history, and the story was told of how, on the opening night of the first American performance, the prompter during the third act became so overcome he threw away the prompt book and retired to a dark corner of the wings where he was subsequently found quietly sobbing his heart out. Maud of course sobbed, too. She was carried away by the beauty and perfection of Modjeska's artistry. She hung about the stage door and haunted the pavement outside the Windsor, hoping for a glimpse of her idol. One afternoon, she took her courage in hand, walked into the hotel, and bravely asked the clerk to send up to Modjeska her calling card on which was scribbled a palpitating request for an interview. Possibly there was something about the earnestness of the message on the cheap little card that appealed to the woman's gracious nature, possibly it was because the weather was stormy and she could not go out for her customary long walk. Scarcely able to believe her ears, Maud heard the bellboy say that Madame would receive her. With racing heart she entered the hydraulic elevator, stepped out on the fourth floor, and walked down the carpeted corridor. Her knees were shaking. They nearly buckled completely beneath her when a maid let her into a room and she got her first glimpse of the diva. Dressed in a lacy tea gown, the great lady was reclining on a chaise longue smoking a cigarette! The cigarette was caught in a small gold clamp attached to a chain on her forefinger, and Modjeska's gracefully lazy gestures in handling it indicated the habitual smoker. The only other woman Maud had ever seen smoke was an ancient Negro crone in Moberly who pulled on a corncob pipe. Modjeska noticed the girl's look of blank astonishment, smiled, and said in her beguiling accent, "You have never before seen a lady with a cigarette?"

"I've never even seen a cigarette!" came the blurted reply.

"So now you have," said Modjeska. "In my country we have the saying, 'One breaks bread with an Arab and smokes with a Pole.'—But don't be alarmed!" She laughed. "I shan't ask you to join me. Come in, sit down, and tell me all about yourself."

Maud did. Modjeska's lovely manner put her more or less at her ease, and in a breathless torrent she told her of the inspiration her performances had been, of how she loved the theatre, loved acting, didn't know whether or not she had any talent but wanted so much to go on the stage, although she was sure her family would never allow her to. Then, with the temerity of young and burning ambition, she asked if Madame Modjeska would like to have her recite something. Modjeska politely concealed a wince. She knew all too well what such expressions of dedicated ardor are generally like. Her impulse was to shy clear of the inevitably awkward situation. But there was something about this girl which arrested attention. She had a charming speaking voice, she had distinction, and she was so desperately in earnest. Besides, it was raining outside.

She lit another cigarette, leaned back on the chaise longue, and told her to go ahead. Maud stood up, gulped, and plunged headlong into the "Potion Scene." At the finish, Modjeska put out her cigarette and told her to recite something else, and by way of contrast the girl complied with excerpts from *Mrs. Jarley's Waxworks.* The lady, for all her limited English, laughed spontaneously at the comedy points, then called for a final selection, and the young performer wound up with "Isabella's Plea"—a risky choice, had she known it, for *Measure for Measure* was part of the Modjeska repertoire. When she had finished, there was a pause. Then Modjeska rose, came swiftly across the room, took the girl's trembling hands in her own slim, tapered ones, and said, "Child, you are gifted. At the end of my season you will hear from me." Then she kissed her on both cheeks, opened the door, and gracefully dismissed her.

Maud went home in a happy daze which lasted for the next two months. She went about her daily affairs hardly knowing what she was doing. She could hardly believe any of it had actually happened to her. The interview, the great artist's apparent interest, the promise that she'd hear from her . . . it all seemed unreal. And when the postman delivered an envelope addressed to her in a fine foreign hand, postmarked New York and bearing on the back a tiny coat-of-arms, that too seemed unreal. The letter read:

My dear Miss Durbin:

We are now making contracts and yours will be sent to you shortly. If you are still decided to go on the stage you will sign it, if not please let me know at the earliest date, as I shall have to engage someone else in your place.

I will not tell you what parts you have to play, because I want to read them with you before you commit them to memory, so that you may have at once the clear understanding of every line in your part. I do not usually take so much trouble with the young actresses, but I am interested in you, and if you follow my instructions, I hope you may make your way in the profession.

It is the beginning which is the most difficult and not always pleasant part of the career, but if you begin well, the result is bound to be good.

My acting manager will tell you when we begin the rehearsals. I think that you must be prepared to come to New

York about September 21st, three weeks before our opening of the season.

With best wishes,
Sincerely yours,
HELENA MODJESKA

Maud instantly wrote back a joyfully effusive acceptance, then told her family. She had reckoned without their attitude. Her mother was grieved but compliant. Her father was indignant and anything but compliant. The whole notion was preposterous. He wouldn't even talk about it. However, he talked about it good and plenty when, a few days later, a letter from Modjeska's manager informed them that Madame was in receipt of Miss Durbin's acceptance, that the season would open October 10 with *Henry VIII*, and that in this production Miss Durbin would recite the Prologue and Epilogue, dressed as a boy herald in tunic and *tights!* William Durbin went livid. For a daughter of his to want to go on the stage was bad enough, but for her to be expected to appear before the public in tights was an outrage not to be endured. It was an insult to the girl, to the family, to that sensitive plant which is apparently so frail it is always having to be defended, Southern Womanhood. He bellowed his flat refusal and Maud tearfully returned the contract. There followed a week of youthful heartache. Then, miraculously, there arrived another letter from Modjeska. That understanding and magnanimous lady had written back:

My dear Miss Durbin:

I am afraid my stage manager's letter has discouraged you and, therefore, I write to you to urge you not to give up the opportunity of making your career . . . maybe the only sure one you have. You may get an engagement in some other companies . . . but, I assure you, it will not be the same.

As to the parts you have to play, The Prologue and Epilogue in *Henry VIII* is the best after Katherine. . . . Anne

Boleyn and the other parts are simply walking ladies . . . while here you have an opportunity of being alone on the stage and speaking to the audience. The costume is a very decent one. It is a herald's dress and it may be long to the knees. Besides, you have a charming part in *Camille* . . . Nichette . . . then Phoebe in *As You Like It.* Margarite Curl in *Mary Stuart* and one of the maids in *Much Ado.* The only part where you appear as a boy will be in *Henry VIII* and it is a loose gown and long enough to save you all embarrassment, or injure your instincts of modesty.

You certainly must know that I can get as many young girls as I wish . . . but I feel my duty to give you all the chances first. If you reject the offer then I shall try to get someone else, but, for your own sake, I urge you again not to stop at trifles, and take this opportunity which may decide your future.

All the costumes I will furnish for you and your hotel bill in New York may be paid from the advance money my husband, Mr. Bozenta, will send you to Denver. I shall also send your ticket or money for your trip to New York. Please answer immediately.

Very sincerely yours,
HELENA MODJESKA CHLAPOWSKA,
COUNTESS BOZENTA

The addition of her title in the signature was a clever and calculated touch. It was a gesture she almost never made, for she was democratically unassuming and took pains to keep the fact that she was a noblewoman carefully out of her professional life, as did her husband Count Charles Bozenta Chlapowski who, when he was in America, insisted upon being plain *Mr.* Bozenta. But she must have figured, and quite correctly, that in this instance the aristocratic touch would be effective. In the same post as this letter came one from Beaumont Smith, Modjeska's stage manager. Beaumont Smith, kindly and pompous, was the traditional "grand old actor of the bad old school." It was said he even ordered his ham and eggs in blank verse. His reply was characteristic:

I can fully appreciate your feeling in the matter as my wife had to go through the same ordeal her first season on the stage. From a social standpoint I can understand, but professionally it is not a sentiment to be considered. You will have to come to it sometime. Madame wears tights and you will find that after the first night in male attire, you won't mind it. Actors look upon these things as a matter of course, and during your novitiate is the time to get used to them.

As Jessica in *The Merchant of Venice* and a dozen others I could name you would have to don the male garment and they are parts in which you would be more prominently thrust forward. When you meet, Mrs. Smith will give you *courage* by relating her first experience in "sock and buskin."

I speak thus as one in sympathy with you, but in no power to alter the cast. Those parts are always played by the lady occupying the position you do in the company. We can't put a man into them on account of age and size. The legitimate repertory is different from any other and you will have to play many male parts before you get through. The parts are supposed to be *boys,* not men!

It all sounded reassuringly respectable. Maud's mother was reconciled. Her father hemmed and hawed for a few days over the two letters, then gave grudging consent.

September finally came round and Maud was ready to start for New York. Her mother decided to go with her, partly for reasons of propriety, partly because she could not bear to cut herself off so soon from this daughter who had grown to be such an indispensable confidante and companion. She made arrangements with the neighbors to keep an eye on the household during her absence, and put the older children in charge of the younger ones. Maud packed her modest wardrobe in a tin steamer trunk, and together they boarded the east-bound train. The seventy-five dollars that Mr. Bozenta had advanced toward travel and rehearsal expenses was augmented by a little fund, gifts of May Franklin and Aunt Mag. The travelers counted over their resources with serious care, and during the four-day journey saved money on meals by eating at station lunch counters. The management had reserved them a room at the Park Avenue Hotel, and Maud found a note at the desk saying:

Dear Miss Durbin,

You will please meet the members of Madame Modjeska's Company on the Stage of the Garden Theatre at 11 A.M. September 19th.

Rehearsal of *Henry VIII.*

BEAUMONT SMITH
Stage Director

Maud's hand trembled as she read the instructions over a dozen times. She and her mother consulted a sympathetic doorman as to the exact location of the Garden Theatre and just how long it would take to get there by horsecar. They unpacked, and Maud in preparation for the next day laid out her homemade peek-a-boo blouse and sent off her best serge mail-order suit to be sponged and pressed. They talked over the question of whether or not she should turn up at her first rehearsal accompanied by her mother, and settled on the plan that her mother should walk in with her, stay just long enough to establish the fact that the young girl was not alone in the great city, then leave.

They set out next morning. Maud's heart was pounding wildly. Beaumont Smith, the stage manager, met them at the door, welcomed them with a gentlemanly courtesy that Mrs. Durbin found most reassuring, and asked them to come in. Madame would be along presently. Shyly they entered the mysterious vastness of the darkened theatre. An acetylene rehearsal light cast a weird glare on the bare stage. In a distant corner a group of people were chatting with the attractive informality of show people who are well acquainted. Maud gazed at them with awe. Her mother, repressing a little gasp, whispered, "Actors!" Mr. Smith said that perhaps they'd like to meet the rest of the company, and led them over to the group, the nearest member of which was a young man who was laughing over some anecdote that a pretty woman was telling him. He had huge brown eyes and black curly hair with romantic gray patches over the ears, and his teeth when he laughed were very white. Looking at him, Maud thought him astonishingly handsome. Too handsome, maybe. He must surely be extremely conceited. Her mental speculations were interrupted by Mr. Smith who, she realized, was in the act of making introductions.

"Miss Durbin, let me present Madame's leading man and co-star," she heard him saying, "Mr. Otis Skinner." My future father looked at her with total disinterest, bowed perfunctorily, and turned back to his companion. Maud decided she definitely didn't like him.

The next three weeks were taken up with strenuous rehearsal. Modjeska's interest in her new protégée increased as she saw with what intelligence and sensitive instinct the girl attacked her work. The gracious woman paid special attention to her, frequently shared with her the hot lunch that was brought in during the midday break, and occasionally drove her back to the hotel in her private brougham. Maud was in a state of eager rapture and her mother, by now convinced that the stage was not a pitfall into Sodom and Gomorrah, was happy, too.

The day of dress rehearsal, a telegram arrived for Mrs. Durbin saying that Dick was desperately ill, she must come home at once. Maud, with an aching heart, accompanied her mother to Jersey City and saw her onto the train. All the way back to Manhattan on the ferry the girl stood by the windy rail and sobbed. In the lobby of her hotel she ran into kind Mr. Bozenta, who spoke to her, noticed her red eyes, but made no comment. In half an hour a note arrived from Madame asking if Maud would please come around to see her immediately. Maud bathed her face in cold water and hastened over to the Clarendon, where Madame, refraining from any personal inquiries, asked her if she'd be good enough to help her out by sewing beads onto her Holbein headdress for Queen Katherine. Reminiscing about it years later in an article published in *The Theatre Arts Monthly,* my mother said:

> All afternoon I sat in her drawing room, thinking I was helping. I know now that I was no help . . . it was merely her motherly way of keeping me from sobbing my heart out. It still astonishes me to recall that she should have had a thought for anyone on the eve of her first performance in New York in an exacting and untried rôle! I later was humiliated to find Nascia, her maid, patiently cutting off my beads and resewing them. My stitches had come through. It was my first lesson in infinite pains. "Things done well and with care" was a Modjeska maxim.

In her first part, Maud acquitted herself very well. She spoke her lines with simple sincerity, her voice was lovely, and in her little herald's costume she looked enchanting. However, her family's horror over the indecency of her appearing in tights had left its mark, and she felt rather as though she were standing before the audience stark naked. After two self-conscious performances, she bought herself, at terrific expense, a pair of boots, hip length and made of soft suède. Modjeska, when she saw them, laughed till the tears streamed down her cheeks. She had never heard of a Tudor herald wearing boots. "But," she added upon seeing the girl's downcast expression, "they really look rather dashing and they must have cost you three weeks' salary. You may wear them."

The star was less indulgent a few nights later when Maud, during the wedding scene in which she doubled as a lady-in-waiting, appeared in a headdress she had made herself, blandly copying it from the one worn by the actress playing Anne Boleyn. Modjeska waited till the curtain came down, then walked across the stage, and with no comment other than an angry snort, snatched the silly pink thing off her head. Maud was appalled. A few nights later, Nascia, Madame's maid, brought word to report at the star's dressing room. She hurried over with trepidation.

> I shall never forget the picture [she wrote]. She was standing before her dressing table, wearing a heavily embroidered black kimono. She had on her red wig and the heavy Holbein headdress, and she was smoking a cigarette! On her wig block was my pink satin and gold lace cap, now transformed into something characteristic . . . she had remade it herself, and in adjusting it to my head, she told me I could wear it, but never again must I commit any such breach of professional etiquette as to copy the costume of another player.

After a short New York run, the company went on the road. It was a strenuous tour filled with split weeks and one-night stands, and Modjeska lived with her husband and maid in the private car with which the management in those elegant days provided them. It was considered a "miniature palace on wheels." The lounge was fitted out like a salon with well-stocked bookcases, a few good prints, and large vases filled with fresh flowers. Madame's sleeping quarters might have been those of a grand duchess; a silver toilet set engraved with the Chlapowski coat-of-arms gleamed on an ornate dressing table and the bed was spread with monogrammed linen, brocade coverlet, and a fur-lined throw. The dining compartment was furnished in similar style. The best of china and napery was used and the meals, prepared by a special Polish chef, were delectable, for Madame and her husband were hearty epicures. During long railroad jumps, Madame conducted her life with gracious formality. Her company manager, her leading man, and two members next in importance were daily invited to the car for luncheon or dinner. Protocol was strictly observed and they sat according to their positions in the troupe. Now and then Maud would be asked to come in, too. She was always placed at the end of the table and her shyness prevented her from joining in general conversation to any great extent. But she listened avidly to everything that was said, and watched with starry-eyed eagerness. Mr. Otis Skinner always sat at Madame's right. He never by any chance addressed a single word in Maud's direction. She thought him excessively "stuck up."

The season ended and Modjeska invited Maud to spend the summer at her California ranch. "Arden," as it was called, was just outside of Santa Ana, where there had been established a small but brilliant coterie . . . a sort of Polish-Californian Brook Farm . . . and the Chlapowskis were the centre of it. There was a constant stream of exciting house guests—writers, musicians, artists, actors. Most of them were fiery and passionately patriotic Poles who, exiled from their country for anti-Russian activities, had fled to America. Charles Bozenta Chlapowski was one himself. He had left the University of Louvain to take part in the Prussia-Poland-Posen rebellion, had spent two years in a Berlin prison and, after his release and marriage to Modjeska, had been hounded out of Warsaw by the police. A constant visitor was Sienkiewicz, the author of *Quo Vadis.* Paderewski, when his tours took him to the Pacific Coast, came out for Sundays, as did the De Reszkes, and Joseph Conrad when he visited America made Arden an objective.

The way of living at Arden was simple. Modjeska, shedding the formality she maintained in the theatre, relaxed in the rôle of an efficient hostess, wife, mother, and grandmother (her son by her first marriage, Ralph Modjeski, with his little boy, was staying with them). She was the perfect *femme de ménage* and her hospitality was lavish. Unexpected guests were frequently dropping in, and often as not they sat down as many as fifteen at table. In which event, Jesús, the cook, who was graced with none of the patient qualities of his namesake, would fling a few pots onto the floor, untie his apron, and stamp out of the ranch house swearing by all the saints of Mexico never to return. Madame, equal to the emergency, would take over the kitchen, where she would prepare a delicious meal of her native dishes, and she and her husband would serve it as serenely as part of the daily routine. Next morning Jesús, suffering from a mixture of repentance and *téquila* hangover, would come meekly home and life would resume its even tenor.

Guests and family shared alike in the household chores. The day began with a lavish breakfast which Madame served herself at a long table on the lawn in the shade of some ancient live oaks. Luncheons were set out in picnic boxes for people to take where and whenever they chose. Everyone went his own way during the day. Modjeska busied herself with household and garden. She sketched, she played with her small grandson, and spent much time composing and illustrating a fairy story for him. She was a gifted watercolorist. Dinner was a semi-informal affair held in the great library of the ranch house built by Stanford White. There followed a fine evening of good talk augmented with music, impromptu theatricals, and sometimes dancing, with the Chlapowskis giving exhibitions of Polish and Russian dances. Tea was brought in at ten o'clock and the evening usually ended with a card game. Madame was an avid whist player. She attacked a game with the concentration and zest with which she attacked a part, and she had a snorting intolerance for a poor partner. One evening when her nephew Wladyslaw Benda (later to become distinguished as W. T. Benda, the illustrator and creator of masks) carelessly lost an obvious trick, she rose, swept the pack up from the table, flung them in the lad's flushed face, and with a dramatic cry of "You are a dunce, sir!" sailed from the room.

The great lady's temper was Slavicly inflammable in spite of the fact that she went on the happily misguided assumption that she always had it under complete control.

"I used to lose my temper very often," she once told a reporter. "So did my husband—but it was not wise for both of us to be excited at once, so we agreed that but one of us should lose his temper on any occasion and the other keep calm."

"And does it work?" the reporter had asked.

"Perfectly!" Modjeska had assured him with a peal of laughter. "You see, Charlie is excited *all* the time!"

Modjeska's interest in Maud continued to be keen. She trained her in a few Shakespearean parts, and Maud was an eager pupil. The girl took long walks about the grounds, earnestly reciting her lines aloud to the fascination of the Mexican gardeners who, thinking her pleasantly demented, nicknamed her "La Loquita." She had the chance, too, of watching Modjeska study a part. It was only for a one-act comedy she and Maud were to do for a local amateur benefit, but Madame set about it with as much care as if it had been for a New York opening. "Over and over we read our parts together," Maud wrote in her reminiscent article, "decided upon the business, and then she set about her own task. She did not memorize her lines—she absorbed the character. Action was always suited to the word, the word to the action, and she studied aloud. By the date of the benefit, her part was as perfect as if it had been in her repertory for years. My immature method had been to commit the lines at once to memory. This was a heinous fault and she scolded me roundly."

Maud made quite a hit in the benefit show. Sienkiewicz gave her a copy of *Quo Vadis* with an inscription in enthusiastic Polish, Howard Pyle, who happened to be in the neighborhood, presented her with a drawing of Captain Kidd, and a young man whose name was not recorded shot ten hummingbirds and brought them to her to use as trimming for a hat. Maud was in a happy glow over her little triumph; she wept tenderly over the slaughter of the hummingbirds, but she did trim her hat with them.

The following fall Modjeska's repertory company went again on tour. It was an extensive and a colorful one. The star took delight in all the chance enjoyments the road had to offer and she was generous about sharing them with the members of her troupe. Maud was always among the favored ones to accompany her. In San Francisco they went, escorted by the police, through the forbidden tortuosities of underground Chinatown, and in Virginia City they had the dubious pleasure of making a hair-raising descent into a gold mine. They played Duluth in January and Madame had them driven in hired sleighs by the light of an icy moon out to the house of some Polish friends whom they roused with a carefully rehearsed serenade. In Milwaukee, the German literati gave a select dinner at the end of which Madame rose, drank their health, and asked if she might show her appreciation of their hospitality by giving them a short Polish recitation. "A note of suspense and drama was struck at once." I quote Otis Skinner, who was one of the guests. "Her liquid voice became by turns melancholy and gay, impassioned, tragic, light with happiness and blighting with bitterness. There was not a note in the gamut of emotions she did not touch. She finished with a recurrent rhythm, fateful and portentous. We were clutched by the spell. We didn't know what it was about, but we knew it was something tremendous. In the silence after she had ended, someone asked: 'What was it, Madame? What was it?' 'Why,' she answered with a sly smile, 'I merely recited the alphabet in Polish.'"

The tour took them South. In New Orleans they were the guests of the French Opera Company who gave them a champagne supper on the stage of the old auditorium. In Savannah, Madame appeared in the third act of *Camille* wearing a black lace gown trimmed with a garland of real camellias which stretched from the shoulder to the end of her long train. "I was out in the beautiful cemetery today," she explained, "and I thought all those dear dead people would feel glad to think I had worn some of their lovely flowers, so Nascia and I gathered them and she pinned them on this gown." She was disarmingly tender about her act of vandalism and wore the delicate loot with an air of reverence.

Otis Skinner was still the leading man. Maud didn't like him any better than she had the preceding year. She still thought him "stuck up." Moreover, he had shocked her sensibilities profoundly by his daring innovation in the costuming of *Macbeth* in which character he had shed his "fleshings," had painted his legs in bolarmenia, and had actually gone on bare-limbed.

Maud hardly ever had occasion to exchange conversation with the handsome leading man. He kept very much to himself. If she met him in the theatre, she scuttled past him barely murmuring a vague how-do-you-do. She found herself ducking around scenery flats in order to avoid him. And she had the uncomfortable feeling that in regard to her, he was doing the same thing. It annoyed her. It also annoyed her that she ever gave him a second thought . . . let alone a third or fourth. The evening of Hallowe'en, they were playing *Henry VIII.* Maud, prompted by some inexplicable impulse, bought a pumpkin, carved it into a Jack-o'-lantern, and during a scene when Otis Skinner, as Henry, was on the stage, ran into his dressing room, turned off the lights, and left the object grinning on his make-up shelf. No sooner had she come away than she wished she hadn't done it. She wished so even more when the leading man's dresser came to her with an expression of extreme seriousness and said, "Mr. Skinner didn't at all like your playing that joke on him." She went on for the wedding scene as a lady-in-waiting, flushed with embarrassment and fury. During a short *pavane* she and the other extras had to execute, she was suddenly aware that Henry VIII had slipped off his throne and was making his way in her direction. He came right up to her, quietly pushed her partner aside, took her hand in a movement of the dance, grinned broadly and whispered, "Who put that Jack-o'-lantern in my dressing room?" squeezed her fingers, bowed elegantly, and returned to his dais. Maud gasped and blushed more crimson than the heels of her Tudor shoes. Her heart was pounding violently.

A few nights later during a performance of *Macbeth,* it pounded again, but less pleasurably. That season Modjeska, in her generosity, had taken along Maud's sister Laura as a member of the company. Laura had no particular talent, but she was blonde and lovely to behold, and she proved very effective in minor parts, one of which was that of the boy apparition in the Cauldron Scene. As this callow spectre, she rose through a floor trap up into the kettle, on an elevator platform device propelled by the property men, until her head and shoulders appeared just above the lime-effected steam of the witches' unpalatable brew, at which eminence she imparted to Macbeth the consoling information about Birnam Wood; afterward, the property man lowered her back to the theatre cellar. Her costume was simple, being a fillet of green leaves and a sheet. The sheet she wore was used by Maud for packing her best costumes in at the bottom of her trunk. There came a week of one-night stands, and Maud, tired and irritable, refused one evening to unpack her entire trunk merely to get out her sister's sheet. It was nonsense going to all that trouble for a tank town. Laura could perfectly well tie a white muslin petticoat about her neck and, as nothing more than her head and shoulders ever showed, the citizens of Galesburg would be none the wiser. Laura reluctantly put on the petticoat and tied the drawstring about her neck. She observed somewhat balefully that the bottom, which billowed in eyelet-embroidery flounces and blue ribbon, came only halfway down her shapely legs, but Maud assured her that no one would see her but the property man, and after all, he was hardened to girls in tights. Maud spoke with the annoyingly casual assurance of the player graced with a superior part. It was hardly a glamorous one, but she had some important speeches to say. She was one of the Three Witches and she wore a beard. Her two sister witches were played by men. One was George Hazelton, later to become a successful playwright, the other a man named Rose, who never became a successful anything. Mr. Rose, a nervous little individual, was the stage manager and went on for bit parts. In *Macbeth,* when he was not "double-doubling-toil-and-troubling" he stood in the wings still in costume with the prompt book in hand. The scene that night got off to an unfortunate start as Mr. Rose, in a flutter of confusion over his dual capacity of prompter and Weird Sister, went on with the typewritten script of the play clutched to his bosom. He became aware of it, and after the curtain was up managed somehow to conceal it under the voluminous rags of his costume. What he failed to conceal, however, were his gold-rimmed spectacles—a smart little pince-nez design with a gold ear chain. Throughout the entire scene they wobbled giddily on the bridge of his artificial nose, the stage lightning showing them up beautifully. Maud and George Hazelton went into paroxysms of giggles. Macbeth strode on and demanded of the secret, black, and midnight hags what was't they did. The "deed without a name" came as an unintelligible jumble of snorts and stifled guffaws. Skinner didn't see what was so funny. Then at the sight of little Mr. Rose conscientiously contributing to the sabbath brew his share of "sow's blood that hath eaten her nine farrow; grease that's sweaten from the murderer's gibbet" and peering into the glowing pot through his pince-nez, the leading man's eyes widened in amazement. They nearly popped out of their sockets when time came for the manifestation of the apparitions and Laura as the Crowned Boy arose, not only into the cauldron, but on up and up until she was completely out of it. Indeed, she seemed to be actually hovering in the murky air well above it, almost on a level with "High Dunsinane" itself and all the while trying with desperate modesty to yank down the flounce and ribbon bottom of her white petticoat. The property man, who had a perverted sense of humor, had not been able to resist the temptation of hoisting Laura into complete exposure. The Galesburg public stared in bewilderment. The Three Witches by now were prostrated with hysteria. Maud's extremely pat line of "Why stands Macbeth thus amazedly?" came in a shrill squeal. Macbeth, too, was almost incapable of speech. Only not through mirth. He was furious. His fury, however, was as nothing to that of Modjeska, who was watching from the wings. When the curtain fell, she stormed onto the stage, impressive in her sleepwalking nightgown, faced the by now quaking witches, snatched the glasses off the wretched stage manager, and stood glaring at them in an awful silence that seemed to last an eternity. Finally she spoke in a voice which trembled with emotion. "Mr. Rose," she said. "You are an eediot! The rest of you are eembeciles! Good evening!," and she swept back into her dressing room, slamming the door behind her.

Maud by now was playing better parts. The critics always paid her special attention and certain of them said she had the qualities of a young American Ellen Terry. In spite of all this, she had no job for the forthcoming season. Modjeska was not touring again. The Russian authorities had yielded to popular demand, and the Chlapowskis were to be allowed re-entry into Poland, where they intended to stay at least a year. Otis Skinner was planning to strike out as a star actor-manager and was forming his own company. His leading lady had already been engaged and there was no indication that he was remotely interested in signing up Maud for second parts. She went back to Denver for a month and was about to start for New York to make the rounds of the managers and agents, when a letter arrived from Otis Skinner saying that the actress he had engaged to play opposite him had been forced by illness to cancel her contract, and would Miss Durbin be interested in replacing her, please let him know by return post. Miss Durbin wrote back that she thought she might be interested, a triumph of understatement. It was with considerable will power that she restrained herself from mailing the letter until time for the post of the following day. Within a week a contract arrived from the Skinner management. She was engaged as leading lady for the season of 1895–96. She was amazed and elated. She was also strangely disturbed.

It was not for several months that Maud was to find out that it had been only through the earnest intercession of Modjeska that the young star had been persuaded into taking the risk of engaging her. Modjeska, who believed in the girl's talent, had taken the pains of going to see him to beg him, as a favor to her, to give Maud this opportunity. She never, of course, so much as hinted that she had had a hand in Maud's good fortune. The day before she sailed for Poland she wrote:

My darling Maud,

I was so happy when I read of your good news. I think it the wisest thing Mr. Skinner ever did, because the parts in the new plays suit you to perfection. I hope you will miss me a little next season, but I also hope it will be a good season for you in all respects. This is a great opportunity for you, and you must grasp it with both arms. Study your parts carefully, never be in a hurry to memorize, but rather dwell on the sentences and never stop repeating until you are pleased with yourself. Accept all suggestions but come to the rehearsal prepared with your own business . . . and when it does not meet with approval, then change. Nothing forms an actor better than work with himself. I mean the constant and mental effort, and loud study, no matter what the neighbors may say about it.

And now I take my leave. Good-bye until we meet again. Many kisses for you and Laura. God bless you and speed you to fortune.

Yours faithfully,
H. MODJESKA

My mother never acted with Modjeska again. But their frendship remained warm and they corresponded at regular intervals until the great lady died. Even after that, her memory was kept glowingly alive by both Mother and Father. She became a patron saint of our family. I felt that she was a lovely and intimate acquaintance and that although I met her only once, very briefly, when I was a child of six, I knew exactly what she was like.

All through my mother's life, so many things reminded her of her great benefactress. They were always lovely things. I remember once she came to me with a book in hand and said, "Listen to this, it's a beautiful picture of Madame," and with tears in her eyes she read from Willa Cather's *My Mortal Enemy*, published by Alfred A. Knopf, the following passage:

> By far the handsomest and most distinguished of that company was a woman no longer young but beautiful in age, Helena Modjeska. She looked a woman of another race and another period, no less queenly than when I had seen her in Chicago as Marie Stuart and as Katherine in *Henry VIII*. I remember how, when Oswald asked her to propose a toast, she put out her long arm, lifted her glass, and looking into the blur of the candlelight with a grave face, said "To my coun-n-n-try!" How well I remember those long, beautifully modelled hands, with so much humanity in them. They were worldly, indeed, but fashioned for a nobler worldliness than ours; hands to hold a sceptre, or a chalice . . . or, by courtesy, a sword.

CHAPTER THREE

Parson's Family

The background of Modjeska's handsome *jeune premier* had been very different from that of the shy young girl he was to marry. Born in Cambridge, the second son to bless the home of a scholarly Universalist preacher and his quiet wife, my father came, on his father's side, of a long line of granite-faced New Englanders, worthy citizens, righteous and God-fearing to a conscientious point when one wondered if it mightn't be a case of the Deity who was doing most of the fearing. His dark-eyed mother had come from upstate New York. Modest, soft-spoken, her union with the Skinner family tree was in the nature of the grafting of a delicate fern onto a giant oak. Whoever married a Skinner became a Skinner; their children were Skinners and there was no nonsense about it.

In comparison with the easygoing spirit of the Durbin family, the atmosphere of the Skinner household was austere. Life was a dedication to a *modus vivendi* set along a rigidly restricted path marked Duty, and the bringing up of children was a business of serious endeavor. My father's boyhood days were spent largely in the observance of stern routine. They were not over-gay. His happiest interludes were the summer months when the family went to Vermont to stay with Grandfather Warren. That impressive old patriarch regarded his grandchildren with much the same mild interest he held for his chickens or his cows, and so long as they didn't bother him they were at liberty to do as they pleased. Vermont for Otis meant freedom and bare feet, berry-picking and fishing. It meant lying in mountainside hayfields catching grasshoppers to watch them "spit tobacco," with the sun at high noon cooking freckles on his nose. At an early age he found he had the happy gift common to most of the Skinner men—an uncanny way with wild animals. His younger brother, William, was to be the Thoreau of the family and possessed of the ability to lure a wild doe to feed from his hand as tamely as a Shetland pony. Otis, too, had the same faculty. I have seen him in later years tickle a woodchuck behind the ear with a stalk of timothy until the animal was foolishly writhing with delight. Vermont meant the annual gathering of the Skinner clan, a large flock that numbered such colorful individuals as dashing Uncle Eugene who, it was whispered, had once toured the country in a minstrel show, but had retired to a life of reform and respectability as Proctorville's leading dentist. Then there was rough old Uncle Bill, a railroad engineer, who during the Civil War had driven the first train through the Dismal Swamp. Small Otis would listen entranced as he told how on a run down to the Northern lines with a heavily loaded ammunition train, going "fast as all git-out," on a one-track stretch, he suddenly saw directly ahead of him the headlight of an oncoming locomotive. After jamming on the brakes with a force that all but telescoped the highly explosive cars behind him, he backed furiously into the nearest siding, brought the train to a standstill, jumped down from the cab, reset the switch, sat down on the embankment, and waited for the passing of what proved to be the planet, Venus.

Summer sped by all too rapidly. In early September, Grandpa Warren bade them all a perfunctory and quite relieved farewell and they returned to Cambridge. Life in a New England clerical household was hardly luxurious. The pay of a Universalist minister was moral rather than monetary, and as a virtue, frugality was an even tie with godliness. There was no frivolous spending for non-essentials. The boys were never given allowances, although now and then the mother, scraping the bottom of the till, would manage to spare them a few pennies, three-cent paper "shinplasters," with which to purchase a few pickled limes or licorice "shoestrings." Even Christmas was hardly the horn-of-plenty festival of *Harper's Young People*. Presents were of a purely practical nature and each boy's stocking contained nothing more extravagant than an orange. Local gaiety was confined to parish-house evenings when young and old gathered to listen to a lecture or musical program, following which the mature ones exchanged decorous chit-chat over a glass of non-alcoholic punch while the juvenile element regaled itself pouring melted maple sugar onto bowls full of packed snow.

Any time for play was negligible and the day of a New England boy was dull with duties, firewood to be chopped, coal scuttles to be carted, passages of the Bible to be got by heart, and errands of reluctant mercy to be run for his mother —bearing her jellies to invalid parishioners. It was my father's job on Saturday afternoons to pick up the family crock filled with molasses-soaked beans from the bakery, where it had been left for proper cooking. The baker would extract the red-hot pot, wrap it in its quilted cozy, hand it over along with a loaf of brown bread fresh from the fragrant oven, and the boy would hurry home through the clear, sharp twilight, sniffing the torturingly delicious aroma of that homely dish which, when rightly done, is alone enough to have made Boston exceptional. Saturday's supper was always baked beans and brown bread; Sunday's breakfast was warmed-up leftovers augmented by doughnuts, frizzled ham, and a slice of cold apple pie. There was need for a hearty breakfast, for Sunday was a day of strenuous devotion. The church was such a distance from the house, they had all to spend the day there. Spiritual activities started at nine for the children with a Sunday-School session of Bible learning and hymn-singing. Otis rather enjoyed the latter. One hymn especially, "I Have a Father in the Promised Land," impressed him as particularly charming because for years he thought the words were "I have a father in the brown ink-stand."

For Otis, a lively, normal child, the day was the apotheosis of excruciating boredom. He was fidgety and inattentive, and given a chance to sit with any companion his own age, raised a good deal of hell during the interminable stretches of his father's sermons to which he never made any attempt to listen. Once, when he had been behaving particularly badly, his father stopped in the middle of a sentence, fixed him with an awful eye, and after a terrifying pause said, "If my son Otis would desist from shooting spitballs in the House of the Almighty, I'd continue with my sermon."

In that era a boy was brought up to honor his father and his mother, and in addition to honoring them, it was usually the case that he loved the latter and feared the former. But Charles Skinner was a very human person, in spite of his New England restraint in most matters. He liked music and the theatre and he adored baseball. In later years his parishioners were staggered to hear of the daily appearance of their pastor in the bleachers of the stadium during the World Series, his silver hair and beard flashing in the sun as he emitted loud whoops of encouragement to the Boston team.

It was only through the death of his baby sister that Otis learned that his Olympian father was capable of profound emotion. Kitty had sickened and died of some one of the virulent children's diseases of the day. The mother bore the tragedy with desperate stoicism; if she found outlet for her grief, it was in privacy. The boy's wandered about the house, pale and silent, and the father locked himself in his study all day and evening. In the small hours of the night, Otis, hearing a sound in the living room, crept to the head of the stairs and peered into the room below. His father was pacing up and down, up and down. His face was distorted with suffering, and he was moaning unintelligible words. In his arms, clutched against his heart, was the tiny dead child.

Charles was the literary hope of the family. He wrote stories and poetry which Otis, being a brother, never bothered to read. His plays were creations of wonder, produced in the cellar with casts made up of his schoolmates, and his mother for an audience. Otis, too, was merely a spectator, because he was considered too young to be reliable in any other rôle. But as the boys grew older, Charles became more and more Otis's guide in matters of awareness, and they shared a great many mutual interests.

Charlie was a music-lover and while they were still living in Cambridge, he'd now and then scrape up enough cash for gallery seats for special concerts in Boston, taking along young Otis, with the stern warning that if he fidgeted, he'd have to go home. And sometimes, rapture of raptures, there'd be a theatrical spree in the way of an afternoon at the Boston Museum. It was considered perfectly proper for the family of a parson to patronize that respectable house of entertainment, for it was a museum—more or less. The foyers and promenades were lined with exhibitions of stuffed birds, pickled reptiles, and the busts of eminent poets. On the balcony floor was a gallery of waxworks of an edifying nature: "Three Stages in the Life of a Drunkard," "Indians Massacring Jane McCrae," "Daniel Lambert, the Fat Man," drinking from a mug the size of a coal scuttle a draught of beer crowned with a foam collar of dusty cotton. An afternoon at the Museum offered, according to the program, "Visits to the instructive Curio Halls. Relaxation in the auditorium's commodious chairs the framework of which is wholly of iron and all of which is elegantly upholstered. And on the stage, a highly moral and dramatic entertainment of drama and farce, with musical olios between the acts." The "highly moral and dramatic entertainments" ran the theatrical gamut of everything from *Macbeth* to *Milly with the Milking Pail;* from *She Stoops to Conquer* to the Great Japanese Acrobat, Tokesan, in his "High Bamboo Celestial Pet Balancing." And Otis, whose all-high standard in the artistic was the duel in the snow of *The Corsican Brothers,* thought everything was wonderful.

The Reverend Charles was offered a new parish in Hartford, and the family left Cambridge when Otis was in his early teens. The boy welcomed the change. Life in the Connecticut capital was less rigid than in Cambridge. But the Skinners knew few people outside the parish, and Otis, for all his good looks and pleasant manner, was shy and slow to make friends. His brother Charlie had flown the nest and had gone to New York to start a career of journalism. Will, the naturalist, was more interested in birds and animals than in people. Otis was lonely. He became an omnivorous reader. There never seemed to be enough available books. School offered little beyond the selections to be found in McGuffey's Eclectic Readers. The family shelves, given over chiefly to works such as Foxe's *Lives of the*

Martyrs and the sermons of William Ellery Channing, contained little in the way of romance beyond the novels of Bulwer-Lytton and the poems of William Cullen Bryant. Young Otis was early initiated into the forbidden delights of the dime novel—Beadle's, Monroe's, and similar publications, with lurid orange jackets illustrated with stirring engravings of virtuous maidens barely escaping defilement over ice floes or Niagara Falls. He hid the copies at the foot of an apple tree and, when he could, pored over them in a leafy hide-out in the upper branches. Dime novels were not the only proscribed reading matter, for the elder Skinner considered the *Boston Transcript* and *The Christian Leader* the only newspapers proper for family consumption. The hired girl, however, was a subscriber to a lively daily journal with comic cartoons and items of scandal and frivolity. After reading the copies, she'd rumple them up and use them as stuffing for her "everyday" bustle. Her "dress" bustle, Madame Foy's standard wire contraption, she saved to wear on her afternoons off, and on those precious occasions Otis would wait till she'd left the house, then cautiously steal into her room, open her top drawer, take out the wad of newspaper, straighten it, and have a fascinating hour of bustle-reading.

My father's interest in books, however, was no indication of his scholarship, which was extremely poor. The standards of the Brown Grammar School were high and he had a hard time keeping up. When he was sixteen, it was mutually and sorrowfully agreed by all concerned that to expect him to graduate with honors was an illusory dream. Even to expect him to graduate at all was an overoptimistic anticipation, my father used to say, with a wry smile. It seemed wiser for him to start earning a living than to continue an education that wasn't taking. He left high school to become a clerk in an insurance company, a position in which he distinguished himself not at all. The routine writing-out of dull policies in a stuffy office was an occupation for which he was spectacularly unfitted, and he quit to take a job in the shipping department of a wholesale commission house. This was hard work, but he loved it because it was physical work and most of the time outdoors. He had to see to the hauling of heavy crates and cases, loading some onto freight cars, storing others in warehouses. Workmen were scarce and he did much of the labor himself, staying out till all hours of the night in all sorts of weather, rising in the dark to go, lantern in hand, into glacial lofts to print addresses with ink half-frozen and fingers numb with frostbite. He had never been overstrong and used to suffer with migraine headaches, but on this rugged course of sprouts he blossomed with health. He always claimed it laid the foundation for the great vitality that was his throughout his life.

It was at this point that Charlie, working as cub reporter for the *Brooklyn Times*, had written, urging him to come to the city for a spree, and the lad had scrimped enough from his salary to purchase a round-trip ticket. The older brother was at the red-brick Grand Central Station to meet the young greenhorn. Charlie had wangled twenty-four hours' leave to show him around. It was a wonderful day. They journeyed the length and breadth of the island in stages and open horse-cars. The Battery, Castle Garden, the Eden Musée, Fourteenth Street with Tammany Hall and Tony Pastor's high-toned Variety House at one end and the Metropolitan Museum at the other. They strolled along Fifth Avenue and gazed at the Astor mansions, Delmonico's, and the Carrara marble palace of A. T. Stewart, catching glimpses through lace curtains of the gaslit rococo glories within, and they watched members of the "swallow-tail Democracy" going into the Manhattan Club. They crossed the street, dodging the fast teams, bobtail cars, and careening delivery wagons, and reached Broadway where they gazed wistfully at the

Hoffman House, too modest to venture into the bar to see the Bouguereau "Nymphs and Satyr." They stood with ghoulish reverence on the spot outside the Grand Central Hotel where Stokes's fatal bullet had pierced the colossal paunch of Jim Fisk; then ate dinner at a modest restaurant, splurging on oysters and a glass of lager. The day ended with the crowning wonder of climbing up to gallery seats at the Lyceum Theatre to see a performance of *The Hunchback of Notre Dame*. They of course arrived way ahead of time, but that was all part of the excitement. They entertained themselves watching the audience fill the balconies under them while far below the dazzling élite paraded in to the *fauteuils* of the parterre. The orchestra, spotless in white tie and tails, struck up the overture, the great chandelier dimmed out as gas footlights shot an aurora borealis on the gilded proscenium and the calciums sputtered on with a loud hiss. The curtain rose on a scene of fourteenth-century Paris and the boy found himself in a world of poets and priests, cutthroats and troubadours, thieves and gypsies. It was an excellent cast, Sol Smith as Gringoire, John Jack as the grotesquely touching Quasimodo, and the lovely Jeffreys Lewis an exquisite Esmeralda. But it was the Claude Frollo of Charles Wheatley which threw the dice for him that night. As the sinister monk stole onto the stage, Otis suddenly saw himself playing the part. The pale face, half-shadowed by the black cowl, was not Wheatley's but his own. He sat forward, his body taut, his dark eyes shining, his lips following the melodramatic lines. During the entr'actes he sat as if spellbound, neither speaking nor moving. His heart was pounding and his mind was a racing runaway. Charles glanced sideways at him and with wise intuition said nothing.

The play ended. [I quote my father's own words.] The gallery crowd moved slowly down the stairway and out into

> the cool night air. We walked down the Bowery to Grand Street. We took the Williamsburg ferry and then home to my brother's humble boarding house in Brooklyn and to bed. But there was no sleep for me.
>
> I stayed on for two more days. What I did, I don't know and I never shall. It is all a blank. At night I took the train back to Hartford.
>
> I had found my life's work.

Once home, he kept the momentous decision to himself. Partly because he dreaded his parents' disapproval and more because this discovery seemed too precious, too much in the nature of a revelation to sully it by sharing it with anyone. It was his great secret of which he spoke only to the outdoors. During his free hours, he'd thrust a dog-eared volume of Shakespeare into his pocket and hike out of town to a stretch of countryside where at a certain bend in the road he'd leap a ditch, vault a fence rail, and with a secluded pasture for an auditorium would declaim Marc Antony to a herd of mildly astonished cows.

He subscribed to the *New York Clipper*, an early version of *Variety*, published weekly and containing on four mammoth pages of eye-destroying fine print the theatrical news of New York and the hinterland. He devoured every word of it, from the leading-column accounts of the latest production at Wood's to the back-page ads of jobless actors, acrobats, and virtuosi of the musical glasses.

It was a thrilling New York season. Sardou had shocked the English-speaking public into disapproving appreciation, and *Frou-Frou*, with Fanny Davenport as the doll heroine, was enjoying a popular run at Daly's, feminine hearts were pounding over Dion Boucicault in *The Shaughraun*, Clara Morris's *Camille* added to the general atmosphere of faded violets and agreeable guilt, and when Clara Louise Kellogg sang "Connais-tu le Pays," the very brownstone fronts seemed to melt.

Otis, toiling away at the commission-house job, felt the need to act as a racehorse feels the need to run. He organized a youthful company of amateurs, among them William Gillette whom he had known at Brown High School. Gillette was older than the rest of them, and his chief interest at the time was in puppets. However, he did allow the group to put on a couple of their plays in the loft of his family's carriage house. Fired by this whiff of greasepaint, Otis screwed up sufficient courage to ask his father if they might give a performance in the vestry basement. To his amazement, his father gave permission and the boys chose for their first production a fearful old comedy called *The Honeymoon*, which caused considerable head-shaking in the community.

His next endeavor was in collaboration with a certain W. L. Cheney, a young friend with musical aspirations and a talent for the harmonica. The two decided to make a professional début in a joint concert and dramatic show, and worked up a select program of music and recitation. They found an auditorium in the outskirts of Hartford for fifteen dollars, and had handbills printed announcing that on September 12 at 7:45 P.M.

BY POPULAR DEMAND

The Eminent Musical Artist Professor Cheney

and

The Favorite Elocutionist and Impersonator Mr. O. A. Skinner
will give their select entertainment of
Readings! Character Sketches! and Harmonica Solos!
Ending up with the Screaming Farce

Around The Corner

with Mr. Skinner as Flipper and Prof. Cheney as Nobbler
in the Young Men's Hall of Newington Junction
Price of admission, adults 25¢, children 15¢, babes in arms free.

They spread the ads liberally throughout the town, but fortune favored them with a damp and blustery evening and an audience of some twenty yokels who neither laughed over the screaming farce nor cried during "The Death of Little Dombey," and who never even applauded the Professor's harmonica interpretation of "Sweet Spirit, Hear My Prayers." The box-office receipts totaled $3.75. Skinner and Cheney packed up their show, placed it in four carpetbags, and silently trudged home through the wet night. It was the first of Otis Skinner's professional heartbreaks.

The flop of his initial venture didn't in the least dampen his theatrical ardor. Resigning from the commission house, he got a job as Hartford correspondent for the *New York Dramatic News,* and for a few months reveled in a delirious orgy of theatre-going, an aisle seat at no cost and a chance to see the leading itinerant stars. The weekly items he had to send in to the periodical were good practice for the books he wrote in later life: *Footlights and Spotlights, Mad Folk of the Theatre,* and *The Last Tragedian.*

For almost a year he had kept his ambitions secret. To tell his parents that he intended to become an actor he felt would be the equivalent of announcing the fact that he was about to take up horse-thieving. But the call of the theatre became irresistible and he decided to tell his father. It took him almost a month to do it. He had a clear picture of his father's outraged denunciation and his mother's reproachful tears. He saw himself leaving home, his youth blighted by a parent's curse, his picture, if there were one, turned to the wall. He chose a Friday for the critical interview, for no particular reason except that Friday seemed more baleful, taking first the precaution of packing a trunk so that if immediate banishment were to take place, he'd at least have something to wear in exile.

He chose the hour in which his father was usually engrossed in preparation of next Sunday's sermon. It was hardly the time for announcing a career, even that of a clergyman, but Otis was going to do things up in fine Byronic style. He flung open the door of the sanctum without knocking, in itself an unheard-of act of desecration. Once inside, he stood for a moment speechless and panting, his hands on the knob ready for a quick getaway. The Reverend Skinner looked up from his writing in quiet surprise, gazed over the gold rims of his spectacles at the wild aspect of his offspring, and said, "Yes, Otis?"

"Father," gasped the youth in the voice of Childe Harold, "I'm going to be an *actor!*"

"What was that?" asked the preacher.

"I'm going on the stage!"

During the ensuing pause, Otis braced himself for an Homeric blow-up. His father, however, merely smiled for a space of silent amusement, then cleared his throat and said in a mild tone, "Well, son, that's quite interesting. I'm very fond of the theatre and it will be nice having someone in the family who can get free seats for your mother and myself. But suppose we discuss it later. I have, as you are doubtless aware, a sermon to write."

His mother's reaction to the news was even more baffling. He had counted on her for sympathetic encouragement and, to his wounded amazement, she burst into peals of derisive laughter.

"You an actor!" she howled. "Why, you can't even talk straight!" It was the only instance he could ever recall of her exhibiting any lack of feeling. It was as if, unaccountably, she had slapped his face. But it made him determined to "show her."

He began writing letters to managers and agents making known the fact that he was ambitious, talented, and available. He answered advertisements in the *Clipper* calling for "gifted young persons who were good dressers on and off the stage," but received no replies except from the producer of a traveling "Tom" show who offered him a walk-on part provided he could "double in brass" in the street parade. He saved up enough money to pay for a heart-breaking trip to New York, where, hat in hand, he cooled his heels in managerial outer rooms, never seeing anyone more important than the office boy. Finally, miraculously, came an offer from one William Davidge, actor-manager of the Philadelphia Museum. He agreed to engage the professional services of Mr. O. A. Skinner in general-utility parts for the season of 1877–78, salary to be seven dollars a week.

The season started in the fall and there was the whole summer to be lived through, with difficulty. The lad studied most of the standard classical parts, none of which, of course, came under the heading of "general utility." But one could never tell when a star might fall ill, or, better still, die of a sudden heart attack, and there would be young Roscius on hand, up in the lines and ready to step into the stellar buskin. His contract, like all of them in those pre-Equity days, called for his furnishing his own wardrobe and he collected what he could of an array of costumes, acquired a few second-hand and very ill-fitting wigs, and purchased enough greasepaint to make up a battalion.

There was the question as to whether or not he'd adopt a stage name. Certainly his own had hardly the romantic lilt of a Dion Boucicault (unless, of course, one happened to know that "Dion," in the case of that beguiling Irishman, was short for "Dionysius"). An agent whom he had interviewed on his fruitless trip to New York had glanced at his cheaply printed visiting card and exclaimed, "Good God, young fellow! You've *got* to be a success with a name like that! Don't know of a funnier sounding one than Skinner, except maybe Otis." The callow aspirant agreed with him, but something in him, perhaps sheer New England mulishness, balked at summarily casting off the hideous and homely title of his forebears. During the early years of his professional life, he had himself billed simply as O. A. Skinner—the A. standing for Augustus which, too, was distressing. After a time, he dropped the A. and became simply Otis Skinner, and when he had brought eventual distinction to that name it ceased to sound so funny.

The summer weeks went by and there was no word from Davidge. The "general-utility" man grew restive and worried. His father, of all people, gave him a slight boost by suggesting that he put him in touch with a certain acquaintance and former parishioner who might have connections in—and the Reverend Skinner made a wry face—"show business." Connections he had indeed and his show was the greatest one on earth, for the parishioner was P. T. Barnum. The fabulous impresario and wizard of the humbug was an enthusiastic member of the church, and in a lively little tract called "Why I am a Universalist," he states with disarming candor, "The Universalist Church is the only one that believes in success." The Reverend Skinner gave his son a letter of introduction and Otis journeyed to Bridgeport and walked from the station to "Waldmere." The amazing entrepreneur, although living in semi-retirement, believed in maintaining the standard of advertising that had made him and his shows famous. As he walked past the outer fields of the Barnum estate, Otis was startled to see a man wearing a turban guiding a plow which was being serenely pulled by an elephant—an act put on daily at the hour the greatest number of trains were passing along the New Haven tracks which bordered the showman's property. Otis trudged up the driveway, past cast-iron fountains and green-painted statues, and on to the wooden Gothic palace before which stood a flagpole topped by a fluttering pennant bearing the initials

"P. T. B." showing, like the pennant over Buckingham Palace, that the owner was in residence. The interior of the mansion was like one of the great man's own sideshow museums. The halls were cluttered with trophy cases, the walls covered with shields, javelins, and "things." Otis looked about him apprehensively, half expecting to bump into the Zebrian Spotted Woman, the Fiji Mermaid, or some of the more educated performing fleas.

Barnum received him with the cordiality of an heroic barker, his hair, white by now, gleamed above a genially florid face. Years of eating and drinking on a scale commensurate with his characteristic lavishness had given him a monumental paunch. The prospective actor stared at him as he had at the other exhibits and exclaimed to himself, "What a make-up for Falstaff!" Barnum asked him to be seated and listened indulgently to his story. Then he rose, went to an ebony desk (a gift, he said casually, from the Maharajah of Somewhere), picked up a mother-of-pearl pen, dipped it into an inkwell—a fantasy fashioned out of a rhino's horn—and wrote, on a sheet of paper with the widest mourning band in all the history of stationery, the following:

> TO WHOM IT MAY CONCERN:
>
> The bearer, O. A. Skinner, esq. is known to me. His parents whom I have known in Hartford Conn, for several years are eminently respectable. Mr. Skinner has an ambition, a talent and a *yearning* for the stage. I have no doubt that he will prove an important acquisition to any theatrical corps which he may join.
>
> P. T. BARNUM

Armed with the letter and new hopes, Otis hastened back to Hartford. Still no word from Davidge, and it was already October. He decided to go to Philadelphia, anyway, and take a chance. He packed his small zinc-covered trunk with his few personal clothes and the motley "wardrobe." His mother helped him, stowing amid his belongings an assortment of books she thought might come in handy . . . Emerson's *Conduct of Life,* the poetical works of Sir Walter Scott, and Otis's school-prize sets of Horatio Alger and Oliver Optic. The family saw him off at the station. He gave his father a manly handshake, young Will a playful cuff, and his mother a brief but very clutching hug. Then he boarded the stuffy wooden coach and set forth for Philadelphia, the theatre, and LIFE. He was exactly nineteen years old.

CHAPTER FOUR

Early Struggles

MY FATHER reached Philadelphia, hurried to the somewhat shabby little theatre at Ninth and Arch Street, and inquired the way to Davidge's office. He was directed up a flight of rickety stairs and waved through a door which gave onto a scene of industry, confusion, and general pandemonium, in the center of which sat Davidge at a huge, cluttered desk, doing a great many things at once. With one hand he was signing a pile of contracts, with the other he alternately thumbed the pages of a manuscript or pawed over some fresh playbills. Now and then he took time out for a pull on a chewed-up cigar or a frantic ping on a bell to summon a harassed messenger boy. All too soon Otis was to learn that this was purely an act. Davidge was anything but the important impresario he pretended to be. He wasn't even a moderately successful one, and the fortunes of his theatre were precarious. He called it "The Philadelphia Museum," aping the Boston one even to the extent of having an exhibition hall of pickled reptiles and some gaudy waxworks, only instead of "The Drunkard's Progress," there was an horrendous replica of "The Last Supper" in which life-sized apostles with staring glass eyes were making merry at a festive meal of onions. The Museum failed to catch on with the Philadelphia public. They spoke derisively of "Davidge's Snake Shop," and attendance at performances was poor. However, on this first encounter with the fourflushing manager, the young tyro was completely taken in. Nervously clutching his hat he walked over to the paper-strewn desk, and shyly mentioned his name and the fact that he understood there was a job waiting for him. Davidge looked up, shook hands with hollow cordiality, and began stalling. It was obvious he had no memory of having written to the boy. The season had started, he explained, he was sorry, but all the positions had been filled. It was too bad, but such was the luck of the game. Perhaps there'd be an opening next fall. And he turned his attention to a script. Otis was discouraged but determined. He produced the Barnum letter. Davidge glanced at the signature, his jaw dropped for a few stunned seconds, then he hawed and said that on second thought there just might be something for him if he'd come back later in the day. He did and Davidge greeted him with a contract and a hearty "Found a place for you, my lad. You open October 30 in *Woodleigh*—part of Jim, an elderly Negro."

The first move was to find living quarters. The salary of seven dollars a week would hardly procure him a suite at the Continental. The theatre was in a neighborhood which came under the heading of questionable, and in an adjoining quarter, in regard to whose character there wasn't even a question, he was able to lease a dingy garret bedroom for the price of a dollar-fifty a week. His landlady was a kindly soul and her house, though dilapidated, was at least respectable. The houses on either side, however, were anything but, and many evenings the bedizened inhabitants peering through grubby lace curtains at the handsome young man striding by would call out invitations or even occasionally toss down a latchkey. It was just as well his family didn't know. His mother wrote him the first week warning him to

> . . . keep good company and keep free from vices to which you will be constantly tempted. I hope you are not one of those that smoke. I don't want you to lose that gold watch on your 21st birthday. As for liquor, shun it as you would sin for it will lead to *every* sin and it would break my heart to have your young life darkened by one false step now. I expect you will continue to make me a proud and happy mother as you always have. I wish you would join one of our congregations in Philadelphia and attend church and get to know the people. They would take an interest in you for your father's sake and for your own too.

Had she but known it, a repertory theatre was a far greater safeguard against vice than church-going. There was time for nothing but work. The house presented two performances daily and the bill was changed every week. In addition to this, on Wednesday and Saturday matinées, known for some reason as "off" ones, a different show of short drama and farce was put on. Rehearsals were squeezed in between times and line-learning was God knew when. Otis was cast in almost every show. By the end of the season he had played exactly ninety-two characters. In the programs for that year one finds his name as appearing in two plays at the matinée and another in the evening. On one double-feature bill he is down as "Solomon Probity, aged 91" in something called *The Chimney Corner,* followed by *The Domestic Drama of Luke the Laborer* in which he had the part of Gypsy Mike. While that evening in *London Jack, or the Maelstrom of Civilization,* his was the distinction of playing "Stoner, Keeper in a Private Madhouse." He appeared as young dandies and doddering Irish immigrants, and "suped" as "Velveteen Knights" or "Brocade Lords." He was even occasionally called upon to fill in as character women . . . old hags or darky comedy wenches, and in the program of *1,000 Milliners Wanted* he is down as both Tom Tipton, a Blade, and Miss Smithers, an Old Maid.

It was grueling work calling for incessant study and scant sleep. What time he was not acting or rehearsing he spent memorizing lines as best he could. He carried with him wherever he went tattered copies of the plays, muttering aloud as he walked along the street, mumbling into the ten-cent stew, coffee, and doughnuts of the shabby restaurants where he snatched his meals. Often as not he was handed, after Saturday night's final curtain, three parts to be got by the rising curtain of Monday's matinée. He paced the floor of his draughty room, a wet towel binding his throbbing temples, his mind a wild jumble of meaningless speeches, and his heart thumping in frenzied dread that he'd never get through. Somehow he always did. He learned how to ad lib, and he caught onto the old stock-company trick of "winging," propping pages of the scene on a handy projection of scenery in the wings where they could be consulted at moments of mental blank. Once when he played a British admiral conducting a court-martial, he never bothered to memorize the part, for he found he could place it in a large ledger on the table before him and read it with effective authority while his thoughts were occupied with the words of the ensuing performance.

There was no time for analysis of a part and any arty concern in regard to aesthetic values would have been considered demented. The objective was to be "up in the lines" by curtain time, then go on and act, getting by somehow, floundering, resorting to tricks, faking, but *acting*. It was slap-bang if you like, and it bore as little relation to fine theatre as the rapidly dashed-off items of an overworked cub reporter bear to fine literature. But it was an experience which formed the basis of a technique that was to carry this young beginner through half a century of distinction. Of that first year he wrote in his memoirs:

> What a school it was! I learned my art crudely, roughly, but by leaps and bounds, driven by necessity to an intuitive grasp of character and the way to express it. To sing; to dance; to fence with foil and broadsword; to kneel; to fall in combat; to work up the crescendo movement of a scene; to sit or to rise; to play fair in a give-and-take episode with a fellow-player; to learn how to make up, and, above all, to do nothing.

His costuming, which he had to arrange himself, was often as makeshift as his more slipshod performances. The scanty wardrobe he'd brought from Hartford had to be augmented with all manner of accessories for which he hadn't the price. His mother helped out by lovingly crotcheting for him her own New England version of Louis XIV lace ruffles and "falls." Modern collars and boiled shirt fronts he himself fashioned out of shelf paper. The tights problem he solved by sewing women's extra long cotton stockings onto the seat of a union suit and dyeing the ensemble the correctly blushing color for conventional "fleshings," a flight of ingenuity which worked well enough until one evening when the stitches burst and amid the howls of audience and cast he had to rush from the stage in a state of chagrin and exposure.

The plays given that season at the theatre on Ninth and Arch Streets would hardly qualify as required reading for the drama student. Except for a rare performance of *Julius Caesar, Much Ado,* or the *School for Scandal,* the classics were not given. Standard tear-jerkers were periodically presented, *Ten Nights in a Barroom* and *East Lynne, Uncle Tom's Cabin* (in which that venerable rôle was in the nineteen-year-old hands of O. A. Skinner), and *The Two Orphans* were done several times, their authorship in every instance being credited to various playwrights. This was because managers and actors had the happily casual fashion of making their own versions. Sometimes the original script was presented under a wholly new title. Whatever copyright laws existed, they were never enforced and plagiarism was as widespread as bootlegging during Prohibition. Anyone could get away with producing a play if he had seen it often enough to memorize the lines or take them down in shorthand. But it was not often necessary to go to that much trouble, for most plays were available in cheap paper editions. Some of the leading itinerant stars, however, went to great lengths to protect their most popular vehicles by means of the "skeleton script." This was a version of the piece complete except for the lines of the principal character whose every speech with the exception of the cue words would be left blank. Much of the "business," especially such movements and effects as the star liked to keep as his own personal prerogative, would also be carefully deleted. This code affair would be sent ahead to the stock company for which the show was booked so that the local cast, though considerably in the dark as to what the play was all about, could be up in its lines. The star seldom put in an appearance before the morning of the opening performance. There would be a quick run-through for lines and places, followed by a patchy dress rehearsal, and that evening the show, as such, would go on. Even so great a luminary as Edwin Booth resorted to the use of "skeleton" scripts. He, however, also sent ahead someone to rehearse each company. This helped only to a limited extent, for apparently when it came to positions and crossings, even the distinguished tragedian was unpredictable. During a subsequent season in another stock company when young Skinner was to play Laertes to his famous Hamlet, he asked the advance director where, during a certain scene, he was to stand. "Oh, any place," was the cavalier reply. "But don't worry, Mr. Booth will find you."

The season at the Museum, while rewarding in experience, as far as pay was concerned was anything but. The stipulated weekly salary of seven dollars was rarely forthcoming and the novice was too shy to ask for it. He was also too proud to write home for funds. The fact that his mother had ridiculed the idea of his ever being an actor still rankled. My father said it was especially hard to steel himself to the homesickness which welled up in him when he read the letters she wrote, asking him to come home, at least for Christmas, luring him with detailed accounts of her mince pies, piccalilly, and johnnycake; begging him to give up this notion of a stage career, offering by way of sublimation some chances to give elocution recitals in near-by towns under the patronage of his father's affiliated clergy. Plugging his ears to such siren songs, he pinched and scraped. His good looks and charm had already softened the heart of his landlady, who let him skip the dollar-fifty-a-week rent of his grubbly little room, and Herr Liszt, the good-hearted proprietor of a German *bierstübe*, occasionally gave him free lager and threw in a sandwich of pumpernickel and *schweitzerkäse*. But such blessings were sparsely intermittent. His frantic schedule called for sturdy sustenance and the third-rate Eat Houses he patronized knew no such word as credit. Recalling that lean season in later years, he used to say that he ate his books. Reluctantly he'd tie up a bundle of the treasured volumes he had brought from home in the zinc-covered trunk, take them over to Leary's second-hand store, and dolefully exchange them for enough to tide him over until the next pinch. Eventually he ran out of books and there was nothing for it but to go brave Davidge in his lair. That breezy mountebank received him and instantly put on his act of the choicest ham. He cajoled, he enlarged upon the benefits the youth was deriving under his aegis, he confided in him his own financial difficulties, showed him a letter from the gas company threatening to cut off his footlights. Otis was polite but insistent. Then Davidge, with a mock-turtle expression of woe, grabbed up the framed photograph of his wife and children and asked his young employee if his heart was so black as to snatch the food out of the mouths of his pretty chickens and their dam. Otis, whose own need for food was so acute he would have accepted it even from so unpalatable a source, said he was sorry about his heart being black but he guessed it was. Davidge with the air of a proud but condemned man produced his wallet and doled him out a few dollars. Thus, warmed by his own magnanimity, his spirits shifted to a mood of genial elation.

"My boy"—and he thwacked him pompously on the shoulder—"in a couple of weeks I'll have a great part for you. In fact, I'm going to give you top billing with the visiting stars!" The part, it turned out, was great according to how you looked at it. The visiting stars were the Frayne Family, a troupe of expert sharpshooters in a vehicle called *Si Slocum, Hero of the Old Southwest*. The climactic piece of resistance was when Frank Frayne as the old Southwestern hero, with back turned, rifle held over one shoulder, and taking aim in a mirror, shot a clay pipe out of the mouth of a Mexican peon, for reasons of plot never quite clearly explained. Otis was cast as the peon. Wearing an immense sombrero pulled down almost to his chin, the pipestem stuck through a hole in the brim and secured between his clacking teeth, he stood in a pose as casual as possible under the circumstances, while, at a distance of ten paces, the celebrated shot drew and fired a bullet which shattered the pipe bowl and a fair number of young Skinner's nerves. The first and second performances went well enough. The fact that he had attained feature billing anaesthetized the young player to the hair-raising possibilities attendant on this moment of acting. Then gradually he stopped acting and began to think, and the pipe, in turn, began to do the acting. By the end of the week it took Frayne three and even four shots to hit the wildly jiggling target. Maybe the young man's terror had in it somewhat of premonition. Frayne, a few seasons later, in a similar act, accidentally killed the woman he was about to marry. Otis read the newspaper account in a cold trance.

Davidge's fortunes went from bad to worse, and in April he closed his theatre twenty-four hours before the sheriff would have done it for him. Otis, still woefully short of cash, picked up a four weeks' engagement at the Chestnut Street Theatre with a short-lived but excellent company. It was a lucky break. He had his first opportunity to play respectable parts with good actors, his salary was enough to keep body and soul not only together but even plumped up a bit, and best of all, his performance of Malcolm in *Macbeth* caught the eye of George K. Goodwin, manager of the Walnut Street Theatre. He went home for the summer, tired but happy. In his breast pocket was a contract for the following season of 1878–79.

Next to the distinguished repertory company over which Mrs. Drew reigned in Arch Street, the Walnut Street was Philadelphia's leading playhouse and the season was a luminous one. Otis Skinner was again engaged for "general utility," a category of parts as catholic as that of the preceding season, only here the calibre of plays and actors was much higher. He was called upon for everything from doubling as both Sextus and Lucius in *Coriolanus* to appearing as what Joseph Jefferson used to call "the dreadful character of *Omnes*." In Chanfrau's production of *The Arkansas Traveler* he took to skirts as an ancient crone, and when Madame

Janauchek trailed her gloomy draperies in a heavily German interpretation of *The Duchess of Malfi*, he was cast as a "Groan of the Dying."

Otis acquitted himself well that season. The Philadelphia critics began to notice him and even his family took less of a derisive attitude. One of his performances was written up in *The Christian Leader*, a source of joyous consolation to his mother. "I have not been so happy," she wrote, "since I had my first pocket in my dress!"

In the spring he played a week's engagement at the Arch Street Theatre under the magnificent dictatorship of Mrs. John Drew. That grand old martinet—"The Duchess" as she was called, well behind her back—wound up her every season with a week of old English comedies: six different plays in six consecutive days, all acted by the same cast who well-nigh broke under the strain of memorizing and keeping hold of their lines and positions. Her leading man did break and bolted after the first performance. Nothing daunted, the indomitable lady snatched her son John Drew off the road from a tour of *Diplomacy*. He arrived home at four in the morning to be met by his mother looking as if she were doing the Sleepwalking Scene. In one hand she held a night lamp, in the other a prompt book which she gave him along with a perfunctory kiss and the bland announcement, "Don't go to bed, John. You open in this tonight." Otis's lot was a series of eighteenth-century beaux, curly, fluttering imbeciles whose flowery capers he took small pleasure in performing. The week passed in a jumble of wigs, swords, lace handkerchiefs, and patched-up lines. The greatest reward of that engagement was the fact that it started his lifelong friendship with that brilliant actor and excellent gentleman, John Drew.

His Philadelphia experience had been a rich one. It was the end of an epoch in the theatre. The local star-supporting stock company was passing out of existence.

> I am glad [my father wrote] that I was able to be in at the death before the old system quite passed away; glad that my novitiate was one of hard knocks that compelled me to swallow my technique in great gulps; glad that in two years I had had to play over one hundred and forty parts; glad of that compulsion of quick study and performance which renders the body supple and the mind obedient; and glad that my dramatic kindergarten was placed among men and women filled with the knowledge of their trade. The Lord keep their memories green! They possessed distinction and they respected the King's English!

Taking in hand his courage and the few dollars he had managed to save, he set out to try his luck in New York, and for at least three months he wore out shoe leather along Broadway, tasting to the dregs the actor's cup of humiliation, the pride-withering agony of waiting day after day, hat in hand, in the bleak outer hallways of theatrical agencies, trying to hide the look of eager expectancy when some office boy emerges through a door marked "Private," assuming an unconvincing expression of haughty indifference on hearing the terse, inevitable, "Sorry, nothing doing today." Fortunately, Otis could bunk over in Brooklyn with his brother, but he had to eat, and Charlie's pay was not sufficient to feed them both. The young man limited himself to two far from square meals a day, makeshift snacks in cellars, "free and easies," or Bowery concert saloons where for ten cents one could get a Western sandwich, a stein of ale, and a chance to lose one's shirt at three-card monte. Week followed week and he still had no prospects. He stubbornly resisted writing home for funds, but it began to look more and more as though he might have after all to throw up the sponge and return to Hartford and a career of clergy-sponsored elocution recitals. At the depth of his despondency he stayed out an entire night, wandering about the great indifferent city, mingling with the strange creatures who prowl through its darkness—ancient charwomen emerging from office buildings, forlorn prostitutes haunting the whiskey wards, lean, mangy cats side by side with bleary bums pawing over the contents of refuse cans. His solitary course led him along the wharves and he walked under the outjutting bows of sailing vessels. The night wind soughed in their rigging, and the anchor lights in their forestays blinked at him like baleful eyes. The air smelled of tar and stale fish and sewage and despair. Suddenly he remembered it was his birthday. He was twenty-one! And what had he to show for himself? His name in the cast list of a number of stock-company programs, and that notice in *The Christian Leader*. The water of the East River looked thick and black and, in his Werther-like mood, he understood why people might want to find oblivion in it. But just then the gray of morning started washing the buildings of their shadows, a soiled sparrow chirped, and a shaft of sunlight struck the gleaming new cobweb of the Brooklyn Bridge. Our Hero decided that instead of effecting his own untimely demise he'd go touch Charlie for some ham and eggs. Charlie was out on an assignment, but, better than ham and eggs, he found awaiting him a notice from an agent. The Kiralfy Brothers had chosen him for their new extravaganza and he was to report the following morning for rehearsal.

Bolossy and Imre Kiralfy had begun their career in Hungary as dancers and gymnasts. Coming to America they went in for producing, at which risky game they had sufficient knack to become enormously successful. Harbingers of Billy Rose, their shows were lavish spectacles, containing a little bit of everything—ballet, singing, melodrama, clowning, and just as much sex as the law and pink tights would allow. This season they had taken over that palace of beauty and red plush, Niblo's Gardens, around which there clung a faint odor of refined brimstone owing to the fact that for many years it housed that sinful and hardy perennial, *The Black Crook.* They were to open with *Enchantment,* a large-scale musical extravaganza complete with melodrama plot, trapeze and flying-ring performers, a "Grand Ballet in the corridors of Babylon," and a sextette of ocarinas. Otis was cast as Maclow, the Beggar of the Mountain. It was a showy part calling for the additional fun of a weird "character" make-up: beetling eyebrows, scraggly whiskers, and a sinister hooked nose which he fashioned out of putty. He had to be killed in the last act, his demise being effected by the simple device of a magician seizing and hurling him over a cliff, after which, instead of expiring instantly, he was to stagger onto the stage and deliver his own death oration. The cliff was twelve feet in height and the Kiralfys told him they would of course see to it that a dummy would be flung over the declivity and he could then go on for his big speech. But in his youth and artistic zeal he protested no, indeed, a dummy would spoil the effect, and he would make the leap himself. The opening night came around and the cliff seemed suddenly to take on the dimensions of the Ausable Chasm. The qualms that assailed him were not soothed by the property man who came up to him with the expression of a chaplain confronting a condemned man and said, "Young feller, just before you do that jump, it may not do any good, but it wouldn't do no harm if you was to say a little prayer." The scene went on and the moment came for the leap. Remembering the ominous advice of the property man, he muttered a sound which started as a whispered prayer and turned in transit into a wild yelp. Two thicknesses of mattress softened his fall, but terror had made him tense and he landed with his knees stiff, in a jolt which all but telescoped him. He staggered to his feet and made his way around a cloth rock and onto the stage, dizzy, shattered, and trying to summon breath for his big speech. Something struck his hand, something clammy, furry, and quite awful. He glanced down and discovered he was clutching his putty nose which, with the whiskers and a portion of the eyebrows still adhering to it, had ripped loose, clearing a path of boyish pink from forehead to chin and leaving him looking like a peeled rabbit. Frantically he whirled around and clamped the thing onto his face again. The disaster had unnerved him and in a panic lest his make-up drop off again, he played the remainder of the scene with his back to the audience, addressing his lines to the cyclorama. It was just as well he did. In his confusion he had stuck his nose on upside down.

Enchantment was a hit and had a long run. The One Hundredth Performance was celebrated as a gala; flowers were presented to every lady in the audience and the programs were printed on satin, of a lurid but festive shade of magenta. The season wound up with a revival of *The Black Crook.* It had been over a decade since that "bewildering forest of female legs" had first horrified and delighted the New York public, inspiring Richard Grant White to describe Pauline Markham as "the woman who has found the lost arms of the Venus de Milo," while James Gordon Bennett denounced the production in the *Herald,* saying, ". . . Nothing in any other Christian country has approached this indecent and demoralizing exhibition. . . . There might have been in Sodom and Gomorrah such a spectacle on the Broadway of these doomed cities just before fire and brimstone rained down upon them." The shock factor had worn off by now, but the piece was good for a yearly revival. My father in his memoirs says little about the production, but to the ladies of the ballet and ensemble, those shimmering nymphs and substantially upholstered amazons, he tosses a bouquet of respectability. They were, it seems, hard-working and rather dull paragons of quiet behavior and theatrical domesticity. Their backstage life was a round of mending and pressing their own costumes, darning the slightly dowdy tights Mr. Bennett had found so evil, and cooking drab little meals over the make-up gas jets of the chorus room. A picture as commendable as it is disappointing.

Otis Skinner's next serious engagement was with Lawrence Barrett. Three years in his touring company, and Otis had his first taste of what, for all its hardships and heartaches, he was to love all his life—The Road. Barrett, who had a country-wide following, played everywhere. Big cities, small cities, fashionable communities, and tank towns. They appeared in every variety of auditorium: smart theatres and shabby "opry houses," fair grounds and lodge halls . . . theatres in metropolitan centres, theatres in lonely prairies, theatres on the sides of mountains, and theatres on pleasure piers jutting out into the ocean. The Chicago he saw was the Chicago of the Gold Coast. New Orleans was still the city of the French Opera, Voodoo dances in Congo Square, and fiery young creoles settling accounts under the Duelling Oaks. Leadville was a set for a "western," its streets a blear of saloons and faro houses, as was Marshall, Texas, where only a few years earlier a drunken sheriff had wounded Maurice Barrymore and killed one of his fellow players. It was rough experience, and at the close of the third year the young actor felt he rated a few seasons on Broadway. When he was offered a contract with Daly, he felt his dreams had come true.

CHAPTER FIVE

Daly's

DALY'S! It's a name to summon up a period, like Delmonico's, Lily Langtry, Saratoga, and Ward McAllister. In 1885, Augustin Daly and his gifted players were at a height of popularity never equaled by any other dramatic corps in the country. Daly's theatre was *the* thing. It was referred to as the American Comédie Française. It had style, it had elegance, it had—to use a much too common word for an all too uncommon quality—glamour. Opening nights were like brilliant receptions which no smart New Yorker would miss. Chauncey Depew, Mark Twain, Stanford White, General Sherman, Thomas Bailey Aldrich, the painter Abbey, crowded in along with the *beau monde* who arrived in ermine stoles and pearl studs, while Daly himself stood by the ticket box to greet his friends.

Daly, however, was the only member of his smart establishment who ever came in contact with the audience. He would never have allowed his actors to do so. Augustin Daly was a dictator and his word was rigid law. His actors were not permitted to be seen in the front of the house, even if they were not in the current bill. He forbade them to walk along

Broadway by daylight and raised his own particular Irish hell if any of them were seen at public gatherings without his permission. For a player to be so indiscreet as to give out a personal interview to a reporter, or even to speak to a newspaper man, meant instant dismissal. Actors, he claimed, as far as the public was concerned, should be part of the illusion of the theatre. Meet them as ordinary flesh-and-blood men and women, and the magic is gone. There is much to be said for the theory. But Daly carried his dictatorship to strict lengths.

> If I were to tell you [wrote the critic Alan Dale] of the severity of the labor imposed by Mr. Daly upon his people, your hair would stand on end. He owns their souls and bodies. Not only does he undertake to regulate their conduct while in his theatre, but he permits his rules to haunt them when they have shaken the dust of his house from their feet. When they are tucked up in their little beds at night, he likes them to remember that they are still members of Daly's Theatre.

His backstage discipline was of almost military rigidness. All visitors were barred. An actor was not permitted to watch scenes in which he had no participation or to wander about the stage behind the set, or to stand in the wings except for the few seconds prior to an entrance. "Places" were announced by the callboy, and being late for a cue meant a five-dollar fine. Once during a certain performance Daly, as the all-powerful exception proving his own rule regarding visitors in dressing rooms, was regaling Ada Rehan in hers with a long-winded story. The callboy knocked for the lady's cue and neither of them heard him. Daly went on with his narrative and the callboy knocked a second time. Again Daly's voice drowned out the sound. The third rap, however, was loud and insistent. Rehan with a gasp of terror leaped to her feet and fled onto the stage breathless and late for her entrance. Daly's laughter over his own story was still clearly audible. Next day, he sent her notice of a five-dollar fine.

Daly was a genius, not creative but clever. He knew the secret of catering to public taste. He knew also how to select the right sort of actor. Of that brilliant corps there was not a weak member. Opposite Ada Rehan, who was in the full bloom of her career, was the young matinée idol John Drew, suave, polished, entertaining, the best-dressed man in New York. Mrs. Gilbert, one of those grand old ladies of the theatre, was lively as a grig in the character parts in which she sparred with Charles Leclerq or James Lewis. For young feminine rôles—care, of course, being taken that they'd never in any way compete with Rehan—there were Virginia Dreher and Edith Kingdon, the future Mrs. George Gould. Daly had snatched May Irwin out of Tony Pastor's for broad comedy bits, and for ingénue, he had discovered a slip of a girl, all delicacy and elfin loveliness, who must have been the dream Titania of all time—Effie Shannon. Even the name of the callboy is not one to pass lightly over; the programs have it down as Master William Collier. In addition to this excellent roster, Daly was shrewd enough to take on a number of stagestruck society girls—"Daly's Débutantes" they were called. He was further shrewd enough to cast them only in small actor-proof parts. As assets their sole value lay in luring members of the Four Hundred to opening nights.

For a period when the standard of elegance was the folding bed and Japanese fans tacked bat-wise on walls papered in embossed gold, the décors of Daly's productions were in remarkably good taste. The scenery was always fresh, the props smartly correct, and the women's gowns were the talk of the town. Daly himself supervised every fitting, just as he supervised each detail of everything that went on in his playhouse. As a worker he was tireless. He demanded similar industry from his people. There being no road try-outs, a play, before it opened, had to be perfect—and it was. He worked his people mercilessly, often rehearsing them from ten in the morning till long after midnight. He drove them to a point when, the challenge of the opening night confronting them, they had the hysterical energy of exhausted troops whipped into forced action. It always worked.

In his choice of plays, he put on what he knew would take with a public that was fed up with heavy classics and run-of-the-mill melodramas. The only classics he risked were easily digested comedies: *The School for Scandal, The Recruiting Officer, Midsummer Night's Dream,* and *The Taming of the Shrew.* His popular specialties were the adaptations he himself made from certain German drawing-room farces which were the current rage in Europe. Purified versions of the products of the Palais Royale, they were gay, inconsequential, and fairly absurd: *Nancy and Co., Love on Crutches,* and *A Night Off*—this last an admirable evasion of the original title which was *Der Raub der Sabinerinnen.* It does not do to read them now.

Daly had a complex character. For all his brilliance and a charm which, when he cared to, he could turn on as easily as a spigot, he had a side which was arrogant, vicious, and petty. He had a bad temper and the dictator's sense of inferiority which made him quick to take offense and slow to relinquish a grudge. He could not brook adverse criticism. With the exception of the *Tribune* (of which William Winter was critic), there was not a New York paper which at some time had not lost his ad on account of some comment he considered slighting. He was an egocentric and everything connected in any way with his theatre he regarded as his personal property. That went for the company too.

Ada Rehan, besides being leading lady, enjoyed the offstage rôle of *grande maîtresse*—although *enjoyed* is a debatable word. For she could not have derived much happiness from the relationship. Daly had a wife. He was a strict Catholic. But even if he had been free, it is doubtful if he would have considered marrying Rehan. To hold the whip handle by keeping a woman of her beauty and prominence in the compromising position an extra-marital liaison involved in those cautious times was a sop to his will to power. It gave him a feeling of prestige. What is more, Daly would never have chosen Rehan for the part if she had not been successful. He loved her the way he loved all costly possessions and he kept her as such. He had seen her first in Mrs. Drew's Philadelphia company and his appraising eye was quick to discern the spark of genius behind her Irish beauty and captivating mannerisms. Deciding she was something he wanted, he had snatched her away and established her in his theatre, where he set about making her over, deliberately destroying her happy-go-lucky spirit, turning her into a conventional *fin-de-siècle* woman of the world—poised, highstrung, witty, and neurotic. Daly became her Svengali. She was helpless without his minutest detail of direction. He showed her everything from the stride of her blazing entrance as the Shrew, to the crooking of her little finger over a teacup in a modern scene with John Drew. He treated her very much as his personal chattel. If they appeared together on the street, Daly walked ahead of her, like an Indian, never speaking to her. Offstage she lived alone, on his insistence. She had no friends, again on his insistence. Any private life she might have enjoyed was sacrificed to the ambition Daly implanted, forced, and nurtured in her. W. Graham Robertson, who knew her in London, says of her:

> . . . bewitching, elusive, irritating, amazing Ada Rehan! . . . Her career was a mystery which to me admits of but one explanation. Daly must have been a great actor who could not act. He was rough and uncouth, with harsh utterance and

> uncultured accent; a singer without a voice, a musician without an instrument. But in Ada Rehan he found his means of self expression; Ada Rehan with her quaint charm and her gentle nature which he could mould to his will.

Ada Rehan was a bitter, distrustful woman and Daly was the cause. Added to the list of his bad qualities was that of being woman-crazy. Not content with the favors of his leading lady, he made a play for nearly every personable young thing he thought might be capturable in his company. Occasionally he succeeded. Rehan was jealous to a psychotic degree, and in Daly a sadistic streak, equally psychotic, prompted him to parade his conquests in front of her, driving her into hysterical rages which secretly delighted him. The side affairs were always short-lived. Having reassured himself as to his powers of seduction, he'd soon tire of the young thing, summarily inform her the adventure was over, and return to Rehan who, wounded and morose, always took him back.

Rehan was at the zenith of a brilliant career as the queen of high comedy. In the theatre, she was the goddess of laughter with a vital magnetism, the full-blown beauty of a Romney, a voice that had the loveliest of lilts and a bewitching charm. She had too that asset of the great actress—manner. Reviewers of the day call her "a figure of dazzling glee and delicious drollery," "a twenty-carat sparkler from start to finish," while William Winter, whose every mention of her gushes to the point of fatuity, writes: "It is chiefly with mirth that she touches the public heart. She can be rich and tender, wistful and delicate—but mostly she sparkles." Her art was one of vitality and endearing magnetism. The exuberant joy of her Rosalind, tearing with the abandonment of a delighted child through the Arden woods, the panther-like fury of Katharine's first entrance, the irresistible funniness of her squabbles with John Drew, completely won over her audience.

While she was in the theatre, her spirits were always high. It was as if she shed her dark moods at the stage door to enter wholeheartedly into the world of comedy, the only one in which she could, for a few hours, be happy. She was usually gay and affable with the other members of the company. Only during the spasmodic periods of Daly's infidelities would she be edgy and difficult, sulking one moment, lashing out at stage hand or actor the next. And for all her *mondaine* polish, there was still left in her much of the engaging quality of the young hoyden from Limerick. As an actress she had one failing which I find particularly endearing, having myself the same weakness to an abnormal degree. This was the tendency to "break up" during a scene. If an actor tripped, or "fluffed" a line, or even so much as winked at her, she'd go off into convulsions of mirth as uncontrollable as the giggles of a small child in church. Sometimes entire scenes would have to be changed because of her inability to get through them without going hysterically to pieces. In Tennyson's *Foresters* she, as Maid Marian, said to John Drew, who was Robin Hood, "Your horn is known and feared through the forest." One evening Drew, prompted by some zany impulse, on the word "horn," quietly covered his nose, which was a fairly prominent one, in an idiotic gesture, setting Rehan off into such fits of hilarity she had to walk off into the wings to sober up. The next night and every night as the same line approached, she'd try desperately to keep a straight face, then inevitably explode and snort through the ensuing words with shaking shoulders and streaming eyes. Daly, who failed to see what was so funny, indignantly rewrote the speech—Tennyson or no Tennyson—and gave her a thundering call-down in front of the cast.

Two members of the troupe who managed to keep their lives outside the theatre uncramped by the Daly jurisdiction were John Drew and Otis Skinner. John Drew, brilliant farceur, elegant gentleman of the drawing-room comedies, was the sought-after darling of the society ones. He was steadily in demand and could take his pick of invitations—balls, dinners, club smokers, race-track luncheons. In his case Daly never protested, partly because he had an idea it would be useless, partly because this glass-of-fashion with his wit and charm was a good advertisement, speaking well for the tone of his establishment. When, however, his new juvenile started going in for extracurricular gaiety, he resented it and said so. Skinner, while not actually telling Daly he could go to hell, politely implied as much and serenely went his own primrose way. Such independence was galling to Daly and laid the foundations for a grudge that was in time to grow to serious consequences. Otis's path was not strewn with such high-toned petals as those which enlivened his friend Drew's. He found his diversion in the strata which enjoyed thinking of itself as "Bohemian," a pleasant world of writers, painters, and fellow actors. The Lambs was the leading professional club at that time, the Players being not yet established. Augustus Thomas, recalling in his memoirs an evening at the Lambs, says:

> It was an honor, privilege and education to be received on equal terms by its then membership which included such men as Lester Wallack, Maurice Barrymore, Richard Mansfield, Nat Goodwin, Steele Mackaye and Robert C. Ingersoll. . . . Fun was spontaneous and unconstrained. At one of the dinners I made my real acquaintance with Otis Skinner. He had come in from a trip on the road, was greeted with shouts and lifted glasses, and because the place on the impromptu programme fitted it, he stood in the doorway, and answering the men's demand, recited Béranger's "When We Were Twenty-One." I shall always remember the romantic picture of that virile Moorish-looking youngster, and the sentiment with which he read "Flo, my Flo, was a coryphée."

And there was plenty of agreeable companionship at Daly's. He, James Lewis, and John Drew were inseparable in the theatre and got to be known as the Glue Brothers. Drew was the leader. A good athlete and sportsman, he organized a company baseball team—himself shortstop, Otis second base, Joseph Holland third, and Willie Collier a spectacular pitcher. Practicing avidly on a Central Park diamond, they worked up enough erratic excellence to take on local teams during the course of the annual road tour. In a glass case in the prop room was a cup commemorating their victory over the Nine of the Chicago Board of Trade.

Daly's, for all its *chic* foyer and elegant front of the house, had many backstage inconveniences, not the least of which was the fact that the dressing rooms were in another building. The stage door was on Sixth Avenue in a tenement which had been refurbished into quarters for dressing rooms. The actors had to come down a flight of stairs, pass through a long wooden corridor clumsily built across an open courtyard, and foot it over an ample portion of the wide stage before reaching their entrances. It took considerable time and one had to leave one's dressing room fully prepared to go on. There could be no last-minute dashing back for any hand prop or make-up repair. In *Love in Harness* the plot concerned a young doctor (played by Otis Skinner) who, fearful lest his pretty wife be taking him too much for granted, pretends, in order to pique her interest, to a past of a lurid shade of purple. As if sent by an eagerly collaborative fate, a fashionable young rake (John Drew, of course) drops in to call, fresh off a steamer from France, most conveniently carrying in his wallet souvenirs of his amorous conquests—a faded rose, a lock of hair, a billet-doux, and further et ceteras. These compromising items he agrees to lend the callow doctor, who leaves them where his wife will not fail to discover them, and one can, if one cares to, imagine the ensuing complications. The planting of the plot in the scene between the two young men depended obviously upon Drew bringing the hand props on with him. One evening he made his entrance to his customary orchestral flourish (Daly, who loved "sneak music," saw to it that each of his leading players went on to a special motif), received his burst of welcome, and launched blithely into his speeches. The moment came for him to produce the wallet and exhibit the mementoes. He felt in one breast pocket and froze slightly. Then he felt in the other and froze completely. His one eye which had a tendency to be slightly walled, shot off at a wild tangent and became glassy. He began to thump himself in all areas of the torso. It was all too clear he had left the wallet back in his dressing room. Skinner watched him in agonized fascination. Then Drew, in a flash of inspired improvisation, came out with, "Dash it, old chap, I must have left the blasted thing in my overcoat—just out here on the hatrack in the hall. Stay there half a mo'." And he dashed off the stage. Skinner stayed, but with Drew having to sprint over to Sixth Avenue and back, he knew it was not going to be for any half mo'. He could hear the sound of Drew's frantic footsteps hurtling off into the distance, and finally dying out completely, leaving him alone on the stage amid a silence that was very awful. He knew he'd have to fill in with something. Leering with the levity of someone who has just heard his own death sentence, he plunged into an impromptu monologue. "Well, well, well! Ha-ha-ha! Good old Geoffrey! Always the same. Ha-ha-*ha!* Upon my word! Yes, *indeed!* He doesn't change, good old Geoffrey doesn't. Not he! Ha-ha-ha!" For what seemed the length of an act of *Hamlet,* he babbled along, striding about the set, inventing meaningless bits of business, picking up objects of bric-à-brac, examining them and putting them down again with the same ghastly "ha-ha-*ha!*" Finally, from off in the dim distance, he could hear the sound of Drew wildly cantering down the wooden corridor, banging through

John Drew, Edith Kingdon, and Otis Skinner in
Love on Crutches
Photograph by Sarony

Maud Durbin as Juliet

Photograph copyright 1897 by F. W. Guerin

the inner door, pounding across the stage, stumbling over scenery braces, and finally nearing the entrance. When at long last good old Geoffrey reappeared from his trip to the hatrack in the hall, he was incapable of speech. Winded and disheveled, he stood in the doorway and for lack of some better way in which to stall for breath, put a finger to his lips, looked mysterious and emitted a long, loud "Sh-h-h-h!"

In the spring of '86 they played London to packed houses and brilliant audiences. Edward, Prince of Wales, came one evening and talked in a loud voice throughout the performance, and another evening his wife, the future Queen Alexandra, came with a young relation who was a Prince of Denmark. John Drew in a whispered *sotto voce* to Skinner speculated he must have come over from his native land in order to collect royalty dues from Henry Irving for *Hamlet*. Things went well that trip and Daly was gay and relaxed. He hired a four-in-hand and drove a group of them to Epsom to see Ormonde win the Derby. He took them all, at his expense, on a twenty-four-hour outing to Stratford, and got up rowing races on the river. The Avon swans surrounded the boat that he, Rehan, Drew, and Skinner were in and Daly became almost hysterical with pleasure. There was an old theatre superstition that swans take instinctively to good actors. "You're good actors! You're good actors!" he cried with the delight of a child, and that evening he gave them a champagne supper at the Warwick Arms.

Following London, they played Glasgow, Edinburgh, and Dublin, and even tried their luck in Germany and France, where it more or less petered out. The Berlin audiences didn't care about seeing their own comedies in translation, and the Parisians shrugged and dismissed them as "*des barbares.*" But Skinner and Drew drank Münchner at the Franziskaner, and splashed in the swimming baths along the

Seine, and felt like smart bohemians fresh out of Du Maurier.

Next season Daly put on *The Taming of the Shrew.* Certain parts, along with their creators, go down in theatrical history as inextricably joined as Siamese twins: Othello and Salvini, Hamlet and Booth, Madame Sans-Gêne and Réjane, and Katharine and Ada Rehan. Her Shrew must have been a joyous whirlwind of fire, pace, and humor. My father said of this rôle:

> Her Kate never, even in its most tempestuous moments, lost its underlying sense of humor. This gained its fullest value in the episodes of violence and extravagance in Petruchio's cottage, in her scenes with Grumio. She seemed to be saying, "It is the funniest thing in the world that I, the haughty Katharine, should be brought to this pass." I doubt if any other actress of her day or before it, ever approached her humor in the part.

To her dazzling characterization John Drew played a brilliant Petruchio. The production was lavish; the play in New York was a furore and Daly decided to risk it in England the summer of '88. It was a bold venture. There was no telling how the British would react to an American company attempting the Bard on native soil. Moreover, the play was not popular and had not been seen in London since the days of the Restoration. As a sage precaution Daly took along William Winter. The critic was well known over there and had a wide acquaintanceship among important theatre people. The local papers were only too glad to print any items he might care to send them, and those items were of course always in the nature of polite boosts for the visiting American company. Daly paid Winter's expenses and occasionally gave him a present, keeping it all on an elaborately non-business basis. The morality of a manager hiring his own private critic is for a more ethical judgment than mine to determine.

Included in the company on that trip was a new one of Daly's "débutantes." Phoebe R. was a middle-western society girl with aspirations and no particular talent for the stage. She was gay and lusciously pretty, and Daly's only palpable reason for engaging her was that she had plenty of nineteenth-century "oomph." She was out less for a career than a good time. The theatre to her was a lark and her own participation in it a considerable joke. Daly realized her limitations and gave her only bit parts. He also realized her attractions and the fact that, for all her conservative social background, the girl had a streak of agreeable wantonness. It was some time since his eye had roved. His situation with Rehan had been going too smoothly of late and was beginning to irk him. He set out to make Phoebe R. his next conquest. Rehan guessed his intentions and went into one of her periods of sullen anger. Her state of emotion was hardly eased when she boarded ship. Daly, who saw to every detail of travel for his troupe, himself allotted the cabin spaces, naming off which members were to double up and with whom, whether they liked it or not. It was his grim idea of humor to force Rehan to share her accommodation with her new rival.

Rehan was a miserable sailor. The weather was stormy and the presence of the girl didn't make her feel any better. She took to her berth and stayed there throughout the entire crossing. The girl, on the other hand, was full of annoying health and spirits. The rougher the sea, the better she felt. Moreover, she regarded "The Governor's" advances as a huge joke. The self-opinionated impresario, unused to being rebuffed in any way, was surprised and offended. He was also seasick. He passed the days in his steamer chair swathed in rugs and black thoughts, his jaundiced eye following the carefree figures of the girl, John Drew, and Otis Skinner as they rollicked about the deck. Phoebe R. had told the two in confidence all about their manager's courtship. She had also given them a hilarious and somewhat cruel account of her cabin mate. Rehan, it seemed, lay in her berth all day, holding salts to her nose, occasionally sipping a glass of warm champagne and refusing to speak to her. Sometimes she'd hear her in the late hours of the night, stifling her sobs in the pillow, and once during a terrific storm, when the toilet articles were crashing off the shelf and the trunks sliding across the floor, a ghastly head rose slowly up beside the girl's upper bunk. The famous red hair was standing out like a witch's, the face the public found so endearing was haggard and distraught, and the white bosom Sargent immortalized in pink satin was heaving beneath a dowdy flannel nightgown. She gazed malevolently at Phoebe, then in a whisper of hatred and deep despair she hissed, "You let that man alone!"

Drew and Skinner found it all highly entertaining. Between them they cooked up a plot to pay Phoebe violent court, partly to annoy Daly and partly because the girl was a toothsome morsel. The plan, in regard to Daly, worked beyond their wildest dreams. As far as young Skinner was concerned, it worked in a different way. He began to take the courtship seriously. So did Phoebe. By the time the ship reached Liverpool, the two were madly in love.

In London, Rehan nursed her jealousy. She was certain that Daly and Phoebe R. were either having or about to have an affair, and Daly let her believe it. The evening *The Shrew* was to open, everybody was edgy. There had been rumors of possible hostility from the press, and a protest in the *Times* demanded to know how a bunch of Yankees dared bring Shakespeare to England. The actors all had first-night nerves. Daly was as jumpy as a freshly decapitated rooster and even the benign William Winter strode about in a state of tense apprehension. Eight o'clock came. The theatre lights blazed and a capacity audience filed in, expectant and gala. The orchestra took their places, the leader rapped with his baton, everyone stood and God saved the Queen. Then the house settled back into its stalls to listen to the overture and glance through the program. The play would start in possibly five minutes. And at that moment, backstage, all hell broke loose. Rehan had come across a note that someone had carelessly dropped on the floor. Noticing it was in Daly's hand, she had picked it up and read, hastily scribbled in pencil: "Enclosed you will find $200. There is more where this comes from." The paper bore neither name nor address, but it was all she needed to confirm her suspicions regarding Phoebe R. With a sob of rage she gathered up the swirling red train of her first-act costume, fled to her dressing room, slammed the door, and announced she was not going on. Willie Collier, the callboy, announced "places" and she told him he could go to hell. The stage manager came around to see what was the trouble and she gave him similar instructions. The overture was nearing its finish. The stage manager sought aid from the diplomat of the company, John Drew, who braved the lioness's den. Rehan didn't tell him to go to hell, but still refused to budge. The orchestra was playing the overture a second time. Daly stormed in from the front of the house to find out what in God's name was holding the curtain. The stage manager told him as best he could and the impresario plunged into the star dressing room to be met by a yowl from Rehan who threw the note in his face, shoved him out, and bolted the door. Seeing the note, he realized what had happened. The message, far from being intended for Phoebe R., had been sent to William Winter, but since his transactions with his personal critic were of a highly confidential nature, he could hardly shout out an explanation before the entire cast. He rattled the knob, he pounded, he threatened, he stormed. Rehan continued to sulk in her tent. The audience was growing restless and the pit had started to applaud. Daly began to entreat. It was a brilliant house, he told her, there was royalty in two of the boxes; it was a crucial night for her and he prophesied that she was about to make the triumphant hit of her career. There was a pause. The bolt slid slowly back and the door opened a crack to reveal Rehan in her flaming gown, beautiful in her fury. In a low, shaking voice she said she'd go on, but on one condition. Daly cried yes, yes, anything. Very well, Rehan stipulated, he must kneel and ask her pardon. This was a preposterous demand to make of an Irish gentleman and Daly recoiled indignantly. Then he heard the sound of a whistle from the pit and the strains of the orchestra starting the overture for the third time. The showman got the better of the Irish gentleman. He sank quickly onto one knee, mumbled an apology, and reached out his hand. Rehan, smiling strangely, took it in her own, held it a moment, then suddenly stooped and bit him to the bone. Daly howled and scrambled to his feet clutching his wound. Rehan strode into the wings, Daly's blood still bright on her mouth, and in homeric tones cried out, "Ring up the curtain!"

Little Effie Shannon watched her first entrance that night. Effie was not in the bill and, in accordance with the regulations, had no right to be hanging around backstage. But Willie Collier had found her a niche behind some scenery and a peekhole where she could watch and "the Governor" would never be the wiser. The play had got off to a slow start. The audience was out of humor over the late curtain and the first few minutes went for nothing. Then came the encounter between Katharine and Bianca. The doors at the back flung open and Rehan, still shaking with passion, burst onto the stage. She had the fire and beauty of an unleashed tigress and she played as she had never played before. With superb abandonment she swept through lines and action, lashed out at Baptista, gave the trembling Bianca a vicious cuff, and with the words "I will go sit and weep till I can find occasion of revenge," which came as a scream from her own heart, she blazed off the set. For a moment the audience sat in stunned silence. Then it went wild in the sort of heroic ovation that is to be heard only in the London theatre. Young Effie Shannon, carried away by the magnificence of the moment, rushed from her hiding place, little caring whether or not she'd be discovered. Speechless with admiration and hardly knowing what she did, she ran across to Rehan, and flung her arms about her. Rehan was standing as if turned to stone. The house was still cheering, but she appeared not to hear. Daly's prophecy about it being the triumphant hit of her career had been fulfilled and meant nothing to her. She looked down into the adoring eyes of Effie Shannon and gradually became aware of her. Then her handsome face broke into a grotesque mask, haggard and distorted. She dropped her head on the girl's shoulder and, in an agony of bitter tears, moaned, "Oh Effie, Effie, I wish I were dead!"

The quarrel was straightened out, Rehan took Daly back as she always did, and that expert showman, who knew the value of a good ham act, went about for a week with his wounded hand heavily bandaged and held in a sling.

The Shrew was the hit of the London season. Sir John Hare gave the company a dinner at the Garrick Club. The guest list contains such names as Henry Irving, Sir Arthur Sullivan, Henry James, the Earl of Cork, Bret Harte, and Ambassador Phelps. Daly refused to attend. He was insulted because the invitations had been sent to the members of his company individually and had not first passed through his hands.

The troupe returned to New York. The Skinner-Phoebe R.

affair was broken off for some reason or other, but Daly, his pride still galled, made up his mind to get even with them both. My father's contract called for one more season under Daly at a weekly salary playing "such parts as the manager sees fit in which to cast him." The manager paid him the salary and saw fit to cast him in nothing the entire season except in two standard revivals which lasted no time at all. The young actor was unable to take any other employment. The pay was adequate and he lived comfortably, but his career was at a standstill. Daly had his revenge. It is characteristic of my father that he bore Daly no ill will. "My memory of him," he says, "is that of a very unusual man. He crossed my horizon at a critical hour of my career. Greater than to any one man is my debt to Augustin Daly." What happened to pretty young Phoebe R. was another story. She skipped the company, joined a second one for a brief time, then married a midwestern millionaire, and within a year committed suicide.

CHAPTER SIX

The Actor Takes a Wife

On emerging into the theatrical world after serving his term of enforced inactivity at Daly's, Otis found to his relief that as a popular *jeune premier* he was once again very much in demand. He was rapidly booked for a number of scattered engagements, the most important of which was with the Booth-Modjeska repertory company where he was employed for second leads: Macduff, Laertes, Bassanio, Mortimer in *Mary Stuart*, and De Mauprat in *Richelieu*. Edwin Booth by now was a broken man. The accumulation of personal tribulation that had dogged his life—his father's insanity, his brother Wilkes's crime that had shaken the nation, the death of his first wife Mary Devlin whom he worshiped and to whose deathbed he had failed to come because he'd been so befuddled with drink he'd not understood the telegram until it was too late, his miserable existence with his second wife, Mary McVicker, a psychopathic—all this had taken a toll of his sensitive endurance. His manner was gentle, kindly, and courteous as ever, but his outlook was one of quiet despair.

> All my life [he wrote to William Winter] has been passed on a "picket duty," as it were. I have been on guard, on the lookout for disasters—for which, when they come, I am prepared. Therefore I have seemed, to those who do not really know me, callous to the many blows that have been dealt me. Why do you not look at this miserable little life as I do? At the very worst 'tis but a scratch, a temporary ill to be soon cured by that dear old doctor Death—who gives us a life more healthful and enduring than all the physicians, temporal and spiritual, can give.

But for all his "inky cloak of black" there was a quality of sweetness and grandeur which left its impression profoundly on Otis Skinner and indeed on everyone who ever played in his companies.

Most people whose interest lies in the theatre have definite ideas about what Booth was like. There is no way of telling whose conception is correct. Even among persons still living who saw him act, opinions differ. My father, who played two seasons with him, formed first-hand impressions that must have been fairly accurate:

> . . . No actor of his time so completely filled the eye, the ear and the mind with an ideal of romantic tragedy as Edwin Booth. Extravagance never marred his work; he was a living illustration of Hamlet's advice to the players concerning the temperate smoothness to be begot in the torrent, tempest and whirlwind of passion.
>
> Like all remarkable actors, he had the power of suggestion. Never losing his own personality in his assumption he yet conveyed the impression that he was the character. It was never with the dominating force of Forrest who is said to have exclaimed, "By God! I AM Lear!" The alchemy of Booth's art was more profound and subtle. . . . Although a small, even a frail man, I could swear that at times in Othello and in Macbeth, he was seven feet tall. But as Shylock, with the copious gabardine he wore, his body appeared shortened to stumpiness. His Iago was lithe, dangerous and radiant with devilish beauty.

I once asked him if he recalled his father's acting sufficiently to say how it compared with his own. He hesitated then said, "I think I must be somewhat quieter.". . . His Hamlet had grown to be such a classic that it turned cold and mechanical at times. But I like best to bring him to mind as Othello and Macbeth. There was that about him infinitely human and at the same time infinitely poetic and lovely. Very much like Booth himself.

My father was writing about his first season with the great man. Booth in those days still had the vitality and keenness of industry which buoyed him above the burden of personal tragedy, a tragedy that never left him and in time wearied his nature and all but extinguished the fire of his artistry.

In 1881, when my father played with Booth for the first time, his spirit had been riding high, he was in his exquisite prime. Playing in his company under his direction, studying his magical technique, my father had learned the things he had been denied in the slapdash school of stock company. Introspection, subtlety, and above all, pace and the value of a pause. Booth, who had yet to become the melancholy recluse of later years, was courteously congenial with the members of his company. He had taken a flattering interest in young Skinner, and often calling him into his dressing room, ". . . he would suggest different and more effective readings. Always he was quiet and gentle. Never insistent. And that was a quality of his acting; poetic symmetry."

My father always claimed it was from Booth he learned the gist of acting, and the fact that any "getting into the mood" is just so much nonsense. This was when he had the chance to play Laertes. That character, as one will recall, is on at the beginning of the play, then doesn't appear again until a good two hours later when, in a state of grief, fury, and drawn sword, he rushes on to avenge the death of his father. The first few nights he had no trouble, being keyed up by excitement and that degree of stage fright which, if it doesn't go too far, can add considerable spirit to a performance. Then he began to lose his punch. The long wait between his first and second appearances seemed to make him go dead. He was trying desperately to "live his part." He would pace the floor of his dressing room, working himself up into an emotional wax. He even reached a point of desperation when he would remove his make-up, change into street clothes, walk frantically about in the night air, evoking inspiration, then return to the theatre just in time to race back into his costume and hurtle himself breathless onto the stage. Booth, who was as wise as he was gifted, observed his agonies for a few days, then one evening sent for him to come to his dressing room. It was between acts and the great tragedian, clad in the "sable garb" of the Dane, was serenely playing solitaire while he smoked a black cigar. "Sit down, Skinner," he said, and Skinner perched uneasily on the edge of a chair. The greatest Hamlet of all time paused to place a red queen on a black king, and take a pull on his stogie before he spoke. Then, "Young man," he said, "I've been watching you and you're killing yourself! You've got some high-toned notion that you're supposed to *be* Laertes! You're going to end up in a lunatic asylum. Relax! During that two-hour wait, read a book, write letters, play pinochle with the stage hands, then come down onto the stage. Loaf about in the wings. Talk to whoever's loafing there too—provided you do it quietly. Don't try to 'work yourself up.' It can't be done. Just wait for your cue, then, when you hear it, *go on the stage and act!*"

The Booth-Modjeska tour was followed by a brief and profoundly mortifying London engagement at the Globe Theatre as leading man in a production of *Romeo and Juliet.* It was the private project of a gentleman who had made a fortune in the paint business and had married a lady with a burning ambition to play Juliet. And her qualifications for the part stopped right there. She was fat, blowsy, and awful, and she uttered the lyrical speeches of that most exquisite of heroines with not only a smashing Cockney accent but also a definite lisp. The opening night the pit gave vent to so much vociferous glee over such gems as "That whith we call a rothe by any other name would thmell ath thweet" that the producer-paint-magnate husband felt it incumbent upon himself to step out before the curtain and make an official statement to the effect that they must please pardon the star's vocal impediment as it was caused by a gum boil!

It was a shoddy, vulgar affair and my father, utterly wretched over being associated with such an absurd production, kept miserably to himself during the run, which was blessedly short. Too humiliated to look up the acquaintances he had made during the brilliant Daly engagements, he ate alone in out-of-the-way restaurants and for his only diversion took interminable walks through districts where no one was likely to recognize him. And yet he himself made a fine impression with the critics and with the London public. When I played there for the first time in 1929, some thirty-nine years after the unfortunate Shakespearean venture, the papers spoke of me as "the daughter of that beloved and excellent actor Otis Skinner who last delighted our audiences with his fine performance of *Romeo*." Surely the London public is the most loyal one on earth!

Otis returned to America and a season with Margaret Mather, that strange, self-educated star whose tempestuous life it would take another book to narrate. And after that, he signed up for the next three years as leading man for Madame Modjeska, during which time he met my mother. It was an ideal engagement and Otis had a range of excellent parts.

Skinner had played a full season with Modjeska before the morning when Maud walked tremulously into the Garden Theatre for her first rehearsal. During the tour he seldom saw her in the theatre or out of it. Father told me that to him, throughout the first months, she appeared to be a shy, studious little person who spent such time as she was not worshiping at Modjeska's feet, either off by herself or making conscientious sightseeing pilgrimages with the older women of the company. On occasions when Madame would invite her to lunch in the private car, she sat at the end of the table listening with shining eyes to the general conversation, but saying nothing. Why Modjeska was taking the trouble to make a protégée of her, he couldn't fathom—except that she seemed a nice child with a pretty complexion and a lovely speaking voice. Beyond that, he dismissed her as just another silly young thing as she had previously dismissed him as being "stuck up."

Indeed, throughout Miss Durbin's first season with the company, the grand young Mr. Skinner was barely aware of her existence. At the beginning of the ensuing one, however, he became slightly more cognizant of it. The girl's summer at Arden had given her poise. She had found that she could hold her own with people of the world. She moved with more assured grace and, in that hat trimmed with the hummingbirds, she was definitely ravishing. And as he became aware of her existence, young Skinner at the same time became aware of the curious fact that she seemed to be avoiding him. If, in the course of a wait in the wings, he'd saunter over in her direction, with elaborate casualness, to be sure, she'd suddenly duck around a scenery flat. The discovery amazed him. It also annoyed him. The young woman was putting on airs. Obviously Modjeska's patronage had gone to her head. Then came the incident of the Jack-o'-lantern and that amused and quite charmed him, and when the impulse moved him to slip away from his throne to give her hand that unexpected squeeze, he found he was strangely excited.

He began too to take notice of the fact that Maud Durbin was a charming actress. Her Phebe in *As You Like It* was a creation of poetic delicacy, and George Hazelton, playing opposite her the jilted Silvius, uttered his "Oh, Phebe, Phebe, Phebe!" with such plaintiveness it was all too clear he was in love with her. Hazelton was not the only one, for, with all her modest simplicity, the girl had admirers aplenty. That did not lessen her in the leading man's estimation either. And yet, when the tour ended and Skinner started making arrangements for the ensuing season in which he planned to venture out as actor-manager with his own company, it never occurred to him to engage the services of Miss Durbin.

It occurred, however, to Modjeska. I have told in a previous chapter of how the gracious lady took the pains to see him in order to persuade him to sign up Maud as his leading lady. It probably didn't require much persuading, although the star felt it necessary to protest a little. After all, Miss Durbin had had only two years' experience and in small parts, would she be up to leads? Modjeska was certain that she would be. A little further demurring and the budding actor-manager said he would take the risk. The next day he wrote the letter Maud found it so difficult not to answer immediately.

The company was to be a touring one. Skinner was not prepared yet to burst on Broadway as a star. There would be a repertory of two plays—*His Grace de Grammont,* a romantic comedy by Clyde Fitch with a Restoration plot, full of lace ruffles, King Charles spaniels, and expletives beginning with " 'od's"; the other was *The King's Jester,* an adaptation of Victor Hugo's *Le Roi S'Amuse* (*Rigoletto,* if you prefer) written by Otis's brother Charles.

They opened in Rockford, Illinois, and went on to Chicago for a successful short run. Then they set out on the road and everywhere played to starvation business. Towns which heretofore had hailed him as the most popular leading man in the country now failed dismally to turn out to see Otis Skinner as a star. In a letter to his brother Charlie written from Chattanooga he remarks wryly that "The vultures are perched on the railings watching the dying forms of plays." Everywhere they went—and they went everywhere—it was the same story. But the youthful actor-manager took it all in his stride and his stride had suddenly become magnificently buoyant because of a wonderful thing that had happened to him. Let the financial wolves howl—let them come right in through the scenery door, he could face them. He could face anything now. He had fallen in love with his leading lady. Really in love . . . for the first time. He had, of course, had his share of amorous adventures. But whatever may have gone before, Maud Durbin was the only real love of his life, and from the start he knew it was to be so. However, for a long time after this momentous realization, he gave no indications of his tumultuous feelings. Maud's feelings in regard to him were tumultuous too, but indefinitely so. She knew that she liked and admired him, that he was gay, intelligent, and kind, and that he was by all means the handsomest man she had ever seen. Beyond that, she did not venture to analyze her emotions. The leaping increase in her heartbeat that took place whenever the star spoke to her, she set down to professional nervousness. As time went on, the increased heartbeat became more leaping and more disturbing. She found, to her annoyance, that she was spending a great deal of time thinking about Mr. S., that she looked forward too eagerly to every encounter with him. Why, she couldn't explain. It was just a notion and she'd get over it soon, she was sure. But the notion persisted and as

Matinée Idol

Photograph by Elias Goldensky

C. O. S. — Age Three

their route carried them on into the balmy South, it became a sweet obsession.

They played a week in that city of visual and gastronomic loveliness, New Orleans. The star, who had always adored the town and knew every nook and corner of it, appointed himself cicerone to his leading lady, and the leading lady was only too willingly led. He showed her the cathedral, the French Opera, the Carré, which in those days was really *Vieux*, Antoine's, where the old gouty-footed waiters served them oysters Creole and buster crabs; he took her through the French market on the levee and they devoured delicious omelets and red wine at Madame Bégue's. The week was magic for them both. At the close of Friday night's performance, a note was placed on the leading lady's dressing table.

"Maudie," it read, "will you come for a walk with me tomorrow? I'll stop by your hotel at ten. Otis."

Ten A.M. is a fantastic hour for theatre people to be doing anything more active than barely starting to wake up, but that Saturday it seemed late enough. Neither had slept and both had been up since seven. Maud was standing waiting for him at the doorway of her hotel, and as he bounded up the steps to take her hand, her cheeks flushed as bright as the camellias she had pinned into her belt. New Orleans was fresh and radiant in the gentle morning sun. The two young people walked in serious silence down the street. Each had a pretty good idea of what was going to happen, but neither felt capable of speech. Finally, Maud timidly broke the tension by asking where they were going, and Otis in his nervousness could think of no better place than the Métairie Cemetery. Redbirds caroled in the live oaks and the Spanish moss swayed above the quaint graves raised like ovens above the ground. At one point they stopped by an ancient sarcophagus, neither knowing exactly why, and each made formal pretense of deciphering the French inscription. A little chameleon with grinning face and pulsating throat skittered into a crack on the side of the crumbling tomb, a church bell chimed the quarter, and Otis asked Maud to be his wife.

The remainder of the tour was a happy blur of love, plans for the future, and bad business. They were together as much as propriety would permit, lunching, taking long walks, and having supper after the show, but then always carefully chaperoned by one of the older women of the company. Such afternoons as they had to be apart, there was a happy exchange of notes or flowers to help ease the pangs of separation.

Dear Little Soul [one of them reads],

It's just because you are faithful and fond and fanciful and freckled and fair that I love you. That's all.

You'll be lonely while I'm at the ball game unless you listen to what the flowers say.

Rest sweetly with all my love,

OTIS

Despite the appalling business, Otis managed to keep his company going until April. They closed on Saturday the twentieth in Corning, New York. Next morning they were married by the Reverend Rob Roy Converse in Christ Church. The church was brand-new and theirs was the first wedding to take place there. The sun shone as warmly as it had the morning of their engagement and a brisk spring wind blew the white robes of the minister as he gave them his blessing from the portal. The young couple walked away toward the station arm in arm. At the turn of the street they paused to wave and the bride blew a kiss to the smiling parson.

The young couple were radiantly happy. They were also completely broke. My mother had no vestige of capital and what small amount Father had been able to save had gone to pay the high cost of his first starring venture. But they didn't care. They had each other and the future was rosy. Otis's nature was one of bland, expansive optimism which lasted his lifetime and was a prime factor in his perennial youthfulness, and Maud in those days had not acquired the neurosis in regard to money matters which in later years led her to live in chronic terror of imminent and abject poverty. What though Otis's first venture had gone on the rocks, next season would see him off and on to the high tide of success. Moreover, if financially he had not yet arrived, his position as a distinguished artist was being recognized. That June Tufts College gave him an honorary M.A., and Maud was in a happy flutter over it. She remained in Proctorsville, Vermont, purring with pride, while he journeyed to receive the degree and to spend a few days with his father, who had been called back to Cambridge. It was their first separation and he sent her the first of those daily letters which, whenever they were apart, he never failed to write throughout thirty-five years of married life.

My Dearest Wife:

It is done, sweetheart. I am an A.M. and your husband is now one of the immortals.

I have thought of you all day long. Your presence has been constantly with me.

After I left you, last night, I stood on the platform for half an hour waiting for the train which was late. It was a weird, uncanny *demi-heure*. The night was so silent, yet so full of sounds. The crickets piped busily; the rival bassos of the Black River Opera Company grated out their deep "*chugs*"; a couple of sleepless whip-poor-wills had a midnight confab speculating on what d–d idiot could be standing down there on the platform under the red light; a somnambulistic bird somewhere near shivered out a few soft frightened notes; the low rush of the waters at the mill dam kept up a constant accompaniment, while every little minute or two some mysterious mechanism within the station released some piped waters that gushed out somewhere with a muffled swish and then were silent again. Lockwood's clock ticked distinctly within his office and all the million stars were out and the bright paring of an old moon hung over the bridge and cast a strange light on the rails.

I stood and waited and wondered if you had gone to sleep again. The train slowed up at the red light and took me on for an hour to Bellows Falls where I waited from 3:15 to 5:30. It was fearfully long, but I thought of you, dear, and my heart kept sending you messages that you would understand.

Father was waiting for me at the station in Boston. His first words were "Did Maud come?"

I hustled home, changed by clothes and we got to Tufts a little after eleven. The chapel was jammed. I sat on the platform with the president, trustees, Governor Greenhaugh and other notables. The gowned and frightened graduates did their little speeches, the diplomas were given out with accompanying chunks of Latin remarks and then the honorary degrees were announced. Pres. Chapin spoke my name, read something in Latin, I got up, the audience applauded, then I sat down and was an A.M. And that's all there was to that. But an awful dinner followed at the gymnasium where everybody made speeches miles long while the guests perspired and were bored. It didn't break up till after four.

Everybody congratulated me and asked after you, my Maudine. Father is bursting with pride. When I got home, I found him sitting in the dark, alone. I haven't a doubt of what he was thinking of.

Your sweet eyes have been haunting me all day, my wife. And you thought I'd be so busy that I'd not miss you. My love, I don't think the time will ever be when business will crowd you from my heart or steal from me the memory of your sweet lips.

Father sends love. I'm going down to the post office with this now so that it'll not delay in reaching you. Goodnight, my Maud. All my heart . . . all my love is yours.

OTIS

In the fall, my father started his second season as actor-manager. If the first season had been bad, the second one was complete disaster. He wanted desperately to try his luck in New York, but that required financial backing and there was no "angel" willing to risk taking a chance on an untried star. It was again the Road, and again barnstorming to empty barns. *Villon the Vagabond* was augmented with *Hamlet*. It was the logical choice for a young star. "Nearly every actor," my father used to say, "is born with *Hamlet* in his blood, or else he acquires *Hamlet*. It's a virus so strong that nothing short of an operation in the shape of an impersonation of the part can remove the disorder. And no good actor has ever failed in the part. It's the most completely human character in the whole range of the drama. You don't conceive it: it is you." His Hamlet was, to judge from the critics, poetic, sensitive, and vital, and Maud Durbin was the most exquisite of Ophelias. Very few people saw them.

From the earliest days of their marriage, my mother exerted great influence in regard to the selection and editing of my father's scripts, an influence that was to continue throughout his subsequent career. He was quick to realize the uncanny correctness of her judgment. One of his letters during the preparations for *Villon* winds up:

> I find your amended manuscript on my return and have only time to say that of course it is a vast improvement. How is it you know so much? As I sat up over my ms. at 4 o'clock this morning the idea of much the same transposition came to me as I find tonight in your ms. *Your thought!* It's a marvellous case of telepathy. I'm done . . . quite out . . . and I'm going to bed, but not before I say good night to the sweetest and most wonderful wife a man ever had.

There followed some five or six appalling years of heartache and disappointment. Season after season of hand-to-mouth trouping. Still no opening in New York. He was branded a provincial star. The term smacked lamentably of "ten-twent'-'n-thirt' " melodrama. They wandered all over the map, barely making it from place to place. Press notices were invariably good, the local intelligentsia were ever loud in praise, but the general public seemed not to know him from Adam. One day in a Kansas City streetcar, Maud overheard a small boy, who was reading passing signs, pipe out, "Say, Ma, what is an Ottis Skinner?" and the mother serenely replied, "I dunno, Son. Probably some sort of farm implement." Sometimes there would not be enough money for transportation and they'd have to lay off for a few days, a week even, in some tank town until Joe Buckley, the ingenious business partner, would manage somehow to bribe a railroad official into letting the company and scenery ride on credit. They traveled by day coach, by river boat, and once by barge. One year they went from New Orleans to Baltimore on a freighter. It was a hair-whitening voyage. The ship was overloaded and nearly foundered in a hurricane off Hatteras; the troupe was deathly sick and one member went temporarily insane and had to be clamped in irons in the brig.

Those were the halcyon days before producers were obliged to put up bonds in Equity which assured touring companies of their salaries and transportation back to New York, and the forlorn theatrical troupe stranded in Chillicothe or Medicine Hat was a surefire joke in every vaudeville sketch. On his struggling way to California one winter Otis received a note from a fellow player who had recently returned from the Coast. "Dear Skinner," it said. "I hear you are about to go West. Don't! The plains are white with the bones of actors who have tried to get back."

It was a tribute to the star that every member of his company stuck loyally with him. There were many weeks when he couldn't meet the salary list. He and Buckley would eke out enough to foot all hotel bills and meals, and somehow at the end of the run he'd manage to pay up back salaries. There was barely ever anything left over for himself and his bride. Any number of times they went quite hungry. But they kept their battered young chins bravely up. Only once did each have a momentary lapse into despair. In Bloomington, Otis had a *crise* in which he vowed he was a failure, that he was merely a third-rate trouper who, like Jo in *Bleak House,* was Always Moving On, and that he'd better throw up the sponge and go into some other sort of profession. And in Selma, Alabama, Maud had her darkest moment. Funds were so low they could not afford to eat in the cheapest restaurant, but Buckley had been promised a cold chicken and some beer, the gift of a benevolent stage hand. He arrived at their wretched little room in the third-class hotel bringing the welcome victuals along with the heart-breaking news that in the last town they'd played he'd parted with a twenty-dollar gold piece, thinking it was a silver dollar. This was too much for Maud, who broke down in hysteria, although hunger got the better of her and she sat on the bed ravenously munching a drumstick and sobbing bitterly into her glass of beer. On both occasions each bore the other up.

But during those hard years, there were rich compensations. Otis Skinner was slowly but firmly building up for himself the loyal road following which was to endure throughout his entire career. He was already an established popular name in Chicago, San Francisco, and Boston, and he felt more sanguine about New York. Then, too, there was the invaluable experience to be gained from the wide repertory of plays he produced and played in. Besides *Hamlet,* there were *Richard III, Romeo and Juliet, The Merchant,* Bulwer-Lytton's *Lady of Lyons,* Henry Arthur Jones's *The Liars,* Browning's *In a Balcony,* Bronson Howard's romantic tear-jerker of the Civil War, *Shenandoah,* a revival of *Fran-*

cesca da Rimini, and Otis's own dramatization of Stevenson's *Prince Otto.*

The road was always colorful and there were many rewarding friendships to be made along the way. Those were the days when Chicago's Forty Club was at its mellow height, and he was on intimate terms with its members—"Bif" Hall, Melville E. Stone, Eugene Field, and George Ade. Ade became a particularly close friend. In a letter written to Maud, who was out of the bill at the time, he says:

> George Ade called today at the theatre and left "Artie" and "Pink Marsh" inscribed to you. I find George is childishly fond of his own books . . . laughs as his own sayings in them, and all that.
>
> Al Ringling invited the members of the company to his show and Ade went with us. The big tent was jammed, money was turned away but we all had the best seats. Ade, Miss Comstock and I went in state in a carriage placed at our disposal by the affable Ringling. We did the sideshows, ate peanuts and were generally jay. Ade was like a kid. He knows all the performers and the secrets of their innermost lives.

There was one happy and profitable interlude between the seasons of stress when Skinner made a short tour in an all-star production of *The Rivals,* headed by that enchanting character, Joseph Jefferson. Otis liked the part of Jack Absolute, he liked the entourage, and of course he adored Jefferson. The old comedian was a wit, a terrific cardplayer, and a wildly enthusiastic painter. He used the company baggage car for a studio. In every town, as soon as the scenery was unloaded and the car shunted off into the yards, he'd climb aboard, set up his easel, get out his paints, and work for hours. He gave Otis and Maud one of his canvases—a charming little landscape of good color and fine composition, rather on the Rousseau-Constable order—a scene in the Catskill woods with a mountain torrent—doubtless one of his imagined sets for *Rip Van Winkle.*

Otis's letters to Maud describe the tour.

I wired you from Albany yesterday that everything was successful and that Mr. Jefferson says it is the best first night's performance of the *Rivals* he ever saw. I think he was sincere. I'm getting the stiffness out of my joints in Capt. Absolute and the part goes well.

We travel in a private company car. We are packed in rather thickly but we live very well. I am commencing to yearn for a bath. Life in the car is extremely cordial. Everyone harmonious and Jefferson is like some funny little good wise fairy. He is a wonder of cheeriness, brightness and entertaining wit. I don't have any privacy, however. The car is always full of people—no place to write. I'm penning this in an obstructed corner with my valise on my knees.

There are a great many spirits aboard—in bottles! They gather around copiously and continuously. I think too many weeks of this would not be to my liking.

Ran into Laurence Hutton who tells me he had a letter from Mark Twain announcing the latter's return to this country and speaking of the fact that though he had "delivered" his last and farewell lecture the week before, he nevertheless had succumbed to an invitation to lecture once more. "In short," Mark concludes, "there is nothing that prevents my becoming a harlot but my sex."

The Jefferson tour was all too short and again he was back at the old heart-breaking grind—hard work, exhausting trouping, no business, and mountainous debts.

Maud during all this period never complained. She felt things would come out right somehow. This was, to be sure, hardly the life she had envisaged, but the man she had married so far surpassed any husband she had ever envisaged, she was content and proud to share his hardships. Her cup of happiness, though storm-tossed, was almost full. There was needed only the fulfillment of two lifelong ambitions to make it slop over. One was a child; the other was a trip to Europe. The child seemed an eventual possibility as soon as business improved—but Europe was a magic mirage as unattainable as El Dorado. That didn't prevent her from dreaming about it, though, or from devouring all the books of travel or history she could find. She'd gaze at every Cunard poster as though it were an old master. Maybe, some day when they were middle-aged, they'd get there.

At the finish of their most financially disastrous season, Otis, realizing that they were both at the end of their physical and emotional endurance, said that they must go away somewhere for a vacation or else they'd have a couple of complete breakdowns. With a little wail, Maud asked where they could go and on what. Otis muttered that he'd borrow the money, he'd manage somehow. They could find an inexpensive place even if it were only for a few weeks. Some days later he announced that they were going up into Canada. He had engaged space on an excursion steamer that was offering a bargain trip up the Saguenay. It wasn't Europe, of course, but at least they'd be on a boat and they'd see scenery if not castles. He'd be able to do some fishing and they'd both have a rest and a change. They might stay a week in Quebec and Montreal, so he advised her to take along plenty of clothes. She'd better include her evening frock too, as they might splurge on one dinner at the Château Frontenac. Maud packed her few dresses in a steamer trunk, Otis assembled his fishing paraphernalia, and they took a train to Montreal. From the station they drove to the Anchor Line dock where they boarded a trim vessel. It was almost the departure hour and Otis insisted they stay up on deck until the boat put off from the dock—there'd be ample time later in which to locate their cabin. The gangplank was hauled up, the hawsers cast free, and, with a deep bark from her foghorn, the steamer backed out into the St. Lawrence and headed downstream. Otis laid his hand over his wife's, which was clutching the rail.

"Maudie," he said, "when you get off this ship you'll be in Liverpool, England."

Maud looked at him for a stunned moment of incredulity. Then she cried out helplessly, "But Otis, dear love, I *can't* go to Europe without saying good-bye to my family!"

"I've said good-bye for you," he reassured her. "They know all about it." And he took her down to their cabin where she found a little stack of bon voyage messages from her mother, her sisters, and her brothers. At that, she collapsed onto the berth and cried and cried. She cried almost incessantly for twenty-four hours. Otis thought she was having some sort of emotional collapse, but she assured him it was only because she was so happy. She continued to cry again at happy intervals clear across the Atlantic.

The trip, of course, was the perfect consummation of what she had so long dreamed of, and when they got back, she knew that her other dream too was to be realized, for she found she was with child.

CHAPTER SEVEN

My First Appearance

I WAS BORN in Chicago. The Durbin family had by now settled permanently there and my mother wanted to be near her own. She was eager to have the baby, but her strength was never robust and she was frightened of what lay ahead of her. My father was off completing a late spring tour and she must have expressed her anxieties to him in her letters, which, unfortunately, were never saved, for his daily communications to her, which fortunately were, are full of a tenderly humorous pampering of her pre-birthing whims, one of which was a craving for cherries.

Dear heart [one of them reads],

Your brave little letter which reached me at Cedar Rapids had a note of sadness which makes me grieve that I can't help you. You mustn't think how long it is, but how short it is going to be now. Don't think, sweetheart, that I could ever be annoyed at you for crying.

I looked all over Fargo today for cherries but none are in the market here. Enclosed is a bill (a 'V'). Send out someone. They are in the Chicago groceries. I saw them.

Tell Cornelia [it was apparently a foregone conclusion that

I was to be a girl] that if she doesn't stop making her mother sad I won't speak to her—and then she'll be sorry.

The day is another of those bright ones, but there is a fine cool north wind blowing that will blow my love down to Chicago to you.

His vigorous letters must have been a daily tonic to her. The pantheistic zest with which he always responded to the four seasons was especially keen that year of happy expectancy. A letter from Mankato, Minnesota, dated April 21, their wedding anniversary, begins ridiculously enough:

Merry Christmas, my sweetheart!

It's springtime—the very first day for spring! I've just come from a long walk, and have seen the early shoots from the trees and have gotten my feet into *green* grass for the first time this year. For two days it has been bleak and cold with lowering skies, and the mercury had an awful weight on its mind. Today is bright with a flecked blue sky and the air full of life and the birds full of fat worms.

I did between five and six miles this morning. Your husband slowly returning to his Appollo (that's got too many *p's* or *L's* or something) like figure. Don't be jealous! You were along—you and your little baby. Oh yes, I've seen the May flowers. Some boys at a way-station were selling big bunches of them. I bought one that was full of the perfume of country and freedom. I was going to pack it and send it to you, but there was no train until next day, and the next day the poor little captive woodland things had begun to droop.

My heart of hearts is yours.

OTIS

P.S. I enclose a notice from the Hazlitt of Minneapolis that has some merit. We always think articles praising us have merit, you know.

To date my start in life by the same device Sterne used for Tristram Shandy, it must have taken place the preceding summer in either France or Holland, for in a letter written late in May my father says:

Cornelia will be true to her nationality. She must wear either the tri-color or the orange and she knows when to come.

I think it isn't far off because I find myself getting horribly nervous and I fancy it is because of a thought or event transference.

Last night I dreamed that it had taken place and it was such a wise little thing! I thought it stood up and talked most sagely to me.

God bless you, my dearest wife. May the new life come as a benediction into ours.

Five days later I was born. Poor Mother, my birth was anything but a benediction. The doctor in charge of the case was not only old, but was paralyzed from the waist down and had to conduct matters from a wheel chair. For Mother to have selected him was characteristic of her habit of engaging the services of professional persons from motives either of friendship or because in her quick impressionability she thought them distinguished. This elderly medico had written a number of essays that had appeared in the *Atlantic Monthly,* so he fell into the latter category. I was an unconscionable time a-borning and in the end had to be produced by a botched-up forceps job. My mother suffered long and cruelly. Father used to tell me how he spent agonized hours riding time and time again on streetcars out toward the suburbs where, becoming panic-stricken, he would jump off, leap onto the next returning tram, and hurry back to the hospital, only to be told that nothing had happened yet.

After her delivery, Mother was desperately ill. Due to some quirk of the old doctor's therapy, she was made to lie immovable for several weeks in a trough-like contraption which Father called her "Mohammed's Coffin." Days were hot and nights were interminable. I was kept in her room where I wailed incessantly. Even in illness and pain Mother was always beautifully considerate of others. To a very old man who was a patient in the adjoining room she managed to scribble an impulsively charming note apologizing for my crying. The aged gentleman wrote back assuring her that she must not be concerned, he could not sleep anyway, and he enjoyed hearing a newborn baby crying. He amused himself thinking about all the things the little girl would live to see. She would see the perfection of wireless, the development of the long-distance telephone; she would see ships that could cross the ocean in five days and aeroplanes that would actually carry passengers. She would live, he said, to see a beautiful and wonderful world. I am glad that two global wars and the atom bomb were not among his prophecies, for that night, to the accompaniment of my wailing, the old man died.

Father had to make a short summer tour in order to defray the hospital bills. His letters overflow with fatuous pride in his new parenthood. One from Washington:

> The journey seemed intolerably long because I was going away from the two dearest things I have on earth. My wife and my baby.
>
> How funny it seems to say the TWO dearest ones. It used to be only one.
>
> I really didn't think we could have such a beautiful little girl as that which has come to us. [Obviously parenthood had warped his vision. I was anything but beautiful, looking, in fact, rather like an Eskimo.] I see her always as I saw her last on Friday night, lying on her side, under her blanket, her little fist doubled up under her chin. And her sweet mother lying in her "mummy-case" with a smile on her face as if she said "And I did that!!!"
>
> Take all my love, dear heart, and when you've taken it, lend it all to Cornelia.

My first few months of existence were passed at the Virginia Hotel. Unable to afford a nurse, Mother took care of me and the care she took was so hysterically meticulous, it very nearly killed me. That was the era when germs had sprung into popular prominence. Everyone was bacteria-conscious to a neurotic degree. The home pasteurizing of milk by boiling it was a craze as widespread as bridge, Boston terriers, and *The Little Shepherd of Kingdom Come.* Mother developed a germ phobia that lasted her lifetime. I was a bottle baby and she was certain that all Chicago milk must be alive with every virus from the common cold to smallpox. Instead of heating it to just the right temperature, she boiled it until there was neither germ nor nourishment left in it. I pined and lost weight and it was only after I had gone in for a series of convulsions that my grandmother persuaded her I was slowly dying of malnutrition which a less scientific, more normal, diet would cure.

Still too frail to wheel the perambulator, Mother used to tip one of the hotel bellboys to wheel me up and down the street on sunny days. The bellboy was an exceptionally alert and attractive lad—and that's not to be wondered at, for his name was Frank Buck. In his memoirs, the amiable adventurer blandly states that I was the yellingest baby in the block and that he could easily have killed me. Perhaps it was his admirable control over murderous impulse which first gave the idea of "bringing 'em back alive."

They took me East in a market basket to stay for a time with Grandfather Skinner. He baptized me. It was an unpretentious ritual held at home. The front parlor was "neated up" to serve as the baptistry while the family sugar bowl was dumped of its contents and impressed into usage as a font. It was characteristic of my grandfather's New England reserve that he waited until the ceremony was over and my name permanently set before announcing in ringing tones that there was no name in the world he so despised as that of Cornelia, and that although he had now conferred it upon me with the Almighty as witness, he had no intention of ever calling me by it. Father, after a moment's stunned silence, weakly spluttered out that he and Maud had chosen the name expressly to please him, as it had been that of his own wife. The old patriarch replied that this merely showed a curious lack of perception. If Otis would take the trouble to think back, he would recall the fact that his father always called his mother Carrie.

"When I was a small boy," he growled, "I shared a school desk with a girl named Cornelia. She was disagreeable and a tattletale. What's more—she smelled!" And he strode from the room.

That was how I came by the coy and somewhat distressing nickname of Bobs, a cognomen which suits me about as patly as would Snooks or Blondie. Bobs was an abbreviation for Bobbles, an even worse flight of parental whimsy—the reason for this being an inability on my part to hold my head up. Whether it was due to weak neck muscles or an abnormally heavy head or possibly a slight tendency to idiocy I don't know, but they told me that whenever I looked up, something would collapse and my head would bobble about like that of a doll in need of repair. It was my grandfather who turned Bobbles into Bobs, and although my head now stays in place, Bobs I have remained to my family and a few intimate friends. It was only after I had committed some heinous misdemeanor that my parents ever called me by my given name. Cornelia became for me the warning of awful reprimand.

In the fall, Mother took me back to Chicago and Father again went on the road. He was not particularly happy on this tour. Business was bad and his letters are sentimentally homesick. From Buffalo and the Iroquois Hotel he writes:

> The orchestra that plays during dinner now is a seven string affair. Thursday night they began in the softest tones to play

> Schubert's "Träumerei." I listened for a moment and then two big tears fell into the stewed tomatoes. I continued to ooze and munch and munch and ooze as long as the selection kept up. I couldn't stop. I kept seeing you and Bobbles. The waiter must have thought I was daft.

For a person who has physically turned into what is unalluringly known as a horse, I was, as a child, peculiarly ailing. My teeth came in with difficulty and high fever, and in spite of Mother's zealousness in regard to germs, I attracted every passing contagious disease. When I was two, I came down with a virulent cold and sore throat. Mother sent for my grandmother, who felt my blazing forehead and said she must get a doctor immediately. The doctor was another of Mother's enthusiasms—well justified, in this instance, a remarkable little woman named Rachel Yarros, a refugee from Russian pogroms who was to make a fine name for herself in the world of medicine and as one of the leading spirits of Hull House. She took one look at my inflamed throat and gravely uttered the word "Diphtheria." She advised giving me the serum at once. Mother distrusted serums almost as much as she distrusted germs. They seemed to her newfangled and experimental. She refused to let me be given the shot. Then my wise little grandmother stepped in. She managed somehow to get her distraught daughter out of the room for a few minutes and, taking full responsibility upon herself, told Doctor Yarros to go ahead with the inoculation. There was no time for consultation with Father. He was off on a fishing trip with his brother Will in the wilds of Maine, they didn't know where, they thought somewhere in the region of Staceyville. A telegram was dispatched there without any hopes of it ever finding him, but by some miracle it reached him and two days later a second message told him that the serum had worked and that I was out of danger. His subsequent letter reads:

Dearest Wife:

Your second telegram was most comforting. I am so far out of the world here. I have the sensation of being in a Dreyfus exile.

Your first telegram came like a thunderclap in a clear sky. And yet, I had the strangest feeling that things were not right on Wednesday, the day our baby had her crisis. We had started our trip into the woods. Toward the end of the day I was up a trout stream quietly fishing. Bill said, "Look at the sun." It was of the most lurid threatening hue. A shiver went through me and all the way to our hang-up on the river bank I paddled with my heart like lead. I didn't sleep that night and at times I could hear the wire bedsprings ringing from the thumping of my heart. It was very strange!

. . . . We slept in a shack. It was fiercely cold. Our canoe was covered with ice the next morning when at five o'clock we began our fishing. . . . We broke camp at 3.30 Saturday afternoon. . . . Then we got into the swift current of the East Branch and shot down to Mattagamon with express speed. We got there at dusk. Someone had ridden over from Stacey-ville with your telegram . . . it was lying on the game warden's kitchen table. I read it and my mind became a blank. I could think of nothing for a while. Then I started for Stacey-ville. Six miles through thick woods, and night had come. Six miles over the worst road ever dreamt of . . . the guides the "dudes" hire have to chop down trees to bridge the sloughs. I tore through the woods and got along by instinct. Everything was a blur. I flew through bogs and sloughs and Bill trudged after me. I could see only one thing, Cornelia's tired eyes. In my ears but one phrase kept ringing over and over again: "Cornelia has diphtheria." How many feet found landing places I don't know. Why I didn't twist an ankle, I don't know. Covered with mud and dripping with sweat we emerged from the woods and reached the farmhouse at nine o'clock. Tracy, our landlord, hitched up his horse and we drove another mile and a half to where the telegraph operator lived. He had gone to bed. We got him up and took him over to the railroad station where by the light of a lantern I wrote my message and left him ticking it out to the operator at Bangor.

No word came from you all day Sunday though the operator "asked" Bangor for it five times during the day. There I was cooped up—tied hand and foot—knowing nothing. I couldn't get a train till Monday morning. At seven I was at the railway station, but it was 8 before the message came. With what suspense I hung over the young man's shoulder as the ticker recorded what you had sent, you may imagine. When he had spelled out "Cornelia much better," I felt everything drop out of me. I didn't care what he wrote after that.

Sit down and fold your hands for a few minutes, my wife. I send my dearest love. You are a brave pair, you and Bobs. Kiss Bobs on her two tired eyes.

OTIS

My father's next engagement was one which he used to say it made him sad to recall. It was a co-starring tour with Ada Rehan in a repertory of *The Shrew, The Merchant,* and *The School for Scandal.* Financially it was highly successful, but emotionally it was depressing and nerve-wracking. Daly had been dead for some years. (And, incidentally, the only bitterness my father ever expressed in regard to that unhappy genius was in a letter written to Mother. "Daly's funeral is today," it says. "It would be mockery for me to attend it. I could not honestly feign grief.") But the loss of that tyrannical, brilliant man who had been her Svengali had left Ada Rehan a mere shell of her former self. She was an aging, embittered woman. Her heart was gone, the fire of her acting had died out, and the sparkling charm that had been her greatest quality flashed only at momentary intervals in her Katharine. Her Portia and Lady Teazle were technically sure, but spiritually dead. She had always been a hypochondriac, and now she was genuinely ill in body as well as in spirit. She was able to attend only three of the preliminary rehearsals, her part being read by the stage manager. Frequently she was barely able to stagger through a performance. She dosed incessantly with tonics and patent medicines and often her breath would reek of valerian. Morose and morbidly shy, she kept to herself, talking with no one. She was civil enough to my father, but it was a vague civility; her brooding thoughts were far away.

Excerpts from Father's letters give more than a hint of the troubles he had with the moody star. They opened *The Merchant* some weeks after the tour had started. The first performance was apparently a nightmare of confusion:

> No one knew where he was. The carpenters were unfamiliar with the scenery. We hadn't an idea of where we were going to be until we had struck the scene. People had a tendency to walk into the Canal and go through solid walls. The orchestra evidently had an idea that it was giving a concert by itself and drums, cymbals and xylophone solos suddenly broke upon the startled ear in the middle of sentimental scenes. Miss Rehan was really in a panic. She fought it off quite bravely until she came to the Trial Scene and then went nearly to pieces. Once or twice I feared she was absolutely gone. I didn't venture to do anything with the scene for fear it would throw her quite off the tracks.
>
> My own performance fell back on sheer method—a pall was over that as over everything. My lines and business were there, but they formed the shell of Shylock, the soul was asleep inside. The fear for the play and for Miss Rehan smothered me.
>
> The lady was most gracious after it was over; she acknowledged defeat but expressed a spirit of determination to win out. She seemed genuine. I hope it wasn't the inspiration of the moment. Perhaps the papers will change her—if she reads them!

Another letter shows Father taking it all in his humorous stride:

> My! but we've a difficult proposition to handle. It's the top-notch of my diplomatic experience and Buckley has his troubles these days. Rehan's traveling companion, an alleged trained nurse or something of that sort, sees to it that her own job is kept fat by constantly fomenting discord and throwing

nervousness and *hell* into the lady. A very funny farce was played in Norfolk the other night. The Characters:

A Wronged Woman . . .	Ada Rehan
A Diplomat	Joseph Buckley
An Attendant Mute . . .	Miss Nelson (Rehan's Nurse)
A Waiter }	By the originals
A Cabby }	
A Dog	A Co-Star

After the performance, Miss R. was told she could not go right to the train but would have to wait till 12.30 when the special boat would leave for the So. RR terminal across the river. Buckley had arranged this time so as to give us (me particularly) a chance for a bite to eat.

The Lady rose in her wrath and demanded to know what cheap way of travel this was that had been selected. Buckley was stutteringly suave and explanatory and denied the cheapness of things, explaining that it was the representative road of the South and especially chosen for her comfort.

Why must she be kept waiting? Why should she not proceed at once to the boat—if boat there must be—and conveyed to the car? Buckley knew that I wouldn't be on hand until the last minute, and also that the boat wouldn't make a second trip; he repeated the fact that the boat was scheduled for 12.30. Well, she would go to the boat anyway—that she would insist on; and thereby hangs the diplomacy of Buckley. This duologue was at the theatre. The scene then shifted to the Monticello where requisitions for hand luggage were made and where bills must be paid. Buckley made several blunders about various things and was unable to get bellboys to move quickly, having insured their slowness by a number of surreptitious dimes. Then there was an error in the bill, or Buckley pretended there was.

Finally Miss Nelson, the nurse, said that they had ordered some chops to be taken with them that they might have them cooked on the train the next day. Buckley, to be sure, hastened to see about them. He rushed in and found the headwaiter. "Any chops for Miss Rehan?" "Yes, sir, all ready, sir." "Are they cooked?" "No, she wants them just as they are." "You cook 'em!" "But——" "Never mind. You cook 'em." "Yes, sir."

The party were in the carriage and Buckley went back and said there had been some misunderstanding, but it was all right, the chops would be there presently. During the nice long wait *The Wronged Woman* had no better amusement than to open up on Buckley about things in general. The hands of the clock were getting toward twelve. *The Wronged Woman* and her dog got out and walked up and down and the Diplomat wrapped himself in silence and Chesterfieldian attitudes. Suddenly a boy appeared:

"Here ye are, Boss. Right off the fire."

"What's off the fire?"

"Chops, Boss."

"You don't mean to tell me they're cooked?"

"Yes, Boss."

The Wronged Woman: "Never mind, Mr. Buckley."

The Diplomat: "Please, Miss Rehan! What do you mean by bringing those chops down like that? Can't you get *anything* straight in this hotel? You take those back!"

"I know, Boss, the gentleman say——"

"We haven't time to listen to you. Do what I told you and bring what was ordered—*raw* chops—RAW! Hurry up. Wait a minute. I don't trust you. I'll go myself."

The Wronged Woman: "Oh, please, Mr. Buckley. Never mind."

"No, Miss Rehan. You stay right there. I'm not going to see you insulted in this way. You've given your order and I'm going to see you get what you want."

"Oh, please! You're awfully kind but——"

"I won't be a minute!"

Exit Waiter followed by Diplomat.

2nd Scene: Inside the entrance door of Monticello.

Diplomat: "Boy, that scolding don't go. Here's a dollar."

Boy grins and chortles in glee.

Five minutes later.

Chops appear as desired. *Wronged Woman* entirely mollified. Party arrange themselves comfortably in carriage.

Diplomat (*approaching driver*): "This lady is very nervous and ill—drive to the boat as slowly as you know how."

Carriage creeps to wharf. In three minutes co-star appears. Boat sails!

Horatius at the Bridge! Davy Crockett and the wolves! Where are they?

Rehan loved only one thing in the whole world and that was a snuffly little Boston bull named Bobs, and she loved it with a devotion as hysterical as it was pitiful. If Bobs were ill—which, as a result of overeating, he not infrequently was—she'd refuse to play her performance unless an attendant veterinary stayed all the while in her dressing room to watch over the dog basket. If, on some short railroad jump where there were no Pullmans, Bobs was relegated to the baggage car, she went with him and sat amid the trunks and crates for the entire trip. After she died, Bobs was an important beneficiary in her will which provided him with a life of ease and, after his demise, a grave and marble tombstone in a select cemetery. Rehan hated small children with the same sort of uncontrollable aversion some people have for cats or snakes. She couldn't stand to be near them. If a baby or a very young child were brought near her, she would have to get away. It must have cost her an effort even to make perfunctory inquiries of her co-star as to the health of his baby—whose presence, to be sure, my parents were wise enough never to inflict upon her. That year I again fell seriously ill—this time with colitis—and again nearly died. It occurred during Father's Chicago engagement and my parents had at least the consolation of being together when the attack was at its height. One evening, after I was definitely on my way to recovery, Mother, to get an hour's change of scene, had run down to the theatre to sit for a while in Father's dressing room. Rehan, having heard of my illness, and seeing her, felt it her duty to say, "Mrs. Skinner, I hope your little Bobs is better."

"Thank you, Miss Rehan, she is," Mother answered. "We feel pretty certain she's going to live."

Rehan in a sudden and surprising impulse of sympathy

seized Mother's hand. "I know how you feel, my dear," she said. "Just the way I do when *my* little Bobs is ill!"

For one horrified moment my gentle mother wanted to strike her. Then she saw the look in the haggard blue eyes and her own filled with quick tears of understanding.

"Yes, Miss Rehan," she said softly. "Just the same way!"

After this second serious sickness, Mama Durbin, who for two years had watched with admirable restraint the over-meticulous upbringing of her grandchild, now stepped in with some common-sense advice. All this fuss about germs and such was nonsense, that was exactly why I caught them. I needed roughing-up—to be taken out of sterile sheets and put into overalls and given a little good clean dirt. And she whisked me out to the suburbs to stay with her for a while in her little frame house in Ravenswood. She turned me loose in the back yard where I made mud pies while Mama Durbin's chickens scratched around me, and Mac the bull terrier licked my face, and my kid uncle Dowell fed me horehound drops, and I thrived with health and happiness. She told Mother that it was fatal for her to take sole care of me, as obviously she couldn't do it without undue fuss and dither. Expense or no expense, they must engage a nurse-maid.

That was how Martha came into our lives. Martha was a sunny, efficient treasure who had recently arrived from Bavaria and who stayed with us for some years until a tailor from Kankakee persuaded her to become his wife. Under her supervision I grew plump and sturdy. I also learned to talk and what I talked with pure "*hoch Deutsch.*" Of English I knew only a few words, and as Mother spoke no German, it made things complicated as, on Martha's afternoons off, she had to resort to a dictionary to figure out what her child was saying. She was delighted with my prowess in a foreign language, an advantage she considered felicitously cultural.

But at the same time it rather hurt her that she could communicate with me only in her own tender Esperanto, which, had she been less modest, she would have realized was more than adequate, while Father, whose German was fairly fluent, was able to talk long and riotously with me. Looking back on it now, I rather suspect Father's German. He had a remarkable flair for accent and could pronounce foreign words with magnificent bravura, while his actual knowledge of languages was almost nil. However, that never really mattered. In France, Spain, Italy, he was invariably taken for a native—he could look like one (some summers in France he even grew a beard), behave like one, and even utter a few noises like one, but there the performance ended. It was a good act, though, and it had its advantages because it impressed other Americans and awed local porters and cab-drivers to the point of not daring to demand larger tips.

We moved to New York and for a time lived in a small hotel on Gramercy Park. My first recollections of any sort are associated with a hat. It was a present some elegant friend of Mother's had brought me from Paris: a white frou-frou number trimmed with a diminutive ostrich plume, a border of tiny rosebuds, and a saucy satin bow tied, Anna Held fashion, under the chin. With it I wore, secured by a cord about my neck, a little muff of questionable white fur on which had been grafted two rather yellow ermine tails. The hat was my pride and rapture and, being so, was held out as bait for good behavior. If I had been particularly holy, I might wear it on those special occasions when that deity known as "mein Vater" would take me for an outing. We called it "giving the hat a treat." The hat would be taken to view the aquarium, to ride the ponies in Central Park (admirable equestrian headgear!), and as climax to a perfect spree, the hat enjoyed the benefits of a hot chocolate at Maillard's.

When I was four I started being yanked about Europe. It was part of Mother's cultural plan to expose me at a tender age to cathedrals, palaces, and art galleries. I don't believe I enjoyed it very much. Of my first trip I have only the haziest memory of two episodes. One was of an afternoon while we were quietly having tea on the terrace of a small *Gasthaus* in the Austrian mountains. All at once there was a burst of terrific excitement: waiters rushed about frantically fixing up a special table with embroidered linen and hideous floral arrangements and the local group of professional yodelers hurriedly assembled. The landlord rushed out of the kitchen mopping his face, stopping long enough to whisper into Father's ear that royalty incognito, an archduke and his two sons, had just driven in for tea. Mother, glowing with anticipation, moved my chair to a position where I might "get a good look at the little princes." I, of course, caught the prevailing excitement and sat waiting expectantly for a reproduction of Sir John Millais's painting of the famous Lads of the Tower. In came a prosaic party of four—an uncompromising British governess, a man who but for his Alpine hat and *loden* might have been one of my Missouri cousins, and two dreary little boys in sailor suits. A lavish tea, heaped with pastries, preserves, and sweets, was placed before them. I watched for a few minutes, then suggested we leave.

"Why?" Mother whispered. "Don't you want to see the little princes?"

"No!" I shrilled in a voice that carried beautifully. "They're not princes—they're just awful boys and they chew with their mouths open!"

Mother, flushing scarlet, clapped her hand over my face,

but Father snorted with amusement and said, "The child's right! They do!"

The other episode I can vaguely recall took place in Paris one day when Father and I were out on a walk near a big cathedral and he all at once asked me if I'd like to see a "waxworks." Remembering Madame Tussaud's in London which I had adored, I fell for the suggestion with eager delight. The place we went to was dark and dull and not at all like Madame Tussaud's. There were no kings being crowned nor any queens being decapitated. Just a number of people lying down in a highly uninteresting fashion. I was disappointed and bored. On returning to the hotel, I told Mother that I hadn't much liked the waxworks my father had taken me to see. Mother asked him which waxworks it was, and upon his reply she unaccountably burst into tears. There followed a curious argument between the two, Mother asking how he ever came to take me to such a place and Father explaining that he'd always wanted to see it himself, we were right there, and he couldn't leave me alone outside, and anyway, it hadn't made any particular impression on me. He was right, it hadn't, for it was years before I learned that the "waxworks" we had visited was the Paris Morgue.

During my early childhood we lived, as Mother used to say, "in a trunk," spending some months in New York, others off on the road with Father, and making occasional visits to Chicago, Europe, or Vermont. It was all the same to me. I cut out paper dolls with equal absorption in a Gramercy Park flat, a Left Bank pension, or a Pullman section, and on Christmas Eve I hung up my stocking with the same trusting optimism whether on Grandfather Skinner's mantelpiece or on the valve of a hotel radiator. The only place I could call home was the Durbin house in Ravenswood. Mother still played now and then in some of Father's productions, and during those periods I would be left in the care of my grandmother whom I adored. Hers was a warm and cheerful household, and I was very happy with them all.

It was especially convenient to be able to park me with Mama Durbin, but Mother more and more felt the need for a home of our own. Since her marriage, she had become less interested in acting and, after my arrival, she completely gave up the idea of ever making an important career for herself. It was a renunciation, to be sure, but it had its compensations. She had been dazzled by the theatre, but dazzled chiefly by what the theatre could bring to a person of her simple background: travel, the cultural amenities of big cities, and above all, the chance to meet and know people who, in her opinion, were "distinguished." It became her favorite adjective of commendation. And now she found, through the life that was opening up to her and her husband, that there were "distinguished" people outside the theatre. *Beyond* and *above* it would more accurately have expressed her point of view. For Mother developed a curious attitude toward the stage. She always loved it and, until the day she died, she was keenly interested in it; but more and more her approach became a detached one. Father's career was of prime importance to her—as later mine was to be—and yet, as time went on, her attitude became one which indicated she felt that while we both made our livelihoods in the theatre, we, as a family, were not quite of the theatre world. Stage celebrities grew to be of far less importance to her than those persons she set up as gods in her private Olympus of the "distinguished." When Mrs. Patrick Campbell came to luncheon, she was pleased and flutteringly apprehensive, but when Professor Baker of Harvard came, she almost burst with pride. And yet I have sometimes wondered if in some ways this was not a self-imposed attitude—one she deliberately chose to adopt after she had made up her mind to leave the stage in order to make a home for her little family. For there were times in later years when I feel sure she missed theatre life and when I believe she speculated about the success she herself might have made in it. I once asked Father if he thought Mother might have become a great actress. After a slight pause he smiled and said, "I think not. She had beauty, taste, and an elusive Terry-like charm, but she was too fearful of what people thought."

CHAPTER EIGHT

The Latch String

One summer, Father, in search of atmosphere for *The Harvester,* an adaptation of Richepin's *Le Chemineau,* with the locale changed from the Midi to French Canada, had taken us for a few weeks to Les Eboulements, a tiny village perched precariously on the banks of the St. Lawrence between Murray Bay and Baie St. Paul, and there we ran into a remarkable lady who was to have much influence on our lives. Her name was then Mary Crawford—she later became Mrs. Charles B. Dudley, wife of the chief chemist of the Pennsylvania Railroad—but I knew her always as Miss Mary. She was one of the first Americans to have a summer cottage in that community of "habitants" and Gilbert Parker characters. The rest of the year she lived near Bryn Mawr where she taught in one of the preparatory schools. She was vital, brilliant, witty, and at the same time disarmingly lovable, and we all three warmed to her at once, Mother and she immediately cementing a friendship which was to prove to be the closest of their respective lives.

"Miss Mary" persuaded Mother to move to Bryn Mawr for the following winter. She lived with her sister, "Miss Bessie," and a brother whom we knew as "Mr. John," on a large pigeon farm halfway between Bryn Mawr and Conshohocken, in a sweep of that gracious Pennsylvania countryside of opulent fields, thick hedgerows, and majestic woods tidily cleared of underbrush. The neighboring farms were large and shipshape, and the barns were those beautiful structures of mellowed stone that are one of the glories of American architecture. Set snugly into hills with entrances on three levels, they had walled cow yards, and the whitewashed pillars that supported overhanging eaves formed corridors like cloister walks. The Crawford farm had seen a time known as better days, at which happy epoch it must definitely have come under the heading of a handsome estate. A tree-bordered driveway led to the main house, a mansion-like product of the middle-General-Grant period. Just inside the entrance gates was a love of a pre-Revolutionary cottage. The Crawfords, in their more affluent days, had used it as a lodgekeeper's house. It was tiny but ideal for a family such as ours. Miss Mary suggested we rent it for a year, with an idea that we might eventually settle in the neighborhood. Father would be either playing in New York or touring somewhere and Mother was loath to be separated from him, but Miss Mary used the persuasive argument that I was a puny child in need of bracing country air. Furthermore, I should soon be starting the process known as education, and we were near that Athens of the Main Line, Bryn Mawr, where was situated not only the college but any number of excellent preparatory schools, and education was to be found on every turning of the right side of the tracks. Mother, who herself was ever avid for culture, was, as far as I was concerned, hell-bent for it. The prospect of my growing up in a seat of learning was one which decidedly pleased. Moreover, Bryn Mawr was near Philadelphia, and for all her Jeffersonian simplicity which in her case had a strong dash of Aaron Burr grandeur, another prospect which (although she would never have admitted it, even to herself) pleased, was that the little nomadic family might at last settle and take root in a community where other roots had taken proud hold flourishing into the *genus Biddle-Cadwallader* and other such magnificent family trees.

And so we settled in the lodgekeeper's house which had stone walls three feet thick, dated back to colonial days in more ways than one, and made up in quaintness what it lacked in convenience. It was one of those little perfections of antiquity "which," the proud owner will tell you, "has no furnace, no electricity, no gas—but you should see our early Dutch bake oven," despite the fact that nobody since the time of Molly Pitcher has thought of putting that device to practical use. The ceilings were low and supported by hand-hewn beams. Two rooms thrown together made a long, picturesque living room with a fireplace at either end. Down two unexpected and uneven treads one stepped, or more often lurched, into a diminutive dining room, off which was an even more diminutive kitchen which as an afterthought had been added on in the form of a lean-to. To reach the two upstairs bedrooms, one opened a sort of cupboard door and clambered up a flight of narrow stairs as precipitous as ship's rigging. The bedrooms too were picturesque and charmingly inconvenient, being directly under sloping eaves, and if you forgot and sat up in bed too quickly, you bashed your head against an out-jutting structure of plaster.

Mother, who hitherto had never lived in anything older than Moberly's clapboard birdcages, was delighted with the place. I don't remember whether I was or not. Probably not. I would have preferred something on the order of a cut-down version of the Château Frontenac. But Mother was charmed by the old doors that wouldn't stay shut, the windows that wouldn't stay open, the undulating floors that made walking a perilous thing. The house boasted not a single knob or modern lock, all doors being secured by wrought-iron bolts and latches which, because of sagging thresholds, frequently failed to connect. The old iron fastenings showing up against the white woodwork added to the character of the place and Mother, who had a fondness for the names of country houses, called this the Latch String.

The tiny abode completely enchanted her. She was guileless and very young. (Curious how difficult it is to realize that at the time of one's childhood one's mother was in the full morning of young womanhood.) That year in the Latch String must have put her enthusiasm to rude test. It was her first experience in housekeeping, a duty which all her life she thoroughly loathed. The nearest store was four miles away, and four miles by horse and carriage. There was no local delivery. For meat, fresh vegetables, and fish we depended upon the visits of rural hucksters who drove a regular route about the countryside in large vans filled with wares which they measured out on huge brass scales. The hucksters were rough, good-natured men who endeared themselves to me by calling me "Sis"—which, for some reason, made me feel quite grown-up. Twice a week, Mr. John or Miss Bessie went to Bryn Mawr for supplies for the big house, and Mother usually went along, sometimes taking me. The leading grocery was Brinton's, a typical, prosperous country store with a scale outside for weighing hay wagons. A barrel of salt herring stood just inside the doorway, and near it a pickle vat added its tang to the rich aroma of the place. The floor was carefully strewn with a light layer of fresh sawdust, and the well-stocked shelves were always tidy and immaculate. Behind the counter was a row of lovely tin canisters, black, shining, and decorated with gold arabesques and gay little paintings—dating from the days of the China Trade. Mother, carried away by the romantic beauty of the old bins, always purchased a surplus supply of spices and condiments, the names of which charmed her and of the usages of which she had only the foggiest notion.

That winter proved to be one to rival Washington's stop-over at Valley Forge. The house, of course, had no furnace and a vicious wind sweeping down over the frozen Schuylkill would cut through the cracks in the ill-fitting door jambs with the keenness of knife blades, blowing out the candles and making the kerosene lamps sputter like fireworks. I even remember seeing the rag-carpet strips rise and fall in the draughty hallway. Open fireplaces heated, or, to be more accurate, made tepid, the ground floor, and a Franklin stove at the head of the stairs tempered the chill of the two bedrooms, while in the icy bathroom a portable coal-oil stove gave forth less heat than smell.

That year called upon my mother's courage, a quality of which, for all her fluttering charm, she had as much as her pioneer forebears. Up to now she had lived in towns amid people and since her marriage she had always had the protecting presence of Father. Now she found herself in a remote and primitive cottage whose only other occupants were my pallid five-year-old self and an Irish makeshift maid-of-all-work named Annie who slept off in the lean-to, was deaf and a little "touched." There was no telephone and no means of communication with the big house where the Crawfords lived, it being a good quarter of a mile beyond calling distance and thick trees keeping it from view. The Latch String was practically flush with the main road which led from Bryn Mawr to Conshohocken. It was a lonely highway. By day farm wagons, a few private carriages, and an occasional clattering motorcar passed our gate, but at night it was desolately still. If an automobile went by, the occasion was one of eerie suspense. One heard it approaching for minutes before it whizzed past the house (whizzing, in those days, must have been all of twenty-five miles per hour), and one listened for minutes to the sound of the motor dying away in the distance.

One or two nights a week, someone on horseback passed at a canter down the deserted highway. We never knew who the rider was or where he was going. The hoofbeats had an uncanny, almost menacing quality and the sound made me cry, partly from fear, partly from the loneliness of a city-bred child bewildered by the awesomeness of country night. Mother, one evening, hearing my whimpering, came to my bedside, candle in hand, to find out the trouble. I told her I couldn't get to sleep, that I hated the sound of the galloping horse. Mother, I daresay, hated it too, but, with her capacity for turning into beauty all that surrounded her, she made of our common dread a lovely thing. She laughed at me, but very gently, and said it was a nice sound, a friendly sound—a sound which a little boy had heard years ago in Scotland. He must have been about my age then and *he* couldn't sleep, but that was because he was sickly. A lonely rider on a galloping horse used to pass his house too, and night after night he'd lie awake waiting for the hoofbeats to break through the moaning of the wild Highland wind. Years later, as a grown man, he had written a poem about it, a poem for tired little girls like me. And she recited Robert Louis Stevenson's "Windy Nights." The candlelight shone warmly on her serene face and her voice was mysterious but reassuring as she whispered . . .

> Whenever the moon and stars are set,
> Whenever the wind is high,
> All night long in the dark and wet
> A man goes riding by.
> Late in the night when the fires are out,
> Why does he gallop and gallop about?

Whenever the trees are crying aloud
And ships are tossed at sea,
By, on the highway low and loud,
By at the gallop goes he.
By at the gallop he goes, and then
By he comes back at the gallop again.

The words mingled with the distant hoofbeats and, lulled by the rhythm, I drifted off to sleep.

To judge by the standards of the average little girl, I suppose I was lonely, but I didn't know it. The fact that there were no other children near us failed to bother me. I was used to playing by myself. I had the run of the vast Crawford farm which had all manner of trees to climb, although I didn't do it very well, and having once reached a lofty altitude, I'd become terrified and bellow for the Crawford gardener to come help me down. There was a great weeping beech with long garland-like limbs falling about it to the ground and making it into a green pavilion. You parted the trailing branches and inside was a delicious retreat where no one could see you, although you yourself could peek out and determine who might be calling you and whether or not it was worth while answering. Giant chestnut trees towered along the Conshohocken road, for that was before the great blight which practically exterminated the beautiful species. On autumn days when the air was like when you've eaten peppermints, it was fun, if slightly painful, to gather a mass of burrs, crack them open with a stone, and bring the nuts home for Mother to roast in the coals of the living-room fire.

In addition to the trees, there were two monumental gateposts to climb. Made of jagged stone and cement, they were probably quite hideous, but perched on the concrete dome at the top, which commanded a fine view of the highway, one had a sense of distinction and power. My sense of distinction and power occasionally suffered a rude setback when pigeon purchasers driving up in express wagons or fume-belching motorcars, mistaking the Latch String for a lodge house and myself for the superintendent's child, would shout at me Hey, sis, would I go find my father, they wanted to buy some squabs. When with injured dignity I'd reply that my father "was in New York—playing," their bewilderment was evident and it doubtless increased when, without enlightening them further, I'd scramble down from my lofty eminence and, with an air of a grand duchess who has just been called "Waitress," would lead the way to the farm buildings. As a matter of truth, I welcomed any excuse for visiting the pigeon lofts. It was a fascinating region and I'd hang around for hours, making myself a nuisance with the hands by asking if they'd please let me "help" (the small child's term for generally getting in the way) with feeding the breeders, crating squabs, and banding the homers. The hands, for the most part, were Pennsylvania Dutch, strange, silent men. And as I was a strange, silent child, we got along well enough.

A delight which never palled was the old carriage house. Automobiles were jiggling their way into popularity, but the Crawfords still clung proudly to their horses. They had a handsome collection of runabouts, traps, express wagons, and surreys. There was even, back in a dark corner, a Conestoga wagon, the cobwebs heavy as Spanish moss hanging from the venerable shafts. The vehicles in constant use were kept over in a shed near the stable, so nobody much came to the carriage house. It was dark and cool inside. There was a strange smell of leather, wood shavings, and old apples. The ground was soft, and no matter how hard you put your foot down, you made no sound. The place both scared and fascinated me. It would have been nice to have had a companion to share the spookiness with, but I hadn't any. So I invented one. She was a little girl my own age and of course her eyes were cerulean blue and her hair hung in yellow ringlets practically to the floor. I can't recall that she had any name other than "My Friend." She must not have been very bright, for she complied with my every wish and suggestion. She thought I was wonderful, which was a good deal more than I did, and I loved her dearly. I would clamber up into one of the traps, usually the dogcart because it was the smartest, My Friend beside me, and gathering up imaginary reins and whip, would call out a lusty "giddy-app" to a mythical steed. This, in my fancy, was a replica of Wilson's Laundry horse, a beautiful creature I had seen over in Bryn Mawr—snow-white and docile, who spent most of his time tethered to a weight, dozing patiently outside the laundry. My particular Pegasus was an obliging animal who, with the speed of light, went wherever he was told. Sometimes it would be to New York to see Father, sometimes to Chicago, to call on Mama Durbin. Sometimes we took a flyer to the moon, although nothing much was doing there. Our favorite outing was a brisk trot over to Persia to have tea with a potentate I called "The Shawl." This took us further afield than the carriage house. Once arrived in Persia, I reined in Pegasus, whose name, I believe, was Prince, tied him to a handy Moslem hitching post, and proceeded to the "Divan of the Shawl," a ceremonial for which one repaired to the Crawford house, entering for the sake of mystery by a seldom-used side door, and tiptoeing into a vast and formidable room known as the "big sitting room," a strange misnomer, for nobody ever dreamed of sitting in it. The furniture was monumental and the tall windows were hung with heavy curtains suggestive of Holy Week at Saint Patrick's. The shades were always lowered, and an adult, on entering the room, must have felt as if he'd been asked in to view the remains. But for me the gloom was totally dissipated by the glorious presence, in a far corner, of a gem of Edwardian horror known as a "cozy-corner"—a small, low couch constructed out of Moorish saddle bags, secluded by a festoon of Turkish carpets arranged like the half-open flaps of a tent and embellished by a galloon of chenille balls and a venerable deposit of dust. In front of the sofa was a tabouret of teakwood and mother-of-pearl, purchased by some member of the family at the Philadelphia World's Fair of 1876. On this reposed an Oriental after-dinner coffee service which I thought the quintessence of all beauty. The pot was a brass and cloisonné affair with a spout in the shape of a cobra head, a matching sugar bowl, studded with large imitation jewels, and eight porcelain cups the size of eyewash vessels which rattled unsteadily in silver filigree holders. In this tasty retreat the "Shawl" held his court. The sofa was his famous "Divan" where he sat, tailor fashion, My Friend and I flanking him on either side and drinking tea out of the eye cups. The sofa was originally intended for two—and a pretty well-acquainted two from the looks of it—and sometimes the three of us felt cramped sitting there, trying to drink from the wobbly cups and not hit elbows. And in that eventuality the Shawl, who was the soul of courtesy and refinement, would do us further honor by electing one of us to sit on his lap. He invariably chose me, and in that position of dignity, we exchanged cultural amenities, he telling me all about Persia and Ali Baba and I responding with information concerning Chicago and my uncle who worked in a soda fountain.

That was Father's first season under the management of Charles Frohman. A translation of Henri Lavedan's powerful piece, *The Duel*, had reached Broadway and Father was anxious to do it. The play, which dealt with a bitter quarrel between two brothers, one a worldly doctor, the other a fanatical young priest, the familiar Latin struggle between Church and State, had been a furor in Paris with Le Bargy making his greatest hit in the rôle of the priest. (It is still occasionally revived at the Comédie Française.) The part of the Abbé Daniel was right up Father's romantic alley and, knowing Frohman controlled the American rights, he wrote the little Napoleon of the theatre asking about the possibilities of securing a script. Frohman's reply was terse and characteristic. "If you want *The Duel,* come under my management and I will produce it for you." Father would have liked continuing as an actor-manager, but the magic phrase "Charles Frohman presents" had already become a byword in the theatre. For a day or two he hesitated, then wired back his acceptance to go under the Frohman banner.

He never regretted his decision. There was an elegance about the Frohman management, the elegance of good plays and of distinguished actors, of productions just lavish enough yet always in excellent taste, the elegance of a devoted clientèle which included the fashionable carriage trade, drama-loving intelligentsia, and just plain public who knew and appreciated top-notch entertainment, the elegance of theatres which *were* theatres, bless them! such as the Empire, lovely with gilt and crimson plush and a great velvet curtain to catch the glow of that breathless moment when the house slowly darkens and the chatter of the audience quiets down to a few expectant "sh's" and THE PLAY is about to begin. The reason for the popularity of Frohman productions was the man himself. He had an uncanny genius for picking out the right script and the right player. He also chose the right director, although, in his quiet, self-obliterating fashion, he himself supervised every word, every gesture, every prop of the production. And that his supervision was so correctly authoritative was amazing, for he was an incoherent and shy little man whose inability to express himself amounted almost to vocal impediment. But perhaps through some sort of telepathy and an actor's intuitive receptiveness, he was always able to make himself understood. Father said that many a time at rehearsal, Frohman would take him aside (he was far too modest to speak out baldly before any cast), and say, "Otis . . . er . . . look. That girl . . . in that scene . . . er . . . Well, I'd like to see more . . . you know what I mean." And "By Jove," Father would conclude, "you *did* know what he meant!" Frohman was proud of his stars and with good reason, for his galaxy at that time included such names as Maude Adams, John Drew, Billie Burke, Ethel Barrymore—to mention only the greater luminaries. He made them feel like stars and never imagined that by doing so he might lose any of his own importance. Moreover, he had a sincere affection for them and they in turn adored him. He took a keen interest in their personal lives. The Frohman roster was like a great and extremely de luxe Broadway Lodge. He seldom appeared in public. Opening nights found him lurking incognito in the gallery, and if ever by some misfortune he found himself forced to make any sort of speech, he used the words of someone else—often lines from plays he had produced.

For Father and Frohman, *The Duel* was the beginning of a long and happy association which lasted until that fateful day when the waters of the Irish Sea closed over the head of the gallant little producer who stood by the foundering rail of the *Lusitania*, refusing to take up room in a lifeboat, quietly speaking his last heroic words which, of course, weren't his but characteristically came from a play by Sir James M. Barrie: "Why fear death? It's life's most beautiful adventure."

The Duel opened at the Hudson Theatre in New York and ran for a successful season. This was a godsend for Mother, for it meant that Father could come home for Sundays. She had never been separated from him except at such brief intervals as when she went to stay with her family in Chicago, and life at the remote little Latch String had called upon her for a deal of readjustment. To be sure, the Crawfords, who adored her, were kindness itself, and she spent a part of every day in their genial company over at the big house. But evenings, not wishing to leave me in the dubious care of daft Annie, she would stay in our solitary cottage, and evenings were long. She read, of course, omnivorously. Father sent her books and Miss Mary procured others for her from the Bryn Mawr library. Novels by De Morgan, Baroness Orczy, and William J. Locke, Agnes Repplier's brilliant essays, and, for occasional frivolity, Carolyn Wells and George Ade. Shaw she read and the plays of Ibsen and Brieux. Rather daring, that. She went in for a little Browning, because she thought she should. The colorful obscurities of that "poet of the soul" were enjoying a flare of popularity. Browning Societies were quite the thing, ladies who claimed they understood the true meaning of *Sordello* held classes for the enlightenment of other ladies, and every amateur soprano was caroling "The Year's at the Spring." When she felt particularly lonely, she took an occasional flyer in mild philosophy in the way of little tracts of the "keep-smiling-the-sun-is-on-the-wall" variety, which settled all problems so nicely in limp leather and William Morris print. She found particular comfort in the writings of Horace Fletcher, the contents of whose optimistic guidebooks to happiness, *Menticulture* and others, boiled down to the fact that, "Worry is a sneak-thief and anger is a highway robber; banish both from your heart and you have found your heaven on earth." As simple as that. Horace Fletcher, in addition to his books of popular philosophy, was the perpetrator of "fletcherizing," a fad therapy which, in its day, had as much success as had, years later, Coué's "every day in every way." . . . "Fletcherizing" was an elaborate term for chewing, or, as it was more politely put, "masticating"; the theory being that for perfect health, one must chew every mouthful of food at least twenty-five times. The fad, though country-wide, was short-lived. One lingered too long over meals; it took all flavor, and I daresay all nourishment, out of things, and people got aching jaws. The fact that Mother had met the eminent Doctor Fletcher and had found him charming gave her implicit belief in his therapy, and for a few weeks she tried vainly to make me "fletcherize." But happily she gave it up when another distinguished physician told her that humans would be better off if they lived more like animals, swallowing their food without overchewing it.

In addition to her reading matter, she gave herself lessons in French, a brave but hopeless struggle she kept up all her life. I never remember a time when either Chardenal's *Grammaire* or someone else's "often-used idiom" failed to repose by her bed despite the fact that it was her own lost cause, for she never learned to speak the language except in the most enchantingly incorrect fashion and with a melodious accent nobody ever understood.

The Morals of Marcus, Hedda Gabbler, or *La Plume de ma Tante,* however, failed to drown out the noise of the wind, or worse still, the noise of silence, and she must have found the time heavy and long. Her solace that winter was Miss Mary, huge, ungainly, and with a face that looked like a cartoon of George Washington, yet one of the most wonderful faces imaginable, alight as it was with wisdom, kindliness, and joyous humor. She was teaching school that year, but many evenings she would lumber across the frozen lawn to the Latch String, like some benign giantess, and sit with Mother, smoking the acrid little cigarettes which she rolled herself, and talking late into the night. Her intellect was on the same titanic scale as her bodily frame. And it was surprising that this was so, for she came of worthy and prosperous farm folk whose education was sound but limited and whose moral outlook was drained of color by that wry-faced church, strict Methodist.

Not the least colorful of daily events that winter was afforded by our only means of conveyance to and from Bryn Mawr and about the neighboring countryside. For this, we depended upon the Crawfords who kindly gave us the use of a runabout and a species of tree-climbing horse named Brownie. Brownie was a small mare who nine tenths of the time behaved with complete docility. She would pull us along at a brisk little clip, responding obligingly to a flick of the whip or a yank on the reins. She stopped when one wanted her to and she stood without having to be hitched. Let her, however, spy an automobile, a steam roller, or a train, and she became a double for Mazeppa's maniacal mount. Raising the shafts with her, a maneuver which hurled the occupants of the runabout backward to an angle of thirty-five degrees, she would soar onto her hind legs while her forefeet pawed the air as if they were on bicycle pedals. After which, she would stand for a brief moment, trembling horribly, and then bolt in any direction her mood fancied. Sometimes it would be across the bordering ditch, sometimes in the direction of the nearest telephone pole, up which she would attempt to shinny. Mother, who had small experience with horses, was game but terrified. I was even more terrified, and not in the least game, for the moment Brownie went into her act, I would close my eyes, cling on to the narrow arm rest, and bawl. In the case of automobiles, which were comparatively scarce, and steam rollers which were even more so, we adopted the safety measure of having me get out of the runabout, stand in the middle of the road, and signal the oncoming juggernaut to slow down. Most motorists, who in those days weren't any too certain about their own means of locomotion, usually complied, as did the steam-roller operators whom a sense of power in regard to causing runaways had made charitable. But engineers of the Pennsylvania Railroad were not so considerate. A trip to Bryn Mawr, or "the Village," as we called it, necessitated crossing under the trestle of the Main Line tracks, and as a train was nearly always thundering down that busy right-of-way, the controlling of Brownie required the skill of a Frank Buck. Frequently Mother and I both got out and held a side of the little mare's wildly plunging bridle. Occasionally she'd break loose and bolt away from us and we'd have to dash after her calling shrilly to astonished passers-by to stop the runaway horse. These dramatic incidents always ended humiliatingly enough in the easy recapture of Brownie who would be found, her frenzy abated, serenely cropping somebody's lawn.

It was Brownie who took us to the Bryn Mawr station Sunday mornings and our terror at her rearing and plunging was mitigated by the rapture of knowing that Father was arriving by the eleven-forty-five local. Throughout my childhood, Sundays meant the homecoming of Father, and Father meant all that was wonderful. The contralto whoop of the Pennsylvania engine rounding the bend was like a fanfare announcing an event as exciting as any act of Barnum and Bailey's. As the train roared into view, I'd hold my breath for fear it wouldn't slow down. Then would come the moment of panic for fear he might not be on board, followed by a gulp of joy at the sight of him swinging down out of the last car I'd expected him to be on, and a catapulting of myself down the length of the platform to meet him with a wild hurtle and a hand eagerly extended for the present he invariably brought me. Father's presents were simple, but to me they were treasures of delight: little dolls dressed in European costume, Maillard's "Langues de chats" in blue boxes with kittens on the lids, books on the *Little Black Sambo* order. He once brought home a harmonica and another time a xylophone—objects of joy for me and torture for Mother, although she put up with them in her zeal for my culture, thinking they might awaken in me some musical talent. Along with the weekly present came a copy of *Life* —the old *Life* of jokes by Sullivant and Otho Cushing, center pages by Gibson, and those Harrison Cady pictures of daily activities in a fabulous insect world where ladybugs wore Mother Hubbards and grasshoppers were resplendent in dress suits, and so much was going on one could gaze at them for hours and still find something new. Not the least of the booty he'd bring me was the week's clippings of two comic strips which he cut for me every day from the dailies. Mother highly disapproved of this, for "Little Nemo" and "The Dreams of a Rarebit Fiend" had not figured in her campaign of learning.

Sunday meant a large midday meal. And to make it more festive, Father usually brought with him a bottle of claret, of which I would be given a little tumblerful carefully watered. The salad course was in the nature of a ceremony, as Father always mixed the dressing. I can't recall a single meal when he was home, even on occasions of formal dinner parties, when Father failed to mix the salad dressing, in a great wooden bowl, patinaed with countless rubbings of garlic, slatherings of the best Italian olive oil, and guiltless of the sacrilege of soap and water. In this he tossed and tossed the lettuce until it was soaked and dripping and, as the French have it, beautifully "fatigued." How often in later years have I thought with longing of Father's salads when there has been placed before me some gag-worthy woman's-club concoction of fruit, mint jelly, and grated nuts, topped off with a maraschino cherry and chilled in the icebox to tastelessness, which is, I suppose, one thing in its favor.

Evening supper was generally oyster stew, or Father's favorite after-the-show meal, a bowl of crackers and milk. Then, for a brief time, he'd read aloud from Grimm or Hans Andersen, and as I grew sleepy he'd lift me up and carry me piggy-back up the steep cupboard staircase, tuck me into bed himself, and hear my prayers. Then he'd blow out the candle and say, "Good night, Person," and go back to Mother and the sweet-smelling fire, and I'd lie listening to the comforting drone of their voices while the sound of the scampering mice and the thudding apples ceased to hold any terror for me.

It was a snowy winter. Was there more snow in those days, or do our memories furnish us with an exaggerated amount? It seemed especially dazzling on Sundays when the Paoli Local, bearded with icicles and panting extra steam, slowed down and Father swung off looking very handsome and like a Richard Harding Davis hero, in a fur-lined greatcoat with a dashing astrakhan collar. The function of that coat was purely ornamental, a "fresh-air fiend" of a throat doctor having told him that a fur coat was disastrous to the voice and that he must throw it away. Father's New England upbringing would never have allowed him to follow to the letter such drastic therapy. Furthermore, the coat was highly becoming. So he compromised by wearing it wide open or hanging from his shoulders like a Prince Danilo cape. Once arrived at the Latch String, he exchanged it for a scarf and a heavy mackinaw, for I'd lose no time in dragging him out to "see my snow," as if I'd whipped it up myself. I had a gay-colored "Flexible Flyer" and I had laid out what seemed to me a definitely perilous coasting track which zoomed down a steep hill, swerved around a pine tree, crossed a ditch, and ended headlong in a fairly prickly hedge. I remember my amazement when Father, Mother, and I, in just that order, "belly-bumper," with Father on the bottom and steering, made the run without mishap on my diminutive sled. Like all children, I regarded my parents as somewhat atrophied octogenarians, incapable of any activity more sprightly than walking.

Father's guidance of my Flexible Flyer was more skillful than his management one Sunday of the Crawfords' smart cutter with Brownie between the shafts. It is doubtful if Father had ever driven a cutter and, while he claimed to know how to handle a horse, he was reckoning without Brownie. We set off, the three of us wedged tightly together from the waist down by a heavy and slightly redolent buffalo robe. Father took up the reins and flourished the whip as only he could do it. It was clear to Mother and me he was going to make a production of it. He let forth a histrionic halloo and flicked Brownie's startled rump which also let forth a halloo after its own primitive fashion, and we started for God knew where. Brownie being unused to sleighbells, they had the effect on her of a self-propelling rocket. Down the road we hurtled, Father somewhat overcome by his success, pulling on the reins, dramatically but to no avail. Mother, whose blind faith in her mate was ever unwavering, turned pale and kept muttering, "Oh, Otis, dear love." I crawled beneath the buffalo robe and shrieked. A few hundred yards from the gate, the road curved at a sharp angle. Father took it as if he were acting *Ben-Hur*, at which point Providence intervened in the form of a snow bank into which the slewing cutter dumped itself and us along with it. No one was hurt, the cutter was undamaged, Brownie stood docile as a pet cow, and Father's only comment was a triumphant "There!"

* * *

That was Maude Adams's second season in *Peter Pan,* and Father, who had a lay-off during Holy Week, took me over to New York to see it. It was a lovely spree, just the two of us. I of course adored the play and like thousands of other children, sobbed bitterly when I thought Tinker Bell might die; then to restore him to life and to prove my belief in fairies, waved my handkerchief like mad—only it wasn't my handkerchief. Father had forgotten to put one in my pocket, so he lent me his which was larger and made more of a show. And like thousands of other children, I all but broke the springs of my bed that night in my optimistic attempts to fly. Another impression of our trip, as vivid as *Peter Pan,* is the memory of a violent stomach-ache brought on by excitement and Father's overindulgence in the matter of a box of somewhat stale Cottonlene chocolate creams which were to be had by inserting a dime into a box attached to the back of the theatre seat in front of us. I apparently grew suddenly green and droopy, and Father, terrified and helpless without Mother, decided to administer the grim childhood cure-all of castor oil, and dragged me into a drugstore to get some. The mere mention of the ghastly stuff reduced me to such woe that the druggist, a compassionate man, sold it to him in the form of a large capsule. We returned to our hotel room and a considerable portion of the evening was spent in trying to get the capsule, which was the size of a pullet's egg, down my small throat. In spite of glass after glass of water, the miserable thing never left my mouth. I tried. And Father tried, gently poking. It only made me gag horribly. Eventually the great pill grew soft like a bloated oyster and Father, in his most dramatic tones, yelled at me, "Quick! It's going to burst!" That was all I needed. I gulped just at the crucial moment, the capsule burst in transit, and in ten minutes I successfully threw it all up and the chocolates along with it, and Father, ever philosophical, figured the remedy had been successful in the long run. One of the chief joys of that trip was the fact that nobody combed my hair. My coiffure was the popular bob, with a large bow tied firmly onto a tightly twisted wisp at one side. Gentle as Mother was, she always pulled, or to be more accurate I went on the theory that she was going to, and my daily hair-fixing was a painful struggle on Mother's part and a series of protesting *ouches* on mine. Father, on our trip which lasted two days, let me sleep in the bow which he perked up as best he could each morning while he slicked my short mane down with his hands and let it go at that. His triumphant remark to Mother upon our return to Bryn Mawr was, "Maud, look at that bow! It hasn't been off the child since you tied it on two days ago!"

Father's New York engagement ended and he started forth for one of those strenuous tours on which he flourished and grew perennially younger. This one took him through what was in those days—and still is, in some districts—the actor's Gehenna: the South, that land of charming people and filthy hotels, of picturesque countryside and antique railroads, where the glory of Southern cooking is confined to private houses and the average restaurant diet for the bilious traveler is an eternity of sticky fried chicken with a few green vegetables cooked in dishwater and salt pork to a state of gray cotton. Father wrote from Knoxville:

Dearest Wife:

When I get through this Southern tour, I shall consider that there is no kind of experience known to the strolling player that I haven't gone through.

I left Savannah quite pleased to think I had escaped the annoyance of the long Sunday's travel and away from the herd. My sleeper was comfortable though hot and I had an hour and a half leeway for my connection at Atlanta. It looked very safe until, just a dozen miles away from the starting point, the Georgia Central engine broke something. I had omitted to allow for the antebellum condition of all Southern railroad equipment. From that time, through the rest of the night, I spent the hours with my watch and my time-table.

Two hours late in Atlanta. Train to Chattanooga gone! No apparent way of reaching Chattanooga before ten at night. Then the freight was suggested. Would I take a chance? It might not get in till midnight but was due at 7.10. I *took* a chance and climbed into a brand new caboose, oozing with fresh paint (the scars of which I am wearing yet) and settled myself aloft in the cupola-like observatory for the day.

We were an hour late in starting, but the freight was light, merely a few empty cars and we had a fast schedule—for a freight train. My tripmates were the conductor, the flagman and one brakeman. The conductor was a young Georgian with a pleasant smile. I handed him my order slip from the superintendent of the Western and Atlantic road which read, "Allow Mr. Otis Skinner to travel to Chattanooga on No. 14 *AT HIS OWN RISK.*" His grin widened and we became friends. The afternoon passed quickly in my upper perch and I learned a lot about signals and blocks.

Floods were all around us—all train schedules were upset and we met a lot of freight trains going in the opposite direction. But we were a *fast* freight and there was a lordly satisfaction in seeing others up on sidings awaiting our passing. I smoked an innumerable lot of pipes and ate a solitary sandwich I had brought from Atlanta. I got weary from overmuch *pushing the train ON* with my nerves and concluded to shave. There was a tin basin and a "tin" mirror and when I got through I was like a battered tin soldier—though none of my wounds were deep. Presently the light faded a gloriously cloud-streaked western sky and a young moon stuck her horn up above a pile of purple vapor. It was like the night I walked to you from St. Iréné.

The conductor soaked some sticks and coal lumps in kerosene and proceeded to get supper on a big stove. The principal item—the "pièce de resistance"—was saleratus biscuit fried in lard, after having been split with the conductor's jackknife. I was glad I had had my sandwich. But the board was spread and illuminated with train lanterns. I was invited down from my roost. I didn't want to seem churlish, so I drank some coffee out of a rusty tin cup. Then resumed my perch. It was sport watching the sparks spit up into the black night —to see the signals flit by and to rejoice that they were all *white* signals, not *red* ones.

The last block had been passed, we were four hours gone and not half of the 140 miles accomplished. I sent a telegram to Buckley to have a car waiting at a certain Chattanooga street crossing and presented the engineer with a pass for two at the theatre along with my griefs, my hopes and my expectations. He did not fail me.

We flew up grades and around curves. I joyed in listening to the labored pump of the machinery and in watching the arc of lights on the engine-cab's rim and the reflected glare of smoke and steam when the furnace was fed by the busy man at the firebox.

I reached my crossing at 8.15 and the curtain went up at 8.30.

It was done. But to-day I'm very tired. I had pushed that train all the way from Atlanta.

But I have your letter and that's balm for all my hurts. And Bobs' dear little message which I think is very fine.

My heart's love,
Otis

Later that spring my Grandfather Skinner died. He had been failing for some time. When it was certain the good old gentleman was going, Father was telegraphed to come. He was on tour by then, but Frohman closed the play for two days in order to allow him to hasten to his father's bedside. Mother rushed up to Cambridge to be with him and I was left in the protection of Miss Mary. Word of Grandfather's death reached us over the Crawford party-line phone. I was in the kitchen at the time, scooping out of a yellow bowl the delicious leavings of batter "goo" for a cake which Emma, the Pennsylvania Dutch cook, had just put in to bake. Grandfather Skinner was to me a nebulous deity whom I recalled vaguely as someone I had once seen on the eminence of a church pulpit, and at that, I doubt if I would have remembered him at all if it hadn't been for his snowy hair and flowing white beard. The news of his demise I received with equanimity. It seemed hardly worth interrupting my scooping of the batter bowl over. Emma, however, who had good Lutheran training in the fitness of things, flung her apron over her head and, although until that moment she had had no idea that I even had a grandfather, burst into a torrent of tears. Amazed and embarrassed, I ran and flung my arms about her, a consolation which merely increased her sorrow, for she wailed all the louder, clutched me to her large bosom and called me her "poor grandfatherless waif." The term roused in me a wave of self-pity and I remember joining her in a loud orgy of sorrow which was cut short by Miss Mary who loomed into sight at the kitchen threshold, shouted at Emma to stop being an idiot, and bore me off to the cozy living room, where she rapidly allayed my sense of bereavement by feeding me fudge and reading me one of the more spectacular of the *Ingoldsby Legends*.

Grandfather Skinner was laid to rest beside his wife and amid his forebears in the little mountain cemetery in Proctorsville. Father had to return to his tour, but Mother went with the family to Vermont and stayed until the last of the sad duties was accomplished. A letter from Washington reveals something of how Father felt.

Dear Heart [he writes],

My thoughts and love have been with you ever since I left Cambridge.

It seems as if the severing of this tie that held me for so many years to the good and tender man, my father, had brought me nearer to you. It is only in the past three days that it has come to me with a realizing sense, what it all meant.

Death's mystery has had its glory for me. That glory has been shed on my love for you.

Father's next route took him out to the Coast. With this sorrow fresh in his heart, it must have been a trying tour for him. But to waste any minutes of being alive in self-pity or regret was not in his scheme of things. His philosophy was a happy combination of Lao-Tse, Epicurus, and Artemus Ward. Life was something to be lived deeply and enjoyed, more so than ever now that sorrow had sharpened the outlines. He busied himself with the interests which the road always afforded him, good books, good scenery, good friends, and, when it was available, good food. During fifty years of intermittent trouping, he never lost his zest for new places or for old places revisited. New Orleans, of course, was one of his loves, not only for its charm, but for its tender associations with the shy young girl who, sitting on a grave in the old French cemetery, had said yes, she would marry him. From there he writes:

Your city and mine, Dear Heart:

I made my pilgrimage to Métairie yesterday. It is always a bright and beautiful day when I go there. The little chameleons are still chasing each other about the tombs of our trysting place. They are no older. Neither is Métairie. Neither is our love.

I had your sweet letter when I returned in the late afternoon.

Did Bobs get all the postal cards? You must tell her about Métairie and about the chameleons and about father and mother.

I went out St. Charles Avenue yesterday to an insistent photographer. As we went along, we passed a series of streets all named after the Muses . . . there must have been nine of them, I suppose . . . Thalia, Clio, Euterpe, Terpsichore, etc. . . . where but in New Orleans could one find such street naming?

He had his fiftieth birthday there that year and he wrote:

It was half a century ago that I came into the world. That is a most terrible state of affairs. I am supposed by popular

> belief to commence the journey that goes down the mountain but I am so d——ed perverse that I am still *looking* up. There are heights still above me and I never could be content to look away from them.
>
> The crown of my fifty years is you, dear wife, and that crown too will go on gathering glory . . . for not being a sensible crown it will never know that time dims and tarnishes.

We spent the ensuing summer back in French Canada at Les Eboulements. Miss Mary being married and living in Altoona, we rented her pleasant, rambling log-and-plaster cottage. Professor and Mrs. Charles M. Andrews were there that season with their children Ethel and John, and for the first time in my six years, I had the steady companionship of other children.

On rainy days, we played in the attic of Miss Mary's cottage. Cousin Charlie had fastened a rope onto a rafter and our favorite game was to grab the end of it, climb up onto an adjoining beam, and swing down. One afternoon, my hand slipped and I landed on the rough attic floor with a violent thud. I had kicked off my sandals and something hurt my left foot, but, in the heat of the game, I hardly noticed it until Ethel and John, their eyes wide with fascination, began pointing. I had landed on an upturned nail and it had gone clean through my instep. From the open gap was pouring a stream of blood and, at the sight, I began to yell equally gory murder. The grown-ups were off on a fishing trip and there was no adult to tend to the casualty. Ethel, who had suffered a recent encounter with a hornet's nest, put the benefit of her experience to use by slapping on a layer of mud, a remedy which could not have done much harm as, happily, my foot was bleeding profusely. We bound it up in a dishtowel and for a couple of hours the three of us sat on the cottage porch watching my life's stream trickle out through the bandage. The Andrews passed the time speculating on how long it would take me to die and I bawled steadily until the joint flow of tears and blood must have dehydrated me completely. The nail on which I had speared myself proved to be a rusty one and by the time my parents returned, my foot was hot and swollen. The following morning, it was puffed up to twice its size and a nasty red streak along my ankle gave every indication of a first-rate infection. The only physician Les Eboulements ever knew was a medical official sent down from Baie St. Paul by the government under the aegis of the Seigneur in the rare times of serious epidemic. Birth, sickness, and death took their natural courses, checked or assisted by native peasant remedies, the *sage-femme,* and the local apothecary whose panaceas were a combination of patent medicines and the herbs and simples used since the time of Champlain and Cadillac. Mother was frantically alarmed and Father was all for sending to Quebec for a doctor. But Mother, along with her germ phobia, harbored an instinctive distrust of all members of the medical profession, unless they had written a book or won a prize, and, even then, she seldom thought they were to be relied upon unless they were women doctors. "Because," she'd explain with her own brand of logic, "they *must* be fine physicians since nobody thinks they are and it's so brave of them anyway." To Father she pointed out the depressing fact that if I were going to get lockjaw, by the time anyone had made the trip from Quebec, my jaws would be well on their way to setting, and, if I was not to be the victim of a virulent affliction, why go to all that complication? She practiced her own remedy which was to keep the wound open and draining and to bathe my throbbing foot frequently in alternately hot and cold basins of bichloride water. After a week of pain and hobbling about wearing a moccasin of Father's, I made an uneventful recovery.

That was the summer Father taught me to read. Our textbook was a little yellow volume called *The Land of Song, Book 1,* a simple collection of children's verses, many of which I already knew, which made it simpler still. I considered it all highly entertaining. Father, as a teacher, was gay and funny and from a standpoint of scientific education, thoroughly unsound. He taught me to read as he read—slowly, painstakingly, and never missing a word, and, to this day, I can't read any other way. For a scholarly man, Father read almost laboriously. But he remembered what he read, often verbatim and with warm affection. To him, a good book was like a good bottle of wine, its flavor to be relished slowly and respectfully in order not to miss a drop of enjoyment. To skim through a great literary work or to guzzle a quart of fine vintage was a boorish discourtesy to author, winegrower, and to one's own sense of appreciation. As a result, he could quote whole passages from his favorite writers, Dickens, Trollope, Mark Twain, and, of course, Shakespeare. But Shakespeare was more than a favorite author. He was God Almighty and his *Complete Works* took the place of the family Bible. And, in addition to *The Land of Song, Book 1,* I learned to spell out the words of *A Midsummer Night's Dream.* Thanks to Heaven and my wise parents, I always had my Shakespeare "neat." No short cuts, no popularized synopses for little folk with expensive illustrations to turn the great lines into a mediocre substitute for Peter Rabbit. A friend of Mother's had given me a "de luxe" edition of Lamb's *Tales,* a well-meaning gesture which Father took as an insult to the Bard and to his child. I was allowed to look at the illustrations which were of the Maxfield Parrish-Edmond Dulac order, but then, lest I be contaminated by the text, the book was snatched from me and hidden away as carefully as if it had been an advance copy of *Lady Chatterley's Lover.* This, as I look back on it, was an unnecessary precaution. For Shakespeare, in the original and spoken by Father in his golden voice, was a joy and an exciting reality. Any substitute would have been like reading the libretto instead of hearing a performance of *Walküre*. I was not at all perceptive, not particularly overbright, but the music, the color, the narrative fascination of Shakespeare's words held me spellbound. The idea that Shakespeare is "difficult" strikes me as fantastic. Then so is *Mother Goose!* Why is "Sing a Song of Sixpence" any more comprehensible than "Full Fathom Five My Father Lies"? And why should tiny tots be forced to lisp the inanities of "Chicken-Licken" when they might be given the experience of picturing in their imaginations the gay facets of that Elizabethan gem, "The Queen Mab Speech"?

Remembering that summer, I can still see the pine-dark Laurentian hills sharply outlined against the clear Canadian sky, the sloping grain fields clinging to the steep sides of slopes which tumbled down into the cold, majestic St. Lawrence. Sometimes they tumbled in earnest for the name "Les Eboulements," meaning "a sudden slide," was not inapplicable and heavy rains occasionally brought in their wake sudden givings-way of the great riverbanks in thundering avalanches of soil and rocks. It was said that persons had been caught in such cataclysms and buried under the débris. The idea fascinated me. I don't believe I deliberately hoped such a tragedy would take place before my eyes, but, in the unfortunate event that it might be God's will, I wanted desperately to be on hand to see. I recall the *habitant* children in their blue smocks tending with long poles flocks of savage geese. And I can still see the man who brought us milk. His cows grazed in a pasture on the mountainside and he used to milk them at sunset, pour the warm foamy liquid into two great buckets which hung from a wooden yoke about his neck, and tramp down a path to our cottage, whistling in the twilight. And most clear of all the remembered images of that far-off summer is Father, his shirt open at the throat, the manuscript of next season's play rolled into his pocket (he always memorized his parts outdoors, striding about some open clearing until, by the time the part was learned, there was a little circle tramped in the grass which children, chancing upon, might have taken for a fairy ring). Father, striding home through a waist-deep wheat field, carrying the great bunch of wildflowers he always pulled for Mother, lovely, rank assortments of yarrow, Queen Anne's lace, vetch, and wild lupin. I was too young to know the meaning of the word "romantic," but at the sight of him, gay, handsome, often singing in what he thought was French, my heart would pound with pride and delight. "That's my Father," I would say to Mother, in case she didn't know. How Mother, also watching him, must have felt, is food for tumbling song. As he'd come up the porch steps, I'd hurtle into his wide-stretched arms, and he'd greet me with a loud "Hello, Person," and swing me up onto his shoulders. I'd hold on by his forehead, and he'd dash with me into the house, always pretending that he was going to bash my head against the door jamb and always ducking just in time, and making me squeal with happy terror. He would be sopping with sweat, but it was lovely sweat, clean-smelling as the fields. I was very much aware of the way my parents smelled. I suppose children are. Father smelled of health and warmth and clean linen and jackets made of homespun. There was about him the scent of good ripe tobacco, never the sickening reek which clings to a cigar smoker, like the atmosphere of a Pullman car. And Mother had a lovely smell of her own, fresh and dainty, with a fragrance of talcum power and lemon verbena. Her clothes were always clean and crisp, and she pinned tiny sachet bags into the bodices of her homemade, ribbon-trimmed corset covers. I used secretly to love being "just a little sick," because it meant sleeping with Mother, and while it was comforting to cuddle close to her soft plumpness (hers was no fashionably decimated figure, for, try as she would to "bant," as reducing was then called, she never lost her pretty curves which were a part of her beauty), what most soothed and reassured me was her gentle fragrance which was there like a protection throughout the night.

Next winter, we returned to the Latch String. But things were very different for me, because I started in on that lap in life's circuit known as School. Miss Mary had selected the one I was to attend, the Baldwin School, where she herself had taught. It stood high scholastically, and was primarily a college-preparatory institution. Mother, of course, had made up my mind that I would eventually go to college. As a matter of fact, Mother made up my mind about quite a number of things, such, for instance, as the fact that when I grew up I would never under any circumstances go on the stage. Just what I *would* do after attaining maturity varied according to her current enthusiasms. And, in turn, her enthusiasms varied according to her most recent conquest in the way of acquaintances whom she considered "distinguished." On forming a close friendship with the artist Violet Oakley, she decided it would be nice for me to become a mural painter, a stimulating notion which lasted until she met Janet Scudder, at which time it changed into the fantasy that I might develop into an eminent sculptress. I even recall a brief but frightening period when, fired by a sudden and burning admiration for Doctor Anna Shaw, she whipped up the idea of my taking up reform and the pulpit. Music and even dancing (the sort, to be sure, known as "aesthetic") entered vaguely into her campaign of my future careers, but never the stage. People, upon meeting me and feeling called upon to say something, would frequently come out with the obvious remark that they presumed little Cornelia was destined to follow in her father's theatrical footsteps, at which Mother would quickly say, "No, indeed, you're *not* ever going to be an actress, are you, Cornelia?" and shyly I'd croak a weak "No, indeed," vaguely wondering why the words came with little spirit.

The Baldwin School was situated in Bryn Mawr, four miles distant from the Latch String. I went to and from the seat of learning by means of whatever horse-drawn vehicle the kindly Crawfords had free to take me. Sometimes it was the runabout, pulled by Brownie and driven by the Irish coachman, Johnnie, who had one eye and an equal portion of brain. I started in the lowest class, which was a sort of advanced kindergarten. We sang little songs, spelled out words in little books, struggled with a few elementary sums on little blackboards.

Never did child look forward to any experience as much as I to going to school, and never was a child so instantly, so bitterly disappointed. The prospect of meeting and making friends with a whole raft of little girls my own age was intoxicating indeed. I met them. And instead of finding them friends, I found them unaccountably belligerent enemies. To begin with, they all lived near one another and, being well acquainted, had already got together in a group formation, which proved to be a tiny tots' equivalent of the more ruthless of the Chicago gangs. They were all firmly in the club. I was "new." Also I was "queer." From constant association with grown-ups, I used long words. I didn't know how to play games, and if truth were told, found most games rather awful. I spoke with a broad *a* and didn't rip out the letter *r* in orthodox Main Line fashion. I was naturally quiet and, being painfully shy, in the presence of these small savages I became almost mute, a condition which they took for a sign that I was "stuck up."

I might, possibly, have managed to make one friend had it not been for Elise Murphy. That was not her name, and I'd call her by her real one with gleeful maliciousness if, a few years ago, I hadn't met her again. Quiet, attractive, the mother of four sons, she has turned into a charming person, but in those days, she was a fiend fresh out of hell. She took one searching look at me and then seized upon me as her victim with a concentration which never let up. She teased me, she made faces at me, she pulled my hair when Miss Knapp, our teacher, wasn't looking. She mimicked my way of talking, to the rapture of her satellites. My name filled her with derisive amusement, and she called me Chameleon Ogre Skinny, an inspirational epithet which her cohorts took up like a chant whenever I emerged for recess. Finding out from me that my mother's name was Maud, she added a further gem of wit to the nasty refrain by quoting the slightly dated slang expression, "Hee-haw, and her name was Maud." Elise, in addition to her other horrid characteristics, had the further vice of being a small snob of a particularly vulgar order. The fact that her parents were rich she took upon herself as a personal accomplishment, and for some reason her wretched little followers shared her attitude. Baldwin was not at all a wealthy child's establishment and even now I can't figure out how she got away with such ostentation. It was probably less awe of her affluence than the fact that she was a successful bully which made her class dictator. To whatever she pronounced as wonderful or loathsome, the rest of the pack bleated supine assent. I, naturally, came under the loathsome heading. I grew to dread the recess bell, which announced liberation for the other girls. For it was during that period, when she was beyond the restraining presence of gentle Miss Knapp, that Elise would perch on one of the horses in the gym, and surrounded by her buddies, would hold her particular variety of auto-da-fé of which she was the self-appointed Grand Inquisitor, and I the culprit. She would ask me, in dulcet tones, to recite the opening lines of the "Light Brigade," and, imbecile that I was, I'd comply until the yells and catcalls over my "Hahlf a league, hahlf a league, hahlf a league onwahd," made me stop in agonized confusion.

One day, which still remains in my memory as "the calico-dress and express-wagon day," was the most miserable of that none too carefree year. Mother had made me a dress which, as I recall it, must have been one of unusual charm and imagination. She had come across the material in the country store near Conshohocken, an ancient, dingy emporium whose shelves were laden with bolts of fascinating dress goods, of almost ante-bellum vintage. For this particular garment, she chose a pretty calico, darkish blue, with an enchanting pattern of tiny stars and crescent moons. For model, she copied a frock from a Kate Greenaway illustration, with puffed sleeves and an Empire-like high waist. It was trimmed at the bottom with two rows of white rickrack. In taste and originality it probably put to shame Elise's modish sailor suits made, as she told everybody, by her mother's Chestnut Street tailor. Mother took great pains with it, I thought it was just lovely, and the first time I put it on, the admiring Crawfords said I was a "picture." Pleased and happy, I went off to school. The picture the Crawfords had in mind may have been one of pristine charm and quaintness, but the one I presented to my Comanche schoolmates was something, apparently, to be equaled in humor only by something out of the funny papers. They nudged one another, they pointed at me, they tittered and Elise passed an ultimate verdict on my frock by calling it "poor-folksy!" The morning passed for me in complete misery and I counted the minutes until Johnnie the coachman would call for me in the runabout and take me away from the hateful place.

Eventually the final bell sounded, and I was called for, not by Johnnie in the runabout, but by Alan in the express wagon. The express wagon was a battered vehicle used for transporting pigeon crates to and from the station, and Alan was a farmhand equally battered. Today he looked worse than usual, his ragged blue jeans were spotted with birdlime, and his chin was furry with a three days' growth of beard. Ordinarily I welcomed a chance to ride in the express wagon. One could sit beside Alan on the driver's seat and feel vastly important or one could sit back amid the pigeon crates, on one's own seat, and feel vastly uncomfortable but adventuresome. Alan was a taciturn son of the soil, a generous coating of which he bore on his person, and he smelled to high heaven, but I thought him rather wonderful. I had not heard of class consciousness and Alan and the express wagon seemed to me as felicitous a means of transportation as any. But today, as I looked out of the window, drawn up beside my rustic equipage was Elise's glistening dogcart with its smart little cob and the groom impressive in the Murphy livery, and my heart, which was already pretty low sank to new depths of wretchedness. I hoped with my soul that I might be able to slink away without being seen, but, quick as a ferret, Elise spotted the wagon and guessed—from my expression—that it was there for me.

"Look!" she squealed with delight, "Cinderella's coach has called for her! See what Chameleon's family send her to school in!" Then her black, malicious eye fell upon Alan and with mock politeness she said: "Is that your father driving it?"

If I hadn't been the small fool of the world, I would have fought back and even now the memory fills me with a desire to take a train to the town where Elise now leads a reformed and exemplary life and amaze her with a long-delayed uppercut to the jaw. However, all I did at the time was to grab my corduroy school bag (Elise's was of the finest leather) and run out of the building, blinded with tears of fury and hurt.

With a child's instinctive shyness at sharing private grievances with parents, I told Mother nothing of what had happened. But she knew something was tearing at my confused emotions when, at supper, I burst into uncontrollable tears. Wisely she let me cry it all out—then gently asked me what the trouble was. All I told her was that I never again wanted to wear that "poor child's dress." From observations I had made she figured out the situation and, after reassuring me, quietly put away the little frock over which she had taken such tender pains.

One day at recess Elise, searching about for new methods of tormenting me and seeing the janitor's ancient bowler hat lying on the gymnasium window sill, called out to me, in her most jeering tones, to put it on. I started to run away, then, a sudden, curious urge to show off got the better of my timidity, I grabbed the hat, put it on at a jaunty angle, and went into a comedy routine to the tune of "Rufus Rastus Johnson Brown." Strange to say, I was pretty good, a fact which amazed the other children and myself even more so. The older girls gathered around and called upon me to do it over and over until the sudden appearance of a teacher put an end to the silly act. Laying aside the somewhat dirty bowler, I returned to the classroom, flushed with success. The little girls were frankly admiring. Even Elise said she never'd thought I had it in me, and for once, I almost felt I "belonged." My triumph was short-lived. That evening as I was doing my homework by the light of a bright student lamp, Mother began curiously leaning over me with an air of horrified concentration. Slowly she reached for my head and drew a thumb and forefinger down a strand of my hair. For what seemed a very long time she examined what she had found, then, suddenly, unaccountably, she burst into a flood of tears. The sight of Mother crying frightened me considerably, and I followed suit without the slightest idea of the reason for such lamentation. I found out soon enough. Mother went after me with a fine-tooth comb, and if God had slipped up on numbering the hairs of my head, Mother made up for the oversight, for she took each and every one, in turn, scanned it carefully, then ran her fingers down it two or three times. The process took up a large portion of the night. Apparently there had been only "one" (we never mentioned "them" by name), but, she said in a quavering voice, you couldn't tell about—and she lowered her voice to the tone of a fugitive from justice—"*nits*." I hissed at her in apprehension asking what were nits and in an almost inaudible whisper she said—"eggs!" Thereupon she soaked my painfully overworked head with kerosene. We both cried some more and by midnight I went reeking to bed. For three days I was kept home from school. The kerosene was applied regularly, until I became a liability for the family fire insurance and I was kept far away from all manner of flame. It was a sorry interlude.

That spring, Father wrote asking Mother to come join him on the road. She didn't need much urging. It would have been more of a vacation for her to have left me behind, but Father's tour was taking him to the Pacific Coast and she decided that travel in places of scenic beauty came under the heading of culture and education. Accordingly, I was yanked out of school. We took the Pennsylvania to Chicago, stopped for a day with Mama Durbin, then went West on that train of the glorious name, the Overland Limited. Neither of us had a very easy time during the journey. Our space was a lower which, when made up into a bed, we both shared. Mother, for purposes of safety, placed me along with her pocketbook on what she called "the inside," a position which jammed me up against the window. In those sturdy days, ventilation came through a nasty little screen slot which spewed smoke and cinders into my snub nose until by morning I resembled a small minstrel who had only half removed his make-up. Mother's idea of a railway trip was to sit quietly in her Pullman seat reading, resting, and taking in the scenery. Mine was to fidget, flounce, and dash from one end of the car to the other. I loved eating in the diner. Mother liked staying in her space with a box lunch. I loathed box lunches. Everything tasted of apples, even the Zu-Zu's, and unaccountably the cracker crumbs always made their way into one's berth at night and mingled soggily with the cinders. Mother's germ phobia had not diminished. If we did eat in the diner, she wiped off plates and cutlery with her napkin, a precaution which all her life she took on trains and in all European restaurants with the exception of those in England and Sweden, countries which she considered safely hygienic. Mother's wiping-off of our eating implements, especially if she first dipped her napkin in her drinking water and then sent for a fresh glass, mortified me deeply. I felt it hurt the waiters' feelings and I'd try to convey by means of shy little smiles that they mustn't mind, *I* liked them anyway. Except at mealtime, my hands were kept unsullied in depressing cotton gloves, my teeth were brushed in bottled water, and every morning a layer of newspaper with a hole torn in it was meticulously spread on "the seat" notwithstanding the fact that a strong breeze from the train in motion frequently blew it off.

We met Father in Colorado and from there journeyed on westward. Mother had purchased a book on geology, a science she decided must be extremely worth while as she had never known anyone who understood it except that wonderful Miss Florence Bascom who taught the subject at Bryn Mawr College and who went about the countryside tapping rocks with a little hammer, and maybe I would grow up some day to be a geologist. Who knew? Well, I for one knew, but I didn't tell her so. The book she had picked out was called *Earth Sculpture*, and from it she persuaded Father to read to us for a half-hour each day. It was a dreary book, much too difficult for me to understand, and I hated it. (Years later, Father confessed that he hated it too.) Father would read obediently, but without much histrionic fire; I would hump up in a corner like an infuriated gnome, my fingers stuffed defiantly into my ears, and Mother would sit, emitting little musical noises of approval, obviously not really listening to a single word.

The stop I remember best along the way was Salt Lake City. Salt Lake meant good show business. Mormons have always been patrons of the drama. Even in pioneer times, for every theatrical performance that played the town, Brigham Young kept several rows of seats reserved for his wives while the stage box was always regally occupied by himself and his favorite, she of the delightfully fecund name, Amelia Fulsome. Up until the last war, the town was well worth a seven days' stand. The week we were there happened to coincide with a great Church conventicle. From all parts of Utah and even the bordering states, the faithful Latter Day Saints flocked to the capital.

There was an organ recital in the Tabernacle every morning which Mother and I attended, it being a sightseer's objective and open to the public, Mormon or profane. What was not open to any but the faithful, however, was and still is, the Temple, that great granite wedding cake, glorious with its six soaring towers and its mammoth brass angel trumpeting the Covenant to all the world.

From our window in the Hotel Utah, Mother watched the religious line-up, and decided it worth joining. She whipped up the fancy that to get inside the forbidden Mormon Temple would be a cultural adventure of the highest accomplishment, like penetrating Tibet. Nobody, of course, but the faithful were supposedly admitted, but as only half the crowd seemed to be in Mormon attire, the rest in ordinary clothing, who would know whether we were faithful or not. Father would probably have dissuaded her, but he had gone out for one of his long walks and there was only myself to disapprove. She was convinced she could get away with it, but to make sure, and going upon the same principle as that of a beggar woman who thinks the presence of a small child will make her case more convincing, she told me to put on my hat and jacket and come along. I inwardly withered with mortification. The line was very slow in moving along and I was sure people were looking at us. After what seemed an eternity we reached the portal to the holy of holies. Mother hissed at me to keep my head down. Just why she thought that would help us get past I don't know, but I obeyed. Perhaps it was a glimpse of my expression of misery, or the sight of Mother and the realization that here was someone who even in the days of sanctioned polygamy would never have been called upon to share her man with any other woman, which arrested the attention of the frock-coated guardian angel. He gave us one searching look, then in a stride, stood blocking the doorway. If suddenly he had pulled out a sword of fire, I would not have been much surprised. But he simply told us to go. His countenance might have been hewn out of Wasatch rock, but Mother cast on it the smile which hitherto had always made lapdogs of tigers, and said, with a little dovelike coo, "How do you do! We've come to worship too." (I hadn't, but I kept that to myself.) The local Cerberus, unmoved by Mother's shy blandishments, merely repeated the simple information that we'd have to go, and, rather in the manner of reprimanded hounds, we went. We didn't tell Father for several days, by which time we were on our way to California.

We spent two weeks in and around that place of charm and wonder, San Francisco. It, to my mind, is the only city in this country possessing that exciting and elusive quality known by the much overworked word of glamour. Certainly it is the one metropolis in America where I wake up mornings with that sense of breathless suspense, of expectant happiness, when I inwardly hug myself and say, "Dear God. I'm in San Francisco!" as I've said, "I'm in Paris!" or, "I'm in Rome!" I think at the age of six I must have loved it, although what remains in my memory is a jumbled kaleidoscope of blue water, swooping gulls, and sudden great soft fogs trailing over the Bay and making it boom forth into a choir of fog horns like giant bullfrogs in a swamp; cable cars running up almost perpendicular hills, Chinese children on Grant Avenue jabbering actual Chinese, which seemed peculiarly clever of them, and sea lions basking on the Cliff House rocks, looking like stoutish ladies in fur dolmans, flapping about so gracefully one wasn't aware they'd been deprived of their feet. I remember seeing trees which actually bore oranges. The reality of them growing like any mere apple, on a tree, seemed to me wonderful. Lemons too came under the same miracle category, and grapefruit, and I saw them all, growing in neat rows as if someone had tidied up the Garden of the Hesperides.

I remember an afternoon at somebody's house where I was being very much bored by the conversation of the grown-ups until a sudden and fascinating diversion took place. There was a sound of distant wind. The chair on which I had been placed and told not to move all at once started itself to do the moving, and the pictures on the walls began amazingly to swing. I was quite charmed by such goings on and couldn't understand why Mother shot across the room to snatch me up in her arms or why our hostess turned pale and told us to stand in a door threshold in case plaster started falling. It was all over in a moment. Father, who was as blandly bewildered as I, was the first to break the silence with an excited "Great Scott! Was that an earthquake?" Our hostess, a charming native Californian, smiled graciously and said, "Not possibly, Mr. Skinner. That was what we call a temblor." It was only a few years since that "temblor" which had destroyed half the city and which, she insisted, had been a "fire." No fire followed this lesser convulsion of nature, no plaster fell, and Mother, after her save-my-child gesture, replaced me a little crossly in the chair. I was delighted. I had been in an *earthquake!*

I remember too an afternoon when a lovely lady came to tea with us at the St. Francis Hotel. She spoke with a foreign accent, her eyes were like dark pools, and there was about her a scent of Parma violets. She laughed and conversed warmly with my parents, particularly with Mother whom she called Maud and with whom she had a tender caressing manner. With me she was delightful. She committed none of the outrages of well-meaning adults such as making me sit on her lap, or regarding me with beaming scrutiny to determine "who she looks like," but she treated me with lovely formality, inquiring after the state of health of each of my dolls and exchanging views on Johnnie the teddy bear's reactions to travel, with great gravity. I fell completely in love with her. After she left, Mother told me that I must always remember her visit. She needn't have, for I felt I always would. The lady was Madame Helena Modjeska.

To have experienced an earthquake was indeed an accomplishment, but my cup of adventuresome happiness slopped over on our homeward trip when, at a desolate spot known as Sand Point, Idaho, our train was wrecked. A switch had been left open, the rails spread, the engine jumped the track and crashed clear through a brick signal tower. The baggage van was smashed to matchwood, four or five cars turned over, but, miraculously, no one was killed, although there were a number of serious injuries. It happened around noon. I had nagged Mother into having lunch in the diner and the fact that in the accident that car tipped over whereas our own Pullman remained semi-upright on the tracks, was to her merely further proof of the preferability of a box lunch. There was a sudden jamming on of brakes, a loud crash, and Mother flung herself across me, presumably to ward off sudden death in the form of an avalanche of plates and cutlery. Her gesture, while heroic, succeeded in upsetting first a bottle of ginger ale, then the sugar bowl, both of which emptied their contents all over me. After considerable heaving about, the diner settled itself on its side, the stove upset, someone shouted "Fire," and things were in wild confusion until a rescue squad smashed open a window and, along with the other occupants, we made our way out through the aperture. In accordance with my customary behavior, during times of danger and tribulation, I began bellowing at the top of my lungs. Mother, pale and trembling, carried me over to a slope of the railroad bank and started gently investigating me for signs of compound fractures. My dress, a scarlet gingham number, was sopping wet and I was covered with a red sticky substance at the sight of which Mother, taking it to be blood, started ripping off the ruffle of her petticoat to make bandages and possible tourniquets. Closer inspection of the sticky substance revealed the fact that it wasn't blood, but a tasty mixture of ginger ale, sugar, and the dye from my frock. My bellowing continued unabated and Mother, by now fearing an internal hemorrhage, asked apprehensively where it hurt most. Nothing was hurting me, I wailed. It was Johnnie, my bear. I had left him behind in the Pullman space and for all I knew he might be dead. It was characteristic of Mother that, in her relief and annoyance, she slapped me. And it was even more characteristic of her that she made her way back through the wreckage, clambered into our half-upset car, and rescued the animal, who had survived the catastrophe without a scar.

CHAPTER NINE

Professors' Row

DURING THE NEXT YEAR, we lived on the Bryn Mawr campus in one of the little houses in "Professors' Row." Daily life was less picturesque than it had been at the Latch String, but the presence of a furnace, a telephone, and electric lights made it decidedly more comfortable. Mother felt she had been released from two winters of frontier existence. We no longer depended upon any fractious Brownie, for we were within walking distance of Lancaster Pike and the stores. Also we were near the station where trains ran every thirty minutes to Philadelphia, and, for her, Philadelphia meant civilization in the way of art exhibitions and matinées of the current theatres (every box office always extended her "professional courtesy"). It also meant the Philadelphia Orchestra to which, with considerable qualms over the expense, she had bought a subscription seat far up in the gallery. The height made her dizzy, but she didn't look, she said, only at the conductor. Carefully she'd peruse the program notes; more than once, she'd confess, reading the ones for the wrong concert, but that didn't blunt her ardor.

She found life on a college campus delightful. It was pleasant to stroll about the grounds, to pause and chat with the young girls or to browse in the library to which she had access. She attended the weekly lectures held in Taylor Hall for the students and faculty, but open to a few outsiders by special invitation. Bryn Mawr has always prided itself on its speakers, and with good reason. In those years, Brander Matthews, Richard Watson Gilder, and that beloved hardy perennial "Billy" Phelps came to talk on letters. Mrs. Berenson lectured on Renaissance Art and Lady Gregory read some of her one-act plays. Charles Coburn brought a small theatrical troupe to give Percy MacKaye's *Canterbury Pilgrims* on an open-air stage in the Cloisters. Mother avidly took in everything. Even when the Philosophical Society imported Hugo Münsterberg to address them on "The Psychological Basis of Pragmatism," she listened with attentive respect "because Doctor Münsterberg was so distinguished," although it is doubtful if she understood him any more than she did Professor Fougères, *adjoint professeur* of Latin at the Sorbonne, whose subject was "La Civilisation celtique révelée par les monuments de la Gaule préhistorique."

What fascinated and even staggered her a little that winter was the local appearance of two eminent (although *notorious* was more the current epithet for them) suffragettes. The Votes-for-Women question was shaking the country at the time and Bryn Mawr, with the great feminist, M. Carey Thomas, at its head, took what was considered the revolutionary stand. The presence on the former Quaker rostrum of Mrs. Cobden-Sanderson, explaining "Why I Went to Prison," and of Mrs. Pankhurst, all the more eloquent for a few weeks' regimen of forcible feeding, shocked a few conservative parents to the point of snatching their daughters out of an institution which countenanced such radicalism. Mother found the controversy most exciting. She herself was not a devotee of causes, although she admired those who were. She probably would never have taken any active part in the issue if her many friends who were "Militants" hadn't persuaded her to join their crusade. She did, with cooing caution, and the most warlike deed she ever perpetrated for The Cause was to help stage an evening of Tableaux of Heroic Women in the ballroom of the Bellevue-Stratford. She thought Equal Suffrage was very splendid and right, but her desire for the ballot never conflicted with the infinite tact with which she managed, even during times when feelings ran high and lifelong enmities were incurred, to keep as her devoted friends the "Antis" whom she knew. Her more belligerent sisters would have thrown bricks through the windows of the Senate. Mother would have tossed a bouquet to the Senator and have won the battle in less time.

Life in the small rented house was agreeable. All the faculty families lived close together and, while there were no dividing fences over which to gossip with the lady from next door, there was a friendly atmosphere to Professors' Row which might have made it an academic duplication of the back yards of Moberly. In this milieu, she found ample opportunity for exercising her talent for charming people. And in regard to this gift let me hasten to say that she never made ungracious use of it. If she was aware of it, and I believe she was, she accepted it thankfully and quite humbly as a blessing such as having fine features or good teeth. She must, of course, have known that she was beautiful, that her manner was disarming, and that her voice was the loveliest in the world, but she was totally devoid of vanity. And yet to charm people came to her as naturally as to say good morning. And she made no distinctions in the all-too-ready victims of her gentle wiles, whether it was Mr. Cascia, the ragged son of Italy who collected our garbage, or that extraordinary woman, the President (although "empress" would have described her more fitly) of Bryn Mawr, Miss M. Carey Thomas. She had a genius and, I guess, a passion for putting herself out for people and her reward was the instant response, the warm unfolding of everyone she met. She thought people were wonderful and they thought she was wonderful because she thought they were and because she was lovely and could bring forth qualities of loveliness in almost everyone. Even the most colorless drabs, starved pseudo-intellectuals whom I secretly summed up as "spooks" and to whom Father referred as "Maudie's stray cats," in her glowing presence took on reflected warmth and color surprising even to themselves. I often wondered why she bothered with these dreary individuals, for certainly they meant nothing to her. In fact, on catching sight of some one of these forlorn females in dowdy tweeds and batik blouses, plodding up the driveway to call, I have known her to shudder and emit a rueful little groan, then regain her composure, hasten to the door, and greet the creature as the one person in the world she most wanted to see.

Among her good friends was Ethel Walker (founder of the school), known by everyone as Diddle, then college secretary. Pretty golden-haired, and tiny, she was a gay and enchanting companion for Mother. She had a smart little horse and runabout and together they went on brisk drives about the countryside, although the rapid increase in motor-cars made for a good deal of hazard. Diddle wrote on the subject a parody of the *Recessional* (Kipling was "*the* thing" in those days). It was a gay little poem and two of the verses went—

Guard of the Motor, Great Chauffeur,
  Master of every road and way,
Who renders useless curb and spur
  And drives to madness roan and bay,
Oh, Goggled Magnate, spare us yet,
  Lest we upset, lest we upset!

Horn-warned, our courage melts away,
Within our cowed hearts sink the fires.
Our horsemanship of yesterday
Is vanquished by exploding tires.
Oh, Skilled Mechanic, spare us yet,
Lest we upset, lest we upset!

At Mother's suggestion, she sent the piece to *Life* and within a week received an acceptance and a check for twenty-five dollars. The two of them squandered the largesse on a spree in Philadelphia, a matinée of *The Witching Hour,* dinner preceded by an Orange Blossom cocktail at the Café l'Aiglon (very dashing, that!), an evening performance of Marlowe and Sothern, and enough left over for a two-pound box of Huyler's to bring home to me.

One of the objects of Mother's bubbling admiration I recall with a good deal of distress. From laudable motives of kindness, I shall call her Mrs. M. She was tall and angular and arty, and she wore her hair in scraggly braids about her head in a fashion she fancied was like Demeter, although it looked to me more like the Boz drawings of Mrs. Gargery. Her husband taught something fairly abstruse in the way of higher mathematics, and it was possibly reaction from this rarefied realm of pure abstraction that had driven her into becoming a devotee of Greek dancing. There was no authority at hand to say just how Greek it was, but Mrs. M. claimed she knew because she had made a study of Minoan vases and had attended every Philadelphia recital of Isadora Duncan's. The vogue for that divinity of motion was at its height. Those who wanted to show they were up on the very latest spoke of her as "Isadorable Duncan." Women, in a wave of emancipation, were shedding their Lily-of-France corsets and, draped in filmy shifts—the best approximation they or the local seamstress could run up on the Singer in the way of something fresh out of Praxiteles—were organizing classes of "aesthetic" dancing. Mother, though slightly alarmed, thought it very brave and progressive of Mrs. M. She encouraged her as she encouraged everybody, and the local priestess of the dance was all for getting up a select Hellenic class, she to be the instructor and her maenads to be composed of Mother, a few faculty wives, and two or three of the more supple women professors. The inspiration was not contagious. The campus ladies gave excuses to the effect that they were not aesthetic types and Mother got herself out of the situation in her lovely, evasive fashion. Not, however, without offering me in her stead as a victim for Mrs. M.'s green altar to beauty. Two other children were led, protesting, to the sacrifice, a pallid Swiss lad whose father taught psychology and a fat phlegmatic girl named Ruth. On a few dismal occasions, we met in Mrs. M.'s dining room. We were clad in homemade tunics whose Attic effect was tempered by a definite exposure of our winter underwear which no devotion to Art would persuade our mothers to dream of allowing us to remove any time between November and April. Barefoot and doleful, we skipped, pranced, waved our small arms, and obediently went through certain gyrations which Mrs. M. assured us would make us feel like Greek children at play when all in the world we cared about being was American children at play. The class was soon disbanded. I don't think Mrs. M. cared for children. Certainly children didn't care for Mrs. M. By way of smoothing out matters, Mother, acting on one of her beautiful and misguided impulses, asked her to hold a sort of soirée in our small sitting room. After all, as she explained when Diddle asked why, Mrs. M. *did* know about Tanagra figures and Doctor M. *was* such a splendid mathematician, and Cornelia *had* been so awkward. The festivity took place on a Sunday night. Mother arranged it so that Otis-dear-love, who was playing in New York during the week, could be on hand to help in the general appreciation of Mrs. M.'s terpsichorean skill. The other spectators were some dozen indulgent neighbors. They sat in an unhappy line along the four walls of the room, not quite knowing where to look, while Mrs. M., with real grapes in her hair and a definite corn on one bare toe, shook the foundations with her version of the *Bacchae*. Slipping out of bed and padding along the upper hallway in my flannelette sleeping-suit, I hung over the stair rail to watch and listen and wonder how grown-ups could be so silly. Father, who managed to slink out of the sitting room, also watched from the stairs. It was the first time I heard him utter the name of our Redeemer—under his breath, and not in a sense of worship.

For me the move to Bryn Mawr was a welcome one. I had the run of the campus and miraculously I had managed to make friends with a few faculty children. Moreover, school had now ceased to be a nightmare. Elise, the bully, had left to attend a more fashionable establishment in Philadelphia, and I was rapidly mastering the technique of getting along with my contemporaries. That fall there was another girl who was as "new" and as "queer" as I had been the previous year, and my first steps on the downward road to worldly wisdom were guided by the revelation that by joining the pack in its mass assault upon this poor little wretch, I was enrolling myself in the none too admirable lodge of my fellow woman.

Just about this time Mother decided to do something about religion, or rather about the accepted manifestation of it. During the small family's nomadic years and the two winters of comparative isolation at the Latch String, churchgoing had never occurred to her. Now in the atmosphere of suburbia, where matters spiritual were more conventionally organized, she decided that Church would be a desirable thing for me, and she looked about for a suitable sect as she might have looked about for a suitable pattern of chintz. I'm not certain, for Mother confided her inner convictions to few people and never to Father nor me, but I should have imagined that she herself would most readily have responded to the *pure serene* of the friendly faith of William Penn. She had friends among some of the Quaker families, gentle, cultured people of sound yet elegant tastes who lived abundantly with peace which, perhaps, is another word for God in their bosoms. But, to her, Quakers belonged to an exclusive portion of Old Philadelphia along with Independence Hall, the Fish House, or State and Schuylkill, and the Radnor Hunt. To ally herself with this quiet breed into which she had not been born would have seemed the act of an interloper and she would sooner have crashed the Assembly Ball than have ventured of a Sunday into a Meeting House. And so she, who was born of a Methodist mother, baptized a Catholic, married to a man of no sectarian convictions whose father had been a liberal Universalist, chose the Episcopal Church, not exactly by the eenie-meenie-miney-mo method, but "because," as she reasoned, "it was the most beautiful literature in the English language and, besides, such nice people are Episcopalians!"

Mother and I became parishioners at the Church of the Redeemer. That is, Mother went to the house of worship in spasmodic surges of piety, although she saw to it that my attendance was regular. This weekly duty I neither minded nor particularly liked. The rector was of the fashionable variety whose manner was more perfunctory than devotional. The unfortunate gentleman was quite deaf and he conducted the service at a pace which gave every indication that he wanted to get the whole thing over with as quickly as possible. Being unable to hear the responses, and having a highly accelerated sense of timing, he would interrupt his congregation in the middle of their every answering sentence. By way of diversion, I invented a little mental game of chance, challenging myself that I couldn't get out all the words of a response before Doctor C.'s toneless singsong cut me short. It was an amicable form of gambling as either I or myself was bound to win. The vocal race required a deep breath and an ability to utter the sentences in wild abbreviation. Thus when Doctor C. called upon the Deity with a throaty "O Lord, open Thou our lips," by starting a beat before the others and rattling out a rapid "Anna moutha show f'rtha PRAISE!" you could about beat him to the "Gloria." You couldn't do it unless you knew the phrases ahead of time and in my zest for the game, I memorized a goodly portion of the Book of Common Prayer. On the infrequent occasions of Mother's attending church, my familiarity with Morning Service amazed and pleased her. She took it to be an indication of juvenile devoutness, and I let her believe it. For a time, my spiritual growth was furthered or, to be truthful, stunted by a brief term at Sunday School. Maybe Sunday Schools are different now. Maybe the let's-all-have-fun spirit of Progressive Education has permeated even those establishments of unmitigated dullness. I wouldn't know. The one I went to was awful. We gathered in a room that was a barn of golden oak. The student body, made up of the reluctant offspring of high-minded parishioners, was divided into classes grouped according to age. Each group clustered in a circle formation, turning dutifully unresponsive faces toward their teacher. The teachers were refined, well-meaning females, some young, some old, and all quite devoid of sex. Our teacher was very plain and smelled like a hymnal. I was assigned to a fidgety little division which was one step up from the kindergarten, but had not yet matriculated into adult chairs. Ours were the sort of coy midget stools nursery-minded grown-ups select for children "because they're cute," heedless of the fact that what the average small child prefers is something on the scale of Saint Peter's throne. Being a creature of beanstalk growth, I resented having to squat on a seat fit for Rumpelstiltskin, my hands dangling to the floor and my knees all but reaching to my chin. I resented too the namby-pambinesses we were taught—hymns such as "Little Lives May Be Divine" when what really caught my fancy was "The Son of God Goes Forth to War," with that delectable verse about the martyrs meeting "the tyrant's brandished steel, the lion's gory mane." I resented it when, led by the droning voice of the teacher, we were made to rattle forth the Twenty-Third Psalm in shrill and meaningless unison. I was happily familiar with that psalm, for I'd heard my father recite it on those rare and exciting occasions when he felt in the vein to repeat from memory a few of the poems. And amid such a category as "Westminster Bridge," "We Are Such Stuff as Dreams Are Made On," and even "Jabberwocky," the glowing words of David didn't seem in the least out of place, while, the dear Lord knows, they did in the doleful setting of Sunday School.

Things took on a more encouraging aspect when it was announced that a play would be given. I imagined it would be something lovely, dealing with fairies and a prince and perhaps a few well-intentioned dwarfs. It didn't turn out quite that way. An inspired little drama whipped up by one of the teachers, it concerned two Chinese children, brother and sister, who had been existing in a lamentable state of heathen darkness until redemption was suddenly revealed to them by the appearance, one at a time, of a series of allegorical figures representing the more important sections of the Prayer Book: Morning and Evening Prayer, Baptism, Visitation of the Sick, etc., each delivering short but moving speeches that were part quotations from the various services and part the authoress's own inspired sentiments. One would think that such a series of exhortations would have sent the children hot-footing it back to the nearest temple, but no, they renounced the faith of their ancestors, entered a mission conveniently located immediately offstage, and, to all intents and purposes, lived piously ever after. I had a fatuous idea that I would be selected to play the little Chinese girl, not because of any histrionic ability, but because I was dark-haired and sallow and my eyes even slanted a bit. But that fat part went to the daughter of a wealthy parishioner. It was hardly a case of type-casting, as the girl had blue eyes and long golden ringlets, but she looked very sweet in her mother's mandarin coat. I had to content myself with the rôle of *Holy Matrimony*, a severe disappointment. I should have preferred *Burial of the Dead*, which was at least dramatic. I don't believe I looked either holy or matrimonial. Spruced up in my own best white dress, with somebody's lace curtain cascading down from a wreath of limp flowers snipped off of somebody else's picture hat, I delivered my lines with the same decorous lack of expression as the rest of the cast. Mother attended the performance. When it was over, she told me I had done very nicely and, on the way home, she said she thought that perhaps by now I had gone long enough to Sunday School.

My next theatrical appearance that season was at Baldwin in the lower-school play and it gave me more of a chance than had *Holy Matrimony*, for I had made off with the part of *Puck*, but not, unfortunately, in Shakespeare's pleasant fantasy. Ours was the brain child of a disciple of the Montessori method and was published in a paper-bound volume entitled *Plays Suitable for Children of the First Grade*. The *mis-en-scène* was a toy shop; the characters were toys and, of course, Puck; the time Midnight. The curtain rose, or rather was yanked open, to disclose a darkened stage around which was dimly visible a line-up of little girls dressed as dolls, manfully trying to maintain varying states of immobility in beaver-board constructions meant to represent doll boxes, but bearing a slight similarity to coffins. Offstage a clock, impersonated by the music teacher with a triangle, struck midnight; the lights flashed on and Puck flew in at the window, resplendent in a jerkin of cloth leaves and a pair of brown tights which, on my skinny legs, saggily belied their name. The window was a bottomless orange crate propped against an aperture in the backdrop and, through it, my particular form of flight gave every indication that Puck hadn't gained much air speed. The gay elf, after landing with a thud, hastened over to the footlights and with finger on lips said "Sh!" to the audience which was already quite silent, then made the rounds of the dolls, waking each with a kiss. When they had come to life in a series of traditional pantomime jerks, Puck gathered them in a circle and again with finger to lips for reasons of mystery never exactly clear, said " 'Tis time for our revels." The revels, which embodied a morris dance, some barely audible songs, and a *pas seul* on the part of the French Doll, were blessedly short-lived. The clock, which fifteen minutes previously had struck midnight, now chimed five. Puck said, "List!" The dolls listed, and Puck with some sorrow announced that 'twas dawn and at that the lights went out. The dolls returned to their coffins and Puck flew out of the window with the soaring grace of a young ostrich. An interested and somewhat agonized spectator of this extravaganza was my father, who happened to be home for a week-end. The presence of a popular matinée idol in the small auditorium created an agreeable flutter in the predominantly female audience. Otis Skinner witnessing for the first time the acting of his only child seemed an occasion rich with portent, and when the play was ended and the curtains had done their best to close, a number of spectators hovered near at hand eager to catch any comment the distinguished actor might let fall. They didn't have to strain their ears, for the comment fell with all the delicacy of a load of bricks. He rose, stretched, turned to Mother, and in that voice which could spread through the topmost gallery clarioned forth, "Well, Maud, she certainly has no talent—thank God!"

Frohman that spring sent Father Paul Potter's adaptation of a colorful script by Emile Fabre, based on Balzac's *Le Ménage du Garçon*. It had been Gémier's greatest success at the Odéon in Paris and, next to *Kismet, The Honor of the Family* proved to be Father's greatest success in America. The part might have been made to order for him and from the first reading of the manuscript his characteristic enthusiasm for all things excellent overflowed in a letter to Mother:

> This is by far the best proposition I've encountered. It is suspensive, intense and compact. The French title *La Rabouilleuse* (The Shrimp Catcher) will have to be changed for there is nothing about shrimps in it.
>
> The man is a picturesque, swaggering Don Caesar sort of fellow, a soldier out of employment after Waterloo—about 1820—and yet the part is one of *absolute colloquialism.* The play doesn't at all resemble the lurid old French "meller" of the Monte-Cristo-Musqueteers order.
>
> It is founded on Balzac's *Le Ménage du Garçon,* a stranger to me—I shall look it up (in English!) but if it is a dramatized novel, it is the best I ever knew.
>
> This swings me back into the romantic a bit, but what a healthful swing! A chance for the freedom of expression which belongs to me but all within reason and normalcy.
>
> NO SOCIAL PROBLEMS (THANK GOD!!!) AND ONE SET FOR 4 ACTS.
>
> I don't know what awaits me in New York, but if I can get everything settled and a sailing opportunity, will you run away to Europe with me on Saturday? *This next Saturday?* The *Caledonia* of the Anchor Line sails for Glasgow that day.

Parking me with the Andrews, they went off to Paris where Father had an orgy of Napoleonic atmosphere. He paid reverent visits to all the places sacred to the memory of the Little Corporal, haunted the tough districts of St. Antoine and Montmartre, and studied "sans-culotte" types in disreputable bistros which he liked romantically to consider "thieves' dens." It was in London, however, while sitting on top of a bus watching a red-nosed cabby in Piccadilly, that he found the model for the pose of that arresting stance which he assumed in the rôle and which remains in the memory of all who saw the play. The cabby was standing with his whip held in the crook of his arm in the manner of a cavalry officer holding his sword on review, while his swaggering body was bent backward until it curved like a letter "S." He copied the posture, using the cane as the man had used his whip, and found the attitude tremendously effective. So did George Luks, who painted him in that pose in a portrait which is in the Phillips Collection in Washington, and so, too, an artist named Victor Hecht whose canvas still hangs in the lobby of the Empire Theatre.

The *Honor of the Family* went through considerable metamorphosis before its New York début. According to Emile Fabre's script, *La Rabouilleuse,* as produced in Paris, was a brutal, realistic treatment of a brutal, realistic collection of people among whom there is not a single admirable character, least of all the protagonist, Colonel Philippe Brideau. This picturesque soldier of fortune is a first-rate son-of-a—— but this was before World War One and *What Price Glory,* so the term was *scoundrel.* The play, on reading it, appeared to be pure drama, melodrama even, and any latent humor it might have had was certainly not apparent in the script. Father studied the part as "straight" and Frohman rehearsed it that way.

They opened in New Rochelle. The first act was talky

and tedious. The plot concerned a number of petty individuals living in the little provincial town of Issoudin shortly after Waterloo. A wealthy and senile old miser, by the name of Rouget, has been beguiled by Flora Bézier, a handsome "fille de joie," to the extent of taking her into his house as a dubious companion. Flora makes herself insolently comfortable, tyrannizes over the silly old dotard, all the time managing to carry on an affair with a handsome and quite worthless commandant, Max Gilet. She and Max plan to elope, as soon as they can lay hands on Rouget's money. All this is related in three quarters of an hour of routine exposition and things have reached a cumulative degree of tedium, when from offstage comes the sound of someone whistling "*Il était une bergère*" in a jaunty, carefree fashion. An instant later, through the broad window at the back, one beholds, striding down the quiet street, the fabulous figure of an ex-military man in a shabby but swankly fitted greatcoat, shoddy boots, rakish beaver top hat cocked over one eye, gray suède gloves out at every fingertip, scarlet handkerchief streaming from his pocket, the button of the Légion d'Honneur on his lapel, an ivory-headed cane adorned with a raveled tassel, a rampant mustache on his sabre-scarred face, and a general air of "I am God Almighty, and who, pray, are you?" The next second he is in the room, demanding an interview with old man Rouget, who, it appears, is his uncle. Flora tells him that Rouget is not to be disturbed. Philippe looks her over from head to foot appraisingly, wipes his nose on the back of his hands, and flashes a brief grin. Then his expression changes to one of brusque determination, and lifting his cane above his head, he brings it down on a table in a whack heard round the theatrical world.

"I will smoke one cigar in the Place St. Jean. When I come back, if my uncle is not home and if you refuse to let me see him, then every one of you can go to hell. Good evening." With which brief speech he leers again, turns on his magnificent, rundown heel, and exits. Curtain. End of the Act.

The night of the try-out in New Rochelle, the audience greeted his entrance with a perfunctory hand, sat spellbound during the whirlwind scene, and after the fall of the curtain remained silent and motionless for several seconds as if stunned by a mass blow in their solar plexes. Father, standing in the wings awaiting the verdict and hearing nothing, thought, of course, that it was all a miserable fiasco, and was slinking off to his dressing room, when he was stopped by the sound of a roar, a roar of great, glorious, unbridled laughter coming from every soul in the audience in one spontaneous yell. They applauded, too, but mostly, they laughed. They laughed, they howled, they whooped. Father, on the other side of the curtain, listened in blank amazement, then, in the voice of a flabbergasted child, said aloud to the air: "Dear gentle God! I guess I'm funny." The shadowy figure of a little man stepped out from behind a piece of scenery. "I guess you are, Otis," said Frohman. And so, Philippe Brideau swept onto the stage like a young tornado to become one of the immortal comedy characterizations of the American stage.

John Mason Brown says of that entrance:

> It took less than a minute . . . but it has lasted a lifetime in the memory of those of us fortunate enough to see it.

Brown saw the 1926 revival. By then the play was creaking considerably, but even to this modern young critic, Otis Skinner's performance was still glorious. He wrote about it as late as 1940, and the following are excerpts from his tender tribute written at the time of my father's death:

The middle of the first act had already slipped by and nothing had happened to catch the eye or rivet the attention. It all seemed too dull . . . and, anyway, this was Christmas.

But just at the moment when you were reaching for your hat or suppressing a yawn which made your eardrums ache, things began to happen. A man swaggered past the window at the back. Yes, this was all, but it was enough to make you swallow your yawn and forget you ever had a hat. Enough, because the brief passing of this man was more than a stage direction . . . it was the creation of a character. . . . Blood had suddenly been pumped into the anemic veins of this old melodrama . . . the blood that is red with the flaming corpuscles of the theatre. A character had been catapulted across the footlights to all of us from the remotest depths of the backstage; from that position at which most of the younger actors are ill-at-ease, but at which the veterans are triumphantly at home.

If at that moment, you suddenly found yourself sitting upright without knowing or caring what had happened to your program; if Christmas had fled your mind, it was because of the brave salty figure of swashbuckling romance which this man cut as he swaggered by the window. From the battered high hat sitting cockily aslant his head, to the cane he had swung with the air of a major-domo, this stout Ratapoil had seemed the most blustering of benevolent villains.

In no time he was past the window and had stomped his way onto the stage, confronting the heartless couple which was conspiring for old Rouget's money. Now we could see him better . . . note those slightly moth-eaten eyebrows, follow the ends of this moustache as they mounted skyward, observe his bulging red cheeks and that nose which seemed a tattered poppy in their midst, and follow that walk of his, which was the finest bluster in roosterdom.

This Brideau's swagger was the swagger all of us have hidden in our hearts. It was a hangover from childhood when within ourselves we were still brave noncomformists, when each of us had rebelled at good behaviour, and, hating the respectable gentry of Nottinghamshire, had given our affection to Robin Hood, and all the other lovable bandits.

"Bang" went Brideau's cane, thumping down on the table like the crack of doom. Out came his warning to the conspirators. Up came a cigar to his mouth, driven home so grandly that it seemed the finest gesture of arrogance possible in this small world. And, with a final, jaunty pat on the top of his high hat, calculated to set it at an even cockier angle, off stalked this Brideau for a stroll.

Any mortal with crutches, a wheel chair or a nurse can come onto the stage. And almost anyone . . . and many modern actors do . . . slink from a door and slip into the nearest chair with a desperate sense of thankfulness. But an entrance is made of sterner stuff.

Call it a kind of pillage, a hold-up staged in public, if you will. Although an "entrance" is a trick, of course, therein lies its special glory when it comes off. It is the theatre of the actor at its most militant. Yet to succeed as this entrance of Brideau succeeded, it demands an actor behind it, no ordinary actor, but a personality and a technician capable of carrying it through.

Reassuring as the New Rochelle opening had been, Frohman was not for risking New York before any play had had a workout of at least two months on tour. The canny little manager knew the wisdom of having his scripts corrected, his actors well broken in, and the performance smooth and certain before submitting a new show to the judgment of the Broadway anvil chorus. Moreover, with his new star, a road tour meant good business, for Otis Skinner had a loyal and adoring following in those regions New Yorkers choose to dismiss as "the hinterland," a territory which, with the exception of Manhattan Island, comprises all the United States of America. The star himself welcomed the extended tour. His letters to my mother brimmed over with his current interests, joys, and sorrows.

In Green Bay, Wisconsin, his afflictions were of a homely nature:

I had my corns attended to in Fond-du-Lac by Prof. —Ewer, the "Corn King."

I had to have someone, so I sought the palace of the King. His office was in a business block, back of his kitchen and living room where the Corn Queen could be heard conversing with her "gossip." A little later the Queen came into the presence of the throne and asked for 25 cents for "them potatoes."

I thought at first the King was a policeman for he had brass buttons and a coffinplate pinned on his vest that looked like a detective's badge, but which on inspection revealed the inscription "Professor Ewer. The Corn King."!

The King was very dirty and so were his methods and his instruments. After heating some awful looking salve on an old knifeblade with a match, and daubing the charred mess on my toe, he bound up my wounds, charged me a dollar and said: "Leave that on there for three or four days till you have to wash your feet again"!

I bowed myself out of the Presence and hurried home to wash my foot. I don't know whether this last deed is *lèse-majesté* or high treason.

Some of the letters are of an intimate nature and refer to the ups and downs, the minor misunderstandings of married life.

Yes, wife of mine, we've gone through our various love epidemics, measles, croup, chickenpox, and mumps of matrimonial life, and like lusty children we've come out all right in the end.

We could not be dearer to each other, if we tried. And after all, to understand each other is not so very wonderful . . . we only have to love each other and we understand. For many, many years I think I've understood you. Perhaps for more than you've understood me, for you put me too high at first and life to you was one long ecstasy. Then you found out one bright morning, that sometimes your husband was a grumpy thing . . . that he didn't always stand up in his halo and beautiful make-up. Then desolation yawned before you till you discovered that grumpiness did not necessarily end in the divorce court and now you can view it with comparative calm: and I, on my side, have learned that grumpiness is not pretty manners.

But then God doesn't do these things very much better himself. For two days it has been wet and wild . . . but something sang a low song down somewhere in my life and lo! today is bright and beautiful!

It is life, dear . . . and in the calm that comes with assured sympathy and confidence and understanding lies the secret of happiness. It takes us a few years to learn to wholly respect Darby and Joan. But how many times Darby and Joan must smile at us.

And let me tell you a secret, dear. Darby and Joan never grew *old.*

OTIS

And always he found time in which to write to me. The following was in response to the information that for the first time in my school career I had received a report card marked "passing," also that I had started to study botany, a pleasant class because we were given window boxes in which to plant whatever we liked, my choice being the at least original combination of petunias and radishes.

My Accomplished Child:

It is very awful for your poor, ignorant, old father to realize that his daughter is so wondrous wise . . . that she has no failures in her report and that she knows all about botany and stamens and things.

Why, bless your heart! *I* don't know *anything* about botany. Isn't that a sad state to be in?

I climbed a mountain near here. I got so high (6100 feet above the sea) that the clouds were at my feet and I knew what it must be like to be an angel.

When I came down I met a snake stretched across the road . . . and he looked at me and I looked at him. And I said: "Mr. Snake, you must die!" So I got some rocks and smashed him to *smithereens.* Do you know what *smithereens* are? I don't, but I *think* they look like baked beans. And Mr. Snake was over 5 feet long . . . that's longer than you. And the joke is I don't know whether he was a *Mr.* Snake or *Mrs.* Snake.

When I come home, I shall eat nothing but radishes and shall wear petunias in my hair.

Your loving
FATHER

And in another letter, this one from Victoria, Canada, he tells me:

Wouldn't you think it would be mighty cold up as far North as British Columbia? It isn't! Yet it's not so far from Alaska. There are roses blooming over in the little park around the Parliament Buildings, and in the garden around this hotel are marigolds and wall flowers. And everywhere the grass is green right down to the still waters of Puget Sound whose little wavelets patter across the street from me. That's wrong, isn't it? Wavelets can't patter if they're *still,* can they?

The Parliament Building has a lot of funny statues on it. Over the front doorway there is a stone coat-of-arms that I thought was the British escutcheon, but instead of the lion and unicorn, it is the stag and the mountain goat that support the Cross of St. George while the lion crouches comfortably on the crown overhead. The animals have got electric lights all about them and the goat has got one right where he *sits down!*

The Honor of the Family reached New York in February at the Hudson Theatre, and the press went overboard. Otis Skinner took the Gotham public by storm and overnight he found himself in the "idol" bracket along with William Faversham, Guy Bates Post, Robert Edson, and Henry Miller. Sentimental ladies sent him "mash" notes or wrote him original poems. He was pronounced "too stunning" and "utterly Mansfieldian" by worshiping "matinée girls," hysterical young things who giggled during love scenes, rattled candy papers during quiet ones, and lay in wait for him outside the stage door armed with memory books. He learned to avoid them by escaping through the front of the house.

He learned, too, to avoid the swarm of invitations, which, the moment a play is an established hit, descend upon the star asking him to attend all manner of extra-curricular affairs . . . social demands, charitable demands, and demands from those aggressively humanitarian champions of Causes who for some reason think the name of a popular actor will add distinction to their sponsor list. Such attempted encroachments upon his free time, he tossed aside with good-tempered exasperation.

> Because I'm an actor I'm asked to all sorts of non-theatrical affairs. Bless me, if I were to accept one tenth of 'em, I'd have no *time* to *be* an actor! Will I speak at an Anti-Trust rally? Will I sit on a platform, while certain indignant citizens lay bare the evils of Yellow Journalism, will I go to a tea to raise funds for combatting hookworm in the Tennessee mountains? I WILL NOT! An actor's place is in the theatre, not squandering his energies on a lot of things about which he really knows very little.

He looked forward to the end of each busy week, and a quiet Sunday at home. He enjoyed life in the little house on the college campus, enjoyed the pleasant faculty folk who were our neighbors. He formed a particular friendship with Doctor Henry Sanders ("Sandy" as he was called by everyone, even his students), the brilliantly caustic professor of Greek. They took long walks about the countryside accompanied by Doctor Sanders's little spaniels, and many evenings sat up late before a winter fire, smoking good tobacco and exchanging good talk. "Sandy's" wit was keen and biting. He disliked the theatre, and Otis Skinner as an actor impressed him not at all. He liked him for the person that he was, and Father, who in turn knew nothing of the didactic world and cared even less, liked him. It was a mellow friendship.

That year I had "started piano," and a dubious amenity to

Father's Sunday at home was hearing me play my "piece." The piece for several months never varied, being an example of juvenile virtuosity entitled "The Goblin's Frolic." Toward spring, by dint of playing in desperate concentration with my tongue well out and occasionally bitten, I managed to get through a few bars of a Mendelssohn "Song Without Words," a title Father said was apt, as no words could possibly conform with the noises I produced from the tortured little upright.

Sunday and the playing of my piece, or rather the not playing of it, might, with less understanding parents, have led to a highly emotional situation. I must preface this by saying that during that winter I had become an omnivorous reader. I wish I could state that my reading matter was the sort which gave marked indications of instinctively esoteric choice, for I cherish a grudge filled with envy against these biographers who claim that their nursery shelves groaned (the verb is apposite) with lovingly thumbed-up volumes of Henty, Scott, Fenimore Cooper, and Maria Edgeworth. My taste in literature was a good deal like my taste in art, which ran riotously true to Harrison Fisher. The furthest I could go in the classics was Howard Pyle's *Knights of the Round Table,* and then only because I could ruin the pages by hand-coloring the black-and-white illustrations. *Sara Crewe, or What Happened at Miss Minchin's* had its moments, but my real delight was that honeychile' of the Old South, *The Little Colonel.* Less genteel, but more absorbing than the *Little Colonel* books was a series known as *The Automobile Girls,* thrilling tales of four stalwart young things who, complete with goggles and linen dusters, toured the country in an open Chalmers, encountering every possible sort of adventure. These I read and re-read, and I regarded *The Automobile Girls in the Berkshires* with the same reverence I now hold for *War and Peace.* Then a schoolmate

"Hajj, the Beggar"

Photograph by Arnold Genthe

Otis Skinner as Philippe Brideau in *The Honor of the Family*

Portrait by Victor Hecht, Photograph from Frick Art Reference Library

started lending me books from her aunt's library and, as Chapman's *Homer* burst upon Keats, *Elsie Dinsmore* swam into my ken. The *Elsie* books, to be sure, belonged to an earlier and more heavenly minded generation, and I don't know what their charm could have been, dealing as they did with a religious fanatic of a child, who spent her days praying, hymn-singing, and reproving her less spiritual contemporaries, with lengthy quotations of Scripture. The author of this morbid series must have known how to cast a spell, for Elsie had a way of carrying piety to extremes as absorbing as those to which Dick Tracy today carries adventure. Her life of sanctimony I found most beautiful. Other children wanted to be like Joan of Arc or Queen Guinevere, or even like Captain Kidd. I wanted to be just like Elsie Dinsmore. For a brief but intense period, I got religion.

As I recall it, the arch villain of those edifying volumes was Elsie's father, whose chief offense lay in an understandable lack of sympathy with his daughter's bigotry. He went to church only once on Sunday, and he wasn't much for letting a meal get cold while his child invoked a long-winded blessing. Although his attitude was a grievance to Elsie, she always forgave him with a sweet "he-knows-not-what-he-doth" expression, which must have been considerably galling to the poor man. The temperamental clash between father and daughter reaches a heartrending climax when on a certain Sunday, Mr. Dinsmore asks his daughter to entertain their luncheon guests by playing the piano. Elsie, her blue eyes full of pious reproach, says she's sorry, Father, but it's the Sabbath. Dinsmore *père,* with increasing annoyance, demands that she play and Dinsmore *fille* meekly insists she can't as Holy Writ forbids her to—although just what portion of the Good Book has vouchsafed her this revelation is not indicated. His patience at an end, the harsh parent orders her to sit at the piano until she gets over the silly notion. She sits, but the notion persists. The rest go in to midday dinner. Elsie, white but adamant, continues to sit. All afternoon she remains on the piano stool, as stubborn a little example of exhibitionism as one could hope to find. Finally, at dusk, she keels onto the floor in a dead faint. Mr. Dinsmore, shaken with remorse, picks up her limp body, undergoes a change of heart, and upon Elsie's recovery promises to join her on the sawdust trail. I found the whole account most inspiring. It occurred to me that I might work up a similar family drama. When Father came home the ensuing Sunday, I met him at the station with a sad, distant smile. The trip back to the house was a scanty half-mile, and together we always made it on foot, walking, singing, occasionally skipping and making pleasant idiots of ourselves. That Sunday, I trod beside him with dragging feet, and downcast eyes, like a dismal acolyte burdened by the sins of the world. There was a steep hill on the campus down which we usually hurtled at deliciously terrifying speed. That day, I asked him if he'd mind going by the steps, and slowly, please. Father looked surprised, but made no comment, although I later heard him telling Mother he thought I was coming down with a bilious attack. The instant we reached home, I made a dash for the piano stool where I sat with folded hands and an expression of meek suffering. Mother and Father, full of the week's news, had much to tell one another, and for at least half an hour neither paid me the slightest heed. Father washed up for lunch, and Mother busied herself arranging the dozen of Thorley's big red roses he always brought her. I sat at the piano unnoticed. By now I had succeeded in working myself into a state of trembling tension. It was hard to see in my amiable father a counterpart of the tyrannical Mr. Dinsmore, but I managed to lash myself into a feeling of righteous resentment mingled with pity over his soul, which I decided was definitely damned. The colored lady-of-all-work announced the fact that soup was on, and Father, who was hungry, turned to me with an eager "Ready, Miss?" Still clamped to the stool which, by now, I was clutching with bloodless hands, I looked up at him and, my voice shaking with emotion, said: "Father, I'm not going to play you my piece today." For a moment Father regarded me with good-humored bewilderment, then emitted a hearty: "Well, thank God for that! And now can we go eat?" And that ended my devotional career.

Mother's circle of friends had widened out beyond the Bryn Mawr College group, and gradually Philadelphia began to take her to its cautious bosom. Elderly ladies, "hostesses of the old school," sent her At Home cards. She was invited to attend the meetings of the Browning Society and was made a member of the Contemporary Club. She was even asked to speak at one of the large and formal gatherings of the latter organization. The meeting was to be a discussion on the age-old topic "Is the Theatre Dead?"—the speakers being Agnes Repplier, Metcalf, the critic of *Life,* John Luther Long, the creator of *Madam Butterfly,* and herself. The prospect delighted and terrified her. It had been years since she had made any sort of public appearance, and for two weeks prior to the event, she went about her daily household chores muttering snatches of what she intended to say, interrupted by periodic expostulations of "Don't speak to me, Cornelia, I'm as nervous as a witch." Her appearance on the platform of the Contemporary Club was a *succès fou.* She could not refrain from writing Otis-dear-love all about it, that very night after she came home.

My darling husband,

I hope you had a great success tonight—and dear, dear love, may I confess that I believe I had! It all seemed so strange, so unlike me, but I felt pleased and grateful.

Metcalf spoke first—interestingly but not brilliantly—then came John Luther Long and I may say he made a fool of himself—which made my speech climatic. I was introduced as the newest member of the Contemporary Club and then, dear love, I got up, trembled a bit but read my paper and had an *ovation!* Otis dear, my gown was so pretty—it was white and I think I looked like a lady. I tried to read my paper as convincingly as I could and I tried to say the Drama is not dead. Everybody heard me and one man got up and mentioned my "silvery voice." Don't think that vain, Otis dear, for it did seem good to one so long dead as I feel I have been. My own voice sounded so strange to me for it was the first time I had spoken out in years.

Agnes Repplier came after me and her speech was keenly brilliant and to the point—that of course the Drama was going to the dogs, for critics had said so since the days of Socrates. She was charming.

Otis dear, do love me because I feel pleased. It isn't for myself. It is because of you. Because I stay on here in this conventional but agreeable community—proud of my little success because it shows where you stand in the estimation of the world. I am your wife. That's all I want to be!

Oh, I haven't told you what a grand house I dined in first. At the Jayne's—a mansion on Locust and 12th Streets. We were twelve—all Biddles, or Wisters or some stately old Philadelphia names. And a dinner for the gods! It was great.

Well I must go to bed, 'tis late and I must come down to earth tomorrow and break in the new maid. She is so pretty but she looks very stupid.

I had your Sacramento letter today. Oh, dear, dear love. You are so far away.

All my heart!
MAUD

Mother wrote and received countless notes, a gracious activity but an exacting one which, I am convinced, proved in later life to be a severe drain on her health. For Mother's notes were no perfunctory scribbles. They were warm and disarming and enchantingly personal. Grant Mitchell said he wanted to frame each of her communications—they were so exquisite. They gave the impression of having been written in serene leisure, although I can see her now sitting in a state of jumpy tension at her cluttered desk, saying in a quavering voice, "If I have to write another note, I shall scream out loud." She didn't scream out loud, but she screamed inwardly, and I used to wonder why on earth she went to all that elaborate trouble. But I was of the dawning generation which can't be bothered with anything as archaic as a note when a phone call will answer the purpose in one tenth of the time and none of the grace. But Mother and her contemporaries wrote notes with a zeal incomprehensible to anyone this side of Boston, the last remaining region where the gentle and somewhat exasperating ceremonial continues to flourish. There were notes asking one to a concert, notes accepting the invitation, then, after the event, a note, even if the hostess lived next door, thanking her for the lovely afternoon. Notes enclosing a receipt for Lady Baltimore cake and notes recommending Maurice Hewlett's "latest," or an article by Woodrow Wilson in the current *Review of Reviews*, notes discussing the exact meanings of Gelett Burgess's newly coined words "bromide" and "sulfide" and "blurb" (the definition of the latter, according to its inventor, being "a noise made by a publisher"). Of the countless notes she received, Mother saved all of the ones written by those Olympian persons who had, in her estimation, "done things." "Things" might mean books, painting, music, lecturing, and lastly, almost grudgingly, the theatre. She also saved communications from a few people who had not exactly done things but who *were* things, and things in their case meant Old Philadelphia, the Garden Club, and Main Line security. It was a flowery period and the notes read almost like love letters. "Dearest Lady," they start off, or "Exquisite Person" or "Heavenly, heavenly Mrs. Skinner." And Mother's replies were in the same ecstatic vein, most of the little missives beginning with "Dear Lady," for hers was a generation which, while prone to sentimental friendships, shied skittishly from the usage of first names until acquaintance had ripened for at least a year or two into warm affection. Then came a nervous moment when one suggested that the other now say Mary instead of Mrs. Smith and the other gladly agreed on condition that Jane be substituted for Mrs. Jones, and when that Rubicon was crossed, the occasion was one of happy emotion.

Although school from a social viewpoint was going much better for me, from a scholastic one, it was going much worse. Out of a class not remarkable for brilliance, I was by far the poorest student. My monthly record showed a noteworthy consistency in the steady failure in all subjects with the exception of English and something called "Sloyd," which was a highly educational way of saying carpentry work. Days on which I bore home my report card, I walked with leaden feet. I dreaded that "scene" with Mother and hoped some dire but more welcome fate would overcome me before I reached the house. An automobile might run over me or I might be kidnaped by gypsies or, if I prayed hard enough, a compassionate God might whip up an earthquake. Once, when my marks had reached an all-time low, feeling that life was no longer worth facing, I stretched myself out on the grass of a vacant lot, placed under my head my school bag, and on my chest the card, securing it against the breeze by a piece of brick, and tried to bring about an untimely end by holding my breath. Whoever in childhood despondency has been driven to similar desperate measures will recall how far from simple is this form of self-annihilation, even if one says, I will this time and takes a deep breath first. After a series of unsuccessful explosions and gasps, I began imagining Mother when she came across my pitiful corpse, and the picture of her anguished remorse was so acute, I scrambled to my feet, grabbed up my bag, and tore home to hurtle myself onto Mother's chest and assure her I was all right. Mother, who had not been in any particular doubts on that score, said obviously I was, but was my report? I produced the wretched thing and it in turn produced the inevitable scene. "Really and truly, Cornelia, when I was your age . . ." it invariably began and ended in making me feel the vilest cretin ever born to dazzling parents. At the finish of the session we'd both be in tears.

For Mother, with her gentle manner, her golden voice, and her Bellini Madonna face, could take the heart out of me as neatly as an apple cutter tunnels out the core of a Jonathan. She wanted perfection from me. She wanted it from Father and from anyone over whom she had influence. And she wanted it in her way. She might lack confidence in herself, but never in her theories regarding the conduct of those close to her. It took me years to understand this, years of bewilderment over Mother's chameleon-like attitude of praise and censure, for her praise was lavish when I was doing nicely along the lines she had so carefully laid out for me, while her deflating censure of the stumbling ventures I perpetrated on independent initiative drove me into spells of whispering savagely to myself, "Just wait! Some day I'll show her."

It was during these periods of inner revolt that I became dimly aware of the fact that I possessed a few ideas of my own, and that they did not necessarily coincide with the ideas which Mother tried, with engaging stubbornness, to implant in me. It was a discovery I kept to myself. I could never have admitted it to her, for in our bond there was much love but little confiding. Mother didn't frighten me; she never really awed me. Certainly not when we were alone, just the two of us, for then she was the gayest and tenderest of companions. It was when we were with those "people who count" that I, watching Mother spinning her shimmering webs of charm, felt gauche and awkward and dolefully convinced that I couldn't possibly be anything but an adopted child. Mother liked having me with her on such occasions. She would have liked showing me off if I'd had anything to show beyond a polite leer and an inability to know what to do with my hands. I would loom awkwardly by her side, gawkily silent except for brief flashes when she'd turn to me with her bright "company smile" and say, "My baby thinks so too, don't you, Baby?" And Baby (I was Baby until the day she died), without the slightest idea as to what it was she thought so too, would bleat a weak "yes." One day, the inner worm turned when a great gawk of a female, who was a bird-lover and as intellectual as she was plain, came to tea. Mother, as always, was cooing in admiration that was genuinely if momentarily sincere. Was there ever such a lovely study as ornithology? Was there ever anyone as distinguished as this lady who knew all about the wonderful subject? The lady was, of course, enraptured. And, as always, Mother's disarming act was filling me with admiration and discomfort. Seeing me sitting there motionless and baleful, she reached out for my hand in her pretty caressing fashion and said, "Cornelia loves birds too, don't you, Baby?" Until that moment I had never given birds a thought either of love or of animosity and knew little or nothing about them. I realized, too, that Mother's feeling of kinship with our feathered friends was as vague as my own and I resented her "going on so" over this hideous individual. To the amazement of Mother, who was used to my supine acceptance of the words she put into my mouth, I cast on the visitor a look of poison, and in a low, shaking voice said, "I hate birds. I just hate them. I like cats because they kill them." The lady said, "Well!" and Mother, with alacrity, sent me to my room, where I flung myself on the bed and in a torrent of tears gave vent to the emotions I failed to understand.

CHAPTER TEN

A House of Our Own

MOTHER NOW FELT that here on the Main Line was a way of living she found sympathetic, a community in which it would be nice to settle, and she persuaded Father to buy a small piece of land on the old Gulph Road near the college. It was not without many qualms that she did so, for she never purchased anything from a handkerchief to a grand piano without an agony of misgivings. Her uncertainties concerning the land, however, were as nothing in comparison with her mental conflicts concerning the style of house to be erected on the site, her decisions shifting from Colonial clapboard to French whitewashed brick and on to Pennsylvania farm stone.

Father returned from tour to find her tremulously poring over blueprints she barely understood. He settled the matter by himself, deciding once and for all upon a simple English-type house of beam and plaster. Then, before Mother could again change her mind, he ordered the architect and builder to start work forthwith and announced that we were all three sailing for Europe the following week.

And sail we did on a Fabre Line vessel of some six thousand tons which bore the highly un-nautical name of the *S.S. Madonna.* A jaunty French craft, rather on the order of an excursion boat, it steamed a gay, unsteady course to Marseilles, touching at Gibraltar, Naples, and Corsica. Mother, with her zeal for "getting everything out of things," presented me with the dubiously welcome gift of a diary in which I was to write a daily entry in order to impress upon myself and possible posterity the cultural advantages of the trip.

June 4

Left New York harber at 1.00. Met the captain. He is very nice. Was read Tom Sawyer.

June 5

Mother seasick. Me seasick. Sea full of swells. Father well.

June 6

Met two children. The captain fixed a swing for us. Swung. Was read to.

June 7

Father and I went out to the bow where a littel land bird had flown on board. And we fed it and gave it water & it ate & drank.

June 9

Saw a chambered nortiless. A chambered nortiless is a littel sea animal that has a bladdar that he puts up and uses it as a sail and sails along the surfis of the water. When he wants to go down he lets the bladdar down. The bladdar is transparent and has pale colors. I would like to have a bladdar.

Starting off from Marseilles, our hegira took us through Arles, where we bumped into the Provençal poet Mistral admiring his own statue in the local museum; Avignon, where, I ate my first bouillabaisse and threw it up in the Palace of the Popes; and Orange, where Mother and I sat on the top tier of a Roman theatre while Father, standing where the actors of the time of Tiberius had declaimed Terence, gave us a stirring rendition of "The Walrus and the Carpenter." Then on to Monte Carlo, Turin, and Venice. My diary entry reads:

June 28

Well when we arrived in Venice we went in a gondola to a hotel & had supper & I got a fishbone in my throat & the waiter got it out with butter.

In the evening we walked in the square where St. Marks cathedral is. All the front of St. Marks is mosik which is tiny pieces of glass all fitted like a jigsaw puzzel. I cannot describe how wonderful it was & how like a jewell it shone. If one really wanted to have it described to you, he would have to go there & see it with their own eyes.

At the Austrian border we separated for a time, Father setting out on a four-day walking tour by himself and Mother and I going to Bozen (Bolzano if you prefer), where we stopped in a small and tidy pension flanked on one side by a cobbled street and on the other by a torrent fresh from Dolomite snow. One afternoon in the light of a late Alpine glow, Father tramped gaily into our room.

He told us he had found a lovely hotel in the mountains & that we'd go there by carridge tomorrow. Then he took me out & had nails put in my shoes & got me a mountain hat & alpine-stock!

June 6

Well we got up at six o'clock & started to drive to the hotel in the mts. Whenever we came to a hill Father, the driver & I would get out & walk up it while Mother sat in the carridge & sometimes she would get out too & walk but then she was always stopping to pick wild flowers & Father & I called her "The 2nd Section."

Well when we got there we went out in the woods for a

walk. The woods was very dark & Father said it was very Grimm (that was a pun). We came back & after supper I & a littel german girl & her brother played dominoes. We had to go to bed with candles. There is a big stove made all out of china & I had a feather bed.

July 11

We drove back to Bozen & I told Father about a fine shop where Mother & I had seen a beautiful carved wooden painted figure. It was a fair lady of the middel ages. Well Father told Mother he wanted to get some tobacco & then he & I went to the shop & Father bought the lady. When we got to our room we opened the box & showed it to Mother for she did not know it until now as it was a present. She is the most beautiful Lady I ever saw & Father says she looks like Mother. That night Mother let me open the box & put the Lady from Bozen on the table by my bed & the light from the street shon in & I could see her just as plain.

July 13

We walked around the town of Innsbruk & saw a church & the tomb of King Maximillion. In Schloss Ambros we saw Maximillion's saddle. It was an old yellow velvet one & it was indeed very worn where the King had sat down. Then we went to a brewry & Father gave me a littel stine of beer.

It was the year of the Oberammergau Passion Play. Our first day in the city of pilgrimage is tersely described:

Went for a walk in the fields where I talked with a little boy with long hair who saie he plays an Angle. Saw the king of Saxony. He wore a brown suit & has sore eyes.

The following morning we attended the Passion Play and my entry in small cramped handwriting covers some twenty-five pages of the diary. Judging by the impressive verbiage and accurate spelling, it is obvious that I must have lifted entire paragraphs out of the Montrose Moses translation of the text, a useful libretto with which all Americans armed themselves.

From Oberammergau we went on to Switzerland and spent a few weeks in Pontresina. Mother, ever hopeful of discovering in me any latent talent (except, of course, acting), bought me a sketchbook and box of paints with which she encouraged me to immortalize the beauties of the Engadine. Father, after one look at the results, decided it would be better to make a mountain-climber of me. Father was a good alpinist and it was not hard to share his enthusiasm for this field of adventure. Beginning with easy ascents, we worked ourselves into trim for some really tough climbs.

Our endurance test was the hike from Pontresina to the Italian village of Poschiavo. It was a distance of nearly twenty miles and we did it in a day. My spindly legs were fairly tough, but the extra weight of my rucksack together with the strain of the steady downhill tramp of the final five miles made them start to buckle. The road was a deserted alpine zigzag. Tears, due to fatigue, hunger, and fear of the onrushing dark, were filling my tired eyes. Father diverted my woe by getting me to join him in a flow of spirited songs and the deep woods re-echoed to the strains of "Marching Through Georgia," "Dixie," "Drunk Last Night," and Father's own version of the "Marseillaise," a bit of which went:

> Aux armes, citoyens!
> Ouvrez vos pantalons!

Three kilometers outside of Poschiavo I collapsed, gasping that I was very sorry but my legs wouldn't work any more and that I was so hungry I could eat dirt. Father laughed, called me a gallant but punctured tire, swung me up on his shoulders, and strode the remainder of the way with me clinging to his head.

Poschiavo was a primitive hamlet with a primitive inn, and Father's request for two hot baths was met with blank amazement. There was, the proprietor explained, neither bath nor lavatory in the *albergo*. Then where, Father pleaded in a moving dialect that was a mixture of German and English spoken with an Italian accent, could his small daughter get the hot bath she required to revive her paralyzed legs? After some dubious head-shaking and a vociferous conference held by the proprietor and his entire family, someone recalled the fact that there was a tub to be found at the house of the priest and if the little signorina would be patient and rest in her room they would arrange everything. And they arranged it. Right in the middle of the parlor. The proprietor led me to the door, and indicating the first fruits of his ingenuity with a triumphant "*Ecco un bagno superbo!*" bowed me across the threshold and backed out of the room. Once inside, I paused in modest bewilderment. Apparently the progress of the tub from the padre's house to the inn had made local history, for the windows were crowded with the faces of the town's entire small-boy population, grinning less in lechery than in happy curiosity. Snorting with indignation, I flounced across the room and banged the shutters closed in a gesture of outraged prudery which plunged the boys into blank disappointment and the room into almost total darkness. I undressed, groped my way to the great metal tub, and tested the water. It was depressingly tepid, but it would, I figured, at least serve to wash off the dust of the mountain road. Fearful of upsetting the huge sarcophagus, I clambered gingerly over the side and sat down only to arise with a yowl of pain. When it came to a method of heating the bath, the proprietor's ingenuity had surpassed itself. He had filled the great receptacle with water and then placed it directly over a low fire and my contact with the sizzling bottom resulted in a blistered one of my own.

Our trip wound on to Heidelberg, where in the shadow of the castle we picnicked on a promontory of the Jettenbühl overlooking the Neckar; to The Hague, where the glories of the Mauritshuis were eclipsed by the luscious horrors of the Inquisition torture chambers; to Strasbourg, where one of the early Zeppelins sailed whining overhead so close we could see German tourists busily taking aerial photographs. Then on to Antwerp, where I gazed in surreptitious fascination at the fountain of the "Mannikin-Piss." At first sight of that well-known effigy of a small boy emitting in a most frank and natural fashion a magnificent jet of water, Mother had cried out, "Cornelia, darling, don't look!" although later she changed her mind and, regarding the naïve monument as artistic instruction in the facts of life, allowed me to buy a small brass statuette of the *chef d'oeuvre,* a realistic little souvenir which worked by means of a tiny tube and bulb. That fall at school a teacher came upon me demonstrating it to an admiring group of pals and was all for having me expelled until I explained that my mother had given me the gadget "because it was cultural"—

The cultural improvements of our European trip served not at all to improve my school marks which maintained their level of near-arrested development. Mother alternately scolded and pleaded and I wept, more readily than usual. I had a nasty headache which made me listless and wretched. Mother, who attributed most of my sombre moods to biliousness, resorted to calomel, but the headache grew worse and she put me to bed. With her curious mistrust of most members of the medical profession, she delayed calling a doctor for several days. But to Father, who was touring *The Honor*

C. O. S. and Mother

C. O. S. and Otis Skinner in *Blood and Sand*
Photograph by White Studio

of the Family, she sent word of my illness. He wrote me a letter which I shall always keep.

Beloved Person:

I did not know when I wrote and asked you about Hallowe'en that you were still in bed. If I had, I should not have been so mean.

I really don't know why we get sick at the wrong time. I really don't know why we get sick at all. If I could answer that mystery I should be as wise as God and it isn't given to any of us down on this earth to be as wise as that, is it? Perhaps when you grow up and become a nice velvet cheeked, snowy-haired, bright-eyed old lady you will know more about it. I'm sure your dense-minded Daddy cannot tell . . . not now!

I remember I used to get sick at the wrong time. Once when the long school term was coming to an end (and they *were* long terms when I was a kiddie) I was looking forward to the first day of my vacation because my mother had promised me I could go barefoot . . . and I *did* go barefoot. But I hadn't been without my shoes for more than a few hours when I put my little heel on a cruel piece of slate and nearly tore it off. The doctor had to sew it up and I had to go to bed and stay there for over two weeks. *And it was Vacation!* I don't think I should have minded so much if school term had still been on. (I'll tell you a secret . . . *DON'T YOU TELL MOTHER!!*) I was a dreadfully lazy scholar!

But you are coming out of your difficulties all right. You always do. You did last summer. You *finished well* after I had begun to think you were "all in." You first astonished me by doing your best work just before we reached the "Popa Kanzel" up from the Latimar. And you walked down the Morteratsch Glacier like a soldier after that fearful tug up the sides and over the snowfields of the Diavolezza. But your greatest achievement was in the five or six miles of that stiff pull over the Bernina. When the village hove in sight, you led *me* a chase!

So you mustn't be discouraged, but do as you always have done and you will find your joys will come in some other time. We always have just so much joy in our lives. We are like pitchers . . . we hold just so much; and sometimes we overflow and sometimes we are emptied out . . . and sometimes they take us and wash us out with soap because we have gotten dirty.

Well, dearie, this is a long letter for me to write you. Perhaps it is because I have lots of time in Louisville waiting for a train. Or perhaps it is because I love you very much.

FAJEE

My headache grew steadily worse, my throat was so sore I couldn't swallow, and when my temperature reached the degree of 103° F. Mother broke down and sent for the doctor. I had typhoid fever. It was a mild case and I came through it uneventfully. I was secretly rather pleased. To have acquired a serious malady struck me as quite an achievement, and besides it kept me out of school. Father must have understood my inner satisfaction:

To my soul's Idol—the most beautified Cornelia

Now don't go and say with old Polonius that "beautified is a vile phrase" because any small and important person who has had typhoid fever: NO! I should write it thus—TYPHOID FEVER—it looks more ferocious that way—and come out of it as splendidly as you have, must be beautified.

I was, however, anything but beautified. The fever, light as it had been, had left me pallid and shaky. Mother took me out of school for the remainder of the year and had me tutored three hours a day by two Bryn Mawr graduate students, as uninspiring a pair of beings as ever made of instruction a dreary activity. I'm sure that in me they found a pupil equally doleful, and when we parted in the spring, it was with mutual relief.

Mother herself took an active part in my home education in the matter of English literature. She made up her mind that I "needed more poetry" and proceeded to administer a weekly dose in a sugar-coated form of her own concocting.

Appealing less to my aesthetic sense than to my venal, she struck a deal with me whereby she paid me to memorize each week one poem selected from the *Oxford Book of English Verse*. The rate of payment varied according to the length of the poem. A quatrain netted me ten cents, a sonnet twenty-five, Shelley's *Skylark* sold for thirty-five cents, while the *Eve of St. Agnes* brought in the heady sum of one dollar. The recital of my poem usually took place each Friday at tea time. Mother, sitting behind a steaming kettle and holding the *Oxford Book,* would verify the words while I stood before her giving forth a galloping rendition with hand outstretched to receive my pay. The selection of the piece of poesy she left up to me. After a few weeks, I tired of the *Oxford Book* and switched to Kipling, Mother acquiescing. From Kipling it was a short jump to Robert W. Service. Those hair-on-the-chest idyls of the Yukon were still enjoying a period of popularity and I thought they were beautiful. Mother knew better, but she resigned herself to such William S. Hart taste for the reason that they were the first poems for which I had shown any spark of appreciation and they at least had a quality of pace and rhythm. So, shuddering gently, she listened to "Sam McGee's Cremation" and the vagaries of that Lady named Lou, the true nature of which person, Mother assured herself, I couldn't possibly understand.

Usually for these weekly recitals Mother was my only audience, but on one occasion two other spectators attended my performance. Those were days when, in a suburban community, the established inhabitants indicated their acceptance of newcomers by paying a call. Most of our neighbors had lost no time in dropping in and making Mother feel warmly at home. But up the road lived two genteel and elderly Quaker spinsters whose courage it had taken three months to screw up to the daring point of entering the house of theatre people. Assured by their acquaintances, however, that the smell of brimstone would not assail their delicate nostrils, one Friday afternoon they timidly rang the bell and handed their cards to Bridget, our wild Irish help, who ushered them into the living room. Mother was delighted. That these quaint Cranfordesque ladies should have conquered their scruples to the point of coming to call seemed to her a charming honor and she was only too ready to show them that actors were not the riffraff they had been led to believe. The scene was auspiciously set. Tea was ready, a dish of buttered scones was keeping hot on the brass hob beside a crackling fire, Mother was wearing her simplest but most becoming frock, and for once, I had not left my roller skates on the sofa. She welcomed the little spinsters, settled them in comfortable chairs, filled their stomachs with an excellent tea and their eyes with her own glowing beauty, and made them feel they were wonderful because she really thought they were. The wizened maidens were enchanted and doubtless began wondering what ever ailed William Penn that he should have frowned upon theatre folk. Things were going well; so well, in fact, that Mother decided to administer the final *coup de grâce* to their prejudices by showing them with what methods of culture and refinement she was bringing up her young daughter.

"This is my Cornelia's day for reciting her weekly poem," she said. "Would you dear ladies care to hear her?" The dear ladies said that indeed they would and one of them admitted that she herself was very partial to poetry recitals, especially when Mrs. Florence Earle Coates, the Philadelphia Sappho, read her own, dressed in those lovely artistic tea gowns. Wondering if after all she were doing the right thing, Mother called me down from my room. With the picture of Mrs. Florence Earle Coates and her lovely artistic tea gown fresh in their minds, my entrance must have come as a jolt. Far from trailing tunics of Fortuny glory, I was attired in a middy blouse, serge bloomers, long black ribbed stockings, and sneakers. Mother began emitting the little cooing sounds she made whenever she felt uncertain—which was whenever I appeared in company. She explained that I had just come home from basketball and hoped they'd understand my clothes. The ladies said that yes, indeed, they did. Under the spell of Mother's persuasive manner, they'd have said the same if I had appeared wearing a full suit of armor. Mother told them how her little girl memorized a poem every week, omitting the sordid detail of my being monetarily rewarded for maintaining my end of the pretty custom. She further explained that she left the choosing of the piece up to me.

"And what is the selection today?" chirped one of the ladies whose poetical knowledge was in all probability limited to the works of Felicia Hemans.

"'The Price He Paid,' by Ella Wheeler Wilcox," I announced and, without further ado, plunged dramatically into the loud declamation of a lyrical gem I had culled from the pages of the *Philadelphia Evening Bulletin.* Whatever inspired me to choose it I can't imagine, for I could not have remotely known what it was about, dealing as it did with venereal disease. But Robert W. Service had given me a zest for "strong" things, and this was certainly strong. It was a rhyming narrative following the rag-and-a-bone-and-a-hank-of-hair formula, the narrator being a young man who had spent his youth sowing a wild and extraordinarily unhealthy crop of oats. That he had fellow oat-sowers is indicated in the second verse:

For I saw men everywhere
  Hot-footing the road of vice.
And women and preachers smiled on them
  As long as they paid the price.

But vice, according to Mrs. Wilcox, goes not unpunished and just retribution visits our hero after he has won and wed a pure and beautiful girl:

> She was going to bear me a child,
>   And when in labor she cried,
> With love and fear, I was wild,
>   But now I wish she had died
> For the son she bore me was blind,
>   And crippled and weak and sore,
> And his mother was left a wreck,
>   It was so she settled my score.[1]

By the finish, Mother, whose cooing had increased at the outset of the ditty, was sounding like a whole dovecote. The two sisters, however, merely sipped their tea and listened politely. They were as innocent of the poem's sultry significance as I.

In addition to the Quaker ladies, there were two other neighbors who viewed our ingress into the community with speculation. Mr. and Mrs. A., a couple who, in regard to the Main Line, definitely "belonged," were well off, well mannered, and the personification of the conventional. Mrs. A. was frighteningly *chic,* and Mr. A. had an irreproachable tailor, a bland smile, and an inability to talk about anything other than his golf game.

Evenings when Father was home, he read aloud while Mother and I sewed. Father's reading was a happy compensation for the uninspiring type of needlework I was set to do. I was allotted either dishtowels to hem or a bunch of stockings to darn. If I finished the work at hand, my reward was to be allowed to run baby ribbon with a bobbin through the eyelet insertions of Mother's underwear, an activity I loved. One evening I had finished both my drab

[1] Reprinted by permission of the W. B. Conkey Company and *The Philadelphia Evening Bulletin.*

assignment and the ribbon-running job. Scattered about me on the sofa were numerous ends of pink, pale blue, and yellow ribbon. My hands being idle, Satan, having no better mischief still to find at the moment, prompted me to gather them up, rise, and walk around behind Father's armchair. His hair was the curly, wiry kind that could be made to do all manner of wonderful things. Still listening to *Nicholas Nickleby* and hardly aware of what I was doing, I separated Father's mop into some eight or ten tufts, twirled them out into little spirals in the style of a clown's wig, and tied a jaunty bow on each upstanding end. By the time I had done, he had a fascinating coiffure of beribboned spikes. Father, accustomed to my fooling with his hair, paid no attention to me, but continued reading. He had reached the chapter about Smike and the horrors of Dotheboys Hall, an account I found so touching I left off my hairdressing buffoonery and returned to my place on the sofa. Just as Mrs. Squeers was feeding the starving schoolboys her notorious porridge "which looked like diluted pincushions," there was a ring at the front door. Our maid was out, and Father, thinking it was a call from some one of our friends, jumped up, and going to the door opened it with a hearty "Come in, come in, come in!" There in the porch light stood Mr. and Mrs. A. and there in the hall light stood Father in his pink, blue, and yellow ribbons. Mother, beholding him for the first time, let out a cry of dismay and I sought an ostrich-like refuge, burying my head under a pillow. Father, however, was anything but fazed. "Welcome to the house of Skinner!" he cried out to the bewildered A.'s. "This is the way my daughter likes my hair and I intend to keep it this way all evening." He did.

One more proof that nobody can predict the potential success or failure of a play merely by reading the manuscript is the fact that when Klaw and Erlanger first approached Father with the script of *Kismet,* he turned it down. Even when that management sent Father, with Mother along, on a rapid round trip to see the Oscar Asche production which was the furor of London, he had little faith in the piece taking with the American public. Just as Father was about to wire K. and E. a final refusal, Mother, whose judgment was at times uncannily correct, stepped in. She knew *Kismet* was a good play. She knew Hajj the Beggar was a part which might have been written to order for Otis Skinner, and with that determination which, for all her delicate loveliness, could be as relentless as the most completely armored fist that ever hid in velvet glove, she made up her mind he must do it. They talked it over heatedly and the discussion lasted all one night. I remember waking in the early morning hours and hearing them. I couldn't make out their words, but the tone of their voices frightened me strangely. Father's was a low, stubborn mumble, as if he were saying the same thing over and over again. Mother's voice was stubborn, too, but it was raised in the clear, insistent note I knew only too well to be an indication that Mother was "getting after" something. Next morning Father telegraphed Klaw and Erlanger he'd do the part. His faith in the play was still wobbly. With Frohman he had always gone into every theatrical venture on a percentage basis. This time, deciding this would be too great a risk, he signed a contract for a set salary. And that was another slip-up in judgment. *Kismet* was one of the smash hits of the American theatre; and during its run, which lasted over three years, Father played for a nominal weekly stipend. Ah, well, as he used to remark about it, there wasn't room on our two acres for a swimming pool anyway.

The part of Hajj the Beggar, a wily rascal, who in a single

day goes from rags to riches, stabs and drowns the Grand Wazir, makes an attempt on the life of the young Caliph to whom he eventually marries off his daughter, strangles his old enemy, and winds up this day of considerable activity back in rags again and sentenced to banishment in Mecca, was the most spectacular one of his career. The lavish production was like an Arabian Nights' pageant and the play was Edward Knoblock's finest. But Father never quite got over his original misgiving, never quite settled into the Morocco sandals of Hajj with the delight with which he strutted in the boots of Colonel Brideau or the comfort with which he trudged in the old worn shoes of Mister Antonio.

Kismet was considered very daring, not the least startling innovation being the harem scene. At the rise of the curtain, the Wazir's favorite wife and a number of less favorite ones were discovered lying about on silken cushions in elaborately voluptuous attitudes while a group of five or more odalisques stood beside a bathing pool. At a given moment these last flung off cloaks and walked down into the water presumably naked, although actually they were covered in pink "fleshings" as all-encasing as suits of Munsingwear. Audiences always gasped at the scene and a few members of the Comstock League wrote letters to the papers about it, which of course helped the box office. Mother tried very hard to be modern and broad-minded in regard to the episode. She admitted it was necessary for purposes of plot to establish the pool in which Hajj had later to drown the Wazir, and that it would be slightly anachronistic for the maidens of a harem to step out in black Annette Kellermanns. Moreover, as she'd explain to whoever was with her, the girls were all such *nice* girls, and their figures *were* young and very pretty —but still—— And during the brief interval between the bathers' shedding their cloaks and their safe submergence in the mantling water, she'd coo a steady plainsong of gentle discomfiture.

After a year on Broadway, *Kismet* played the road for two more seasons. The spectacle required five scenery cars, and as the cast numbered some seventy-five members, they traveled like the circus in a special train. It was tough touring. The jumps were difficult and theatre conditions made for all manner of hardships. One of the most serious problems was the pool, and not the least to bear the brunt were the girls who had to bathe and Hamilton Ravelle who had to be drowned in it nightly. It was a metal tank contrivance lowered so that its rim came flush with the level of the stage. The water was heated by a system of steam pipes which worked or not according to local facilities. Except during the harem scene, the aperture was covered over with wooden lids built solidly to form part of the floor. At one matinée in Chicago, the lids were removed and a cloud of steam hissed up like a gush of Old Faithful. Someone had left the pipes on overnight and the water was at a temperature correct for cooking a lobster. The curtain was supposed to rise immediately following a short musical interlude. There was a moment of panic. The girls who were lined up for their cue had the expressions of early Christians suddenly confronted with the stake, and Hamilton Ravelle told everybody what he thought of them in no unblasphemous terms. But stage hands are persons of resource in all emergencies. One group dashed next door to a saloon, another waylaid a passing ice wagon. Cakes and barrels of ice were dumped into the scalding tank only to melt like butter in an oven. The wait was growing critical and the audience was applauding impatiently. More ice was procured. The stage manager tested the water and gave the bathers the consoling information that at any rate it wouldn't kill them. He was right, it didn't. But it parboiled them to the degree that they emerged a bright cerise which showed angrily through their pink fleshings. Hamilton Ravelle, whose state of cerise was equal to that of his fury, swore he'd never play the part again. He was always swearing that. But of course he did play it, and the next night, the steam pipes having been turned off completely and the water having on the surface a delicate skim of ice, he had to be revived with hot blankets, slugs of whiskey, and a salary raise.

The company toured the West. A letter scribbled on the Overland Limited says:

> We are speeding across the plains, dear heart, and it's chill and snowy. There is nothing quite so desolate and forlorn that some moment of the day cannot add a little loftiness and glory to. Charlie's hour was night . . . mine I think always has been the late mellow afternoon before the land becomes red with sunset. The vastness of this Nebraskan and Wyoming stretch is so like the ocean always to me, and this afternoon brought our sea days back. Immensity always brings you near to me.
>
> I had three hours' hard and furious sleep last night. Then I woke in my berth at two o'clock and staid awake. Dawn was quite glorious in the desert. The tumble of eroded cliffs were jewels in the sunrise. I watched them out of my window. I find staying awake at night isn't so bad if you don't fight it. Worry can tire you as much in the daytime as it does at night. The trouble is we generally carry our worries to bed with us and in the waking hours we reach over and grab them to our bosoms.

The tour swung South. In a letter postmarked New Orleans, and still containing a small, dried rose, he says:

> This rose bud was ravished from a cemetery lot at Métaèrie. Some old French citizen fertilized it no doubt. I didn't look to

see who he was. The blossom was fragrant and bright and I took it, and no one saw me but an observant chameleon.

The iron chairs by the walk are growing shabby and perhaps ours has succumbed to rust and decrepitude. The lineal descendants of the chameleons who listened to our vows are growing scarcer. But it is still a sweet spot. The dead ladies and gentlemen are very quiet, but they were most hospitable and they remember us very well.

Sunday:

This morning I went to *Mass!* I've done so many genuflections and crossings that I feel most chastened and Catholic. It's a wonderful thing, the Mass! You can't escape its influence if you've the least bit of idealism and imagination in your system. The marvelous part of its appeal is that it is the expression of a big swinging *belief*. It is the impersonality of it that is so wonderful . . . like being a part of the ocean or a marvellous sunset or a big play. Something vast is surging about you that is not controlled by priests. You know that the priest isn't any better than you are. I can readily understand anyone's conversion to Catholicism. It is the only religion that has kept its poetry, its imagination, its uplift and its childlike belief.

Outside in Jackson Square, General Jackson remains firm and fine rearing on his bronze horse. Around his pedestal the violets and cannas are blooming as well as a few degenerate hollyhocks. There is sleep and kindliness in the air and the General keeps guard over a few tramps dozing on the benches.

My love . . . my dear love to you, bride of the long ago.

OTIS

The second season wound up in Boston. Father writes from the Copley-Plaza:

Believe me, dearest wife, I had a thrill on getting into Boston. It was one of those unexpected things. New England has been calling me for some days but I didn't hear her voice until today and it startled me. Just my Yankee blood having a little maelstrom.

I went for a long walk, for it has been a beautiful Easter day. I saw some wonderful and fine array, ranging from such combinations as willow plumes and tan shoes to ladies whose skirts looked as if their owners were about to run a sack race.

I tried to get into Trinity Church, but a smiling but firm cop stood at the door with a flaming sword and told me that God was busy with a few of his personal friends inside and there wasn't any use in my being fussy. So I came back to the hotel and read *John Barleycorn*. Rather putting one over on God, don't you think?

And tonight I heard the Oratorio of "Elijah" by the Handel and Haydn Society at Symphony Hall and got $2.50 worth of more thrill. I'm sure some of the singers have warbled since the Peace Jubilee. And the audience was such a bunch of Boston frumps who looked so hard-headed I wondered if Mendelssohn's measures moved them too. At any rate it was Oratorio night, and it was the Handel and Haydn and they all came out and got into street cars or walked home. Verily there are no frills about Boston.

It was the last stand of a strenuous tour. The star was run down and tired. He developed a nagging earache which grew daily worse. He had a fever too. The management begged him to close, but the actors "play-must-go-on" spirit, which is a combination of gallantry, stoicism, and plain pigheadedness, made him determined to finish the season. He played the final performance with a temperature of 104°, staggered onto a train for Indianapolis, and his good friend, Doctor Lafayette Page, who got him onto the operating table just in time to prevent a virulent mastoid from penetrating the brain. It was a narrow escape, but he made a quick recovery and the interim of convalescence amid his many warm, entertaining Hoosier acquaintances was pleasant. Booth Tarkington, a lifelong friend, Meredith Nicholson, Mrs. Benjamin Harrison, William Bobbs, the publisher, all made him feel at home. And he visited occasionally with that crotchety poet of the frost on the pumpkin, James Whitcomb Riley, whose qualities were anything but those his homespun verse endorsed.

> I lunched today with Riley, sympathetically but difficultly, for you have to *entertain* Riley. I think I must have told him all the stories I know by this time, so I am a little shy about continuing our friendship.
>
> The only spark of the spirit of the old Riley yesterday was after we had left the house and were in his automobile and I mentioned Walt Whitman. The old man blazed with indignation. "That damn evangelist walking about the streets with his collar undone and his brisket showing!" he snorted, and he quoted one of Whitman's grosser poems and generally damned the sweet singer of Camden.
>
> Yesterday the last bit of adhesive came off and today my wound is dry and bared to the wind and sun. If it were only around on my cheek I could star in a German University town as a man who had defended his honor but not his face.
>
> A wonderful thunder-storm has just passed over cooling the parched Indiana air. I've been out on the porch reading Wordsworth to a poetic young interne, and now I'm going for a walk for the storm has blown over and the earth is fresh.

The operation left him physically depleted and the third and last season of *Kismet* was a nightmare. Father was a miserable sleeper even under the best of circumstances. That year he seldom averaged more than four hours a night. "I had a wonderful sleep last night!" one letter says, "S*E*V*E*N whole hours! That is so rare an occurrence I have to write about it." The part of Hajj had begun to tell on his nerves. It was longer than Hamlet and more strenuous than d'Artagnan. He was dead tired. Tired and filled with a strange uneasiness, over what he could not have said. One letter is headed:

> Washington's Damn Birthday! Thank God there are no other national heroes fit to be celebrated by matinées! When the old boys and girls . . . the Garricks-Kembles-Siddons'-

Keans electrified the world, they only played a few times a week. No wonder they were great and had time to hobnob and get drunk.

I enclose a lot of stuff. . . . Mostly a weariness of the spirit.

As the tiring season wore on, he found himself victim of one of those emotional snarls which at some time or another hits nearly every actor. I suppose today it would be called "occupational neurosis" or "performance fatigue." One of the first manifestations of it is that one starts forgetting lines. Such psychoses are not confined to the stage either. Gentlemen of the cloth say it is not at all unheard of for a minister suddenly to forget the Lord's Prayer.

This type of terror is one of the worst in the world and my father suffered a private Gehenna. Suddenly, for no apparent reason, he started either going blank or mixing up speeches into senseless jargon. After three years, he would have said he knew the part backward. And saying it backward was about what he found himself doing. Before the show he'd go over the text flawlessly; then, with determined confidence, he'd make his entrance and sooner or later the hideous moment of oblivion would hit him like a knockout blow. The ghastly thing continued for several weeks. He thought, of course, he was losing his mind if indeed he hadn't already lost a fair portion of it. He grew more and more frantic. He went for long walks in neighboring countrysides, the *Kismet* manuscript in hand, studying the part from start to finish as if for the first time. He took violent exercise. He even, at the suggestion of one of the members of his company, went to a mental healer—a mortifying experience which at least helped to restore his sense of humor. This was all prior to these brave new days when, at the least jangle of a nerve, people run yammering to the nearest psychiatrist. He had to work out the solution for himself and he did. How he did is a story of his own private philosophy and innate New England common sense. I rather think a certain amount of quiet, unsensational religion entered into his solving of the problem. He wrote to Mother of his fears and hopes:

We certainly need some sort of belief. If it does nothing further, it saves us from our own weaknesses and cowardice. And we don't have to hypnotize ourselves or lash ourselves for it to accomplish its purpose.

I had become afflicted with a hideous self-consciousness of my lines and action. I found myself thinking ahead for a line or two wondering what I said in such and such a speech and when that particular speech arrived, I got cold and panicky.

Then it began to occur to me. I have been merely putting my faith and belief in fear, and not in the power of good which must be the governing power of everything human, physical and spiritual. To believe that there is more intangible but potent good than active evil bearing our lives is a simple start and an easy one which needs no monstrous exertion of will power. To eliminate the will altogether comes as a startling revelation and has a very soothing effect on the nerves.

I find it works. That is a sort of primer.

Now if a word or two gets twisted, I don't bother about it. The most significant part of the whole affair is, *nothing awful really ever happened!* But the number of bridges I crossed was astounding. Strange this groundless apprehension that comes through the separation of mental activity from the work in hand. The ceaseless turning of the wheel is hypnotizing. Do but see that the wheel turns, however, and the influence of its turning vanishes.

When one shakes the idea of cant, man-made religion, popular experimental psychology and above all the notion of a *personal omnipotent being,* one begins to see things more clearly.

One word haunts me—LAW. Summer succeeds winter, the planets keep their rhythmic course about the sun. The seed bursts its shell and becomes a tree. The bird sits upon its egg and produces life. There is the great mystery of death and the profounder mystery of birth. I am an integral part of this LAW, and so long as I am in harmony with it, nothing of ill consequence can befall me.

I'm afraid my creed is either too simple or too complicated to become a cult.

My heart is more quiet and it is all yours,

OTIS

P.S. Old Mr. G. came to call. I am obsessed by his teeth. When he talks to you, they drop down from upstairs and his voice gets under the plate so you think he's talking to you from a cave!

CHAPTER ELEVEN

Warm Springs and World War One

I CANNOT REMEMBER a time when the Warm Springs in Bath County, Virginia, was not a part of my life. I loved it, even as a small girl, with a tender, almost possessive affection. During the bleak Pennsylvania winters I'd long for the old Southern resort with a bitter-sweet "kennst du das Land" nostalgia, dreaming of the blue folds of the Alleghenies, the mountain hayfields shimmering in intense noon, the ice-clear torrent which twined itself caduceus-like in and out of the red dirt road through Dunn's Gap, cooling the splashing hoofs of the horses that pulled the hired surreys. I'd remember those other streams, spills from the hot sulphur springs, which wound their way through lush valley pastures, steaming like outlets from a gentle inferno. I'd close my eyes and see again the mountaineer cabins of plaster and rough-hewn logs, and the rambling boarding house of Miss Summers Anderson with its ancient garden (pronounced "gyarden," of course) a jumble of boxwood, hollyhocks, broken brick walks, and appealing disorder; I'd imagine myself walking through the little village in Germantown Gap with its general store which sold everything from horehound drops to mowing machines . . . its stock was the accumulation of generations, moldy bottles of Peruna and Cardui, bolts of antebellum calico, and a dressmaker's dummy which might have served for fitting the gowns of Mrs. Jefferson Davis.

While the winter wind howled around our Bryn Mawr house, I'd think of the hot powdery Virginia roadsides and the barefoot types one passed on the way, wiry farmhands, vacant-eyed mountaineers, and magnificent Negro patriarchs, and how they'd all pause to say "Good evenin'!" even if it were barely after midday. But chiefly I'd long for the old resort itself. It was a place rife with traces, faded as its chipping whitewash, of the former splendor of the days when it had been the elegant spa which, in the days of Washington Irving, according to one of his fellow Knickerbocker wits, offered "all the airs, graces, paraphernalia, caprices and elegancies of the most fashionable assembly . . . with as many gay equipages and gay people as at Ballston or Long Branch." It had been nearly a century since the lordly stagecoaches, with chain-locked wheel, had lumbered down the mountain highway bearing parties of swank Carolinians who were arriving to flush their aristocratic kidneys of the year's accumulation of juleps. The place had started to lose its popularity by the eighteen-thirties and since then had run genteelly downhill. It was shabby and battered, but still sweet and lovely, like an aging belle who has seen better days but is ever adored. Thinking about it, my breath would catch, recalling the excitement that welled up in me when the hotel bus used to turn in at the shaded driveway and draw up at the foot of the high double stairs which led to the great pillared porch of the main building, a rambling edifice like a whitewashed and smaller version of the United States Hotel at Saratoga. I'd remember the warmth of recognition with which I'd see again the other buildings, charming, slightly dilapidated structures—the

Colonnades, which had been the hotel proper when Thomas Jefferson patronized it (a faded ledger showed his account for food and lodging for himself, servants, and horses as well as how much rum he had consumed), the comfortable vine-covered frame bungalows—"family cottages" they were called—and the rows of connecting one-room structures, former slave quarters, which had been charmingly made over into accommodations for single guests. It was nice to think about summer days in the immense bare dining room, the fans like lazy windmills turning silently in the ceiling and a young apprentice waiter standing at each of the large round tables for ten (there were no private ones) shaking a fly switch of shredded colored paper. And my mouth would water with the memories of Sunday-night suppers, spoon bread, piping hot biscuits running with yellow butter, "crumbs of comfort," damson preserve, and the rest of those amenities which have made calomel the medicinal badge of the South. Soft nights with a moon-bright sky turning the mountains into profile scenery, fireflies sparkling about the cast-iron fountain in the centre of the driveway, tree toads sounding like sleighbells, and, at a distance up the hill and back of the hotel, from the servants' quarters the sound of singing—laughter, too, sometimes, but always deep, rich singing.

And then there was the pool. I'd often dream I was back swimming in that pool. As a matter of fact, there were two of them—the gentlemen's and the ladies'. They were crude circular structures, like circus tents made of wood. Inside they were some forty feet in diameter and the only light came from an open aperture in the roof. The bottom of each pool was covered with the stones and pebbles of the original springs and the walls were the ancient construction which had lasted since the days when General Washington bathed there. Wooden steps, green and slippery with feathery, subaqueous moss, led down into the water. There was never anything to compare with that water. Soft and delicious, it welled up at a temperature of 98° F., "the temperature of the human heart," as Percival Reniers has said, in great crystal bubbles which, if you knew where to stand or tread water, ran up your legs and body tickling exquisitely. It was the clearest liquid in the world and under it one's skin looked like blue marble. The perfect way to swim, of course, was in one's skin, the way the gents did in their establishment; but such paganism was not countenanced in the ladies', where everyone wore the regulation Warm Springs suits. These were shapeless, step-in numbers of bright calico, fashioned like baggy rompers and fastening over the shoulders with tape. As garments of modesty, they were purely theoretical, for, being extremely loose, the slimmer females occasionally swam right out of theirs, while the fat old dames, whose athletic activities were restricted to a rhythmic and majestic dunking, frequently found their bosoms floating out to the surface like misplaced water-wings. This was because the water, as Aunt Fanny used to say, "was so buoyous."

Aunt Fanny, who was in charge of the women's bathhouse, was a great lady, graced with all the dignity of Africa, and all the humor and wisdom, too. She was very old. Exactly how old she would never tell, but she remembered only too searingly clearly the occasion when she was taken from her mother and sold at the New Orleans block to a planter up the river. Age had in no way modified her. Spry as a cricket, she ran the place, bossing everybody with that endearing severity which is the prerogative of the well-loved Mammy, dealing out suits and towels, ordering you into your dressing cubicle when you'd stayed overlong in the enervating water with a peremptory "You come straight out, chile. Yo' lips is gettin' blue!", wrapping you in a sheet after you'd shed your suit, drying and rubbing down your back with her beautiful old brown hands. Once when a New York society woman prudishly protested that she preferred to omit that particular touch of attention, Aunt Fanny silenced her with "Go 'long, honey! Nakedness ain't no treat to me!" She taught countless small children to swim. Securing them with a lasso arrangement she made of long linen strips and holding one end, she'd walk along the narrow platform, trailing the child through the water and shouting down instructions. The moment of graduation was when Aunt Fanny removed the belt, gave the little one a smart clip on the rump, and ordered it to "git on out to de rope"—which sanctuary ran across the middle of the pool. The water was deep and the rope seemed an eternity away, but to disobey Aunty Fanny was the equivalent of disobeying General Pershing. Terrified, but game, the child would start and, to its wonder and delight, would for the first time experience the miracle of swimming. Once or twice during the course of her years of instruction, a kid had become panicky and had started to founder, whereat the old lady, starched petticoats, bandanna, and all, had jumped into the water and struck out like lightning in a rescuing overhand.

We first got to know the Warm one early spring when Father, who was in search of a get-away-from-it-all place in which to study a part, had seen a magazine ad of the historic old resort, thought it worth taking a chance on, and had written to the proprietor, a Mrs. Eubank. A charming reply assured him there would be accommodations for us, although, the letter warned, it being ahead of the season, the hotel was not officially opened and we'd be the only people. If we took the Chesapeake and Ohio sleeper to Hot Springs there would be a carriage waiting to drive us to the Warm, where breakfast and welcome would be waiting. We'd have to be tolerant if the horses looked like goats, their coats were still winter length.

The surrey, the shaggy horses, and a smiling black coachman were at the station to meet us. It was a bitter cold day in early April and we drove the four miles through a thick snowstorm. I added to the joy of things by coming down with one of my violent nosebleeds. As we turned a bend in the road, my nosebleed let up. So did the snow. The sweet, ample Warm Springs Valley opened out before our eyes and seemed to take us to its heart, and then and there we all three fell in love with the place. Father fell in love with it even more when, upon stepping onto the porch of the main hotel, Horace, the head waiter and major-domo, an impressive old man whose magnificent side whiskers gave him the air of a colored Lord Dundreary, stood in the doorway bearing a tray on which gleamed three exquisite mint juleps. "Mis' Eubank's compliments," he said, "she figured you'd be right chilly after that drive." That Mrs. Eubank had not also figured on my tender years was all to the good as far as Father was concerned. He never before or since had a drink before breakfast, but that morning he downed his julep and mine and was grateful.

Mrs. Eubank was a widow lady who ran the place less as a proprietor than as a royal matriarch. She was a semi-invalid, suffering in the traditional manner of certain elderly Southern ladies from one of those chronic indispositions the nature of which is never made clear to anyone, not even to themselves. She seldom stirred from the frame cottage which served as her palace. Her Star Chamber was the wide veranda where she issued all daily orders and from where she had a fine view of the hotel, the kitchens, the offices, and a secluded side porch where, on moonlit nights, the old lady could determine who was petting whom.

We three loved the Warm for many reasons. Father gloried in his solitary walks about the mountainous countryside, in the sun-mottled glades where he could study aloud and undisturbed next season's part, in the sybaritic waters of the ancient pools. He felt relaxed and at home amid the amiable coterie who liked and admired him for what he was and never lionized him as an actor, although when trippers from the Hot or White Sulphur drove over for the day, local cicerones were apt to point him out proudly as "our Celebrity," and that was all right too. There were good and entertaining friendships to be had—George Barr McCutcheon, Charles Belmore Davis, brother of Richard Harding, Ben Valentine, the Richmond man of letters, and the novelist Mary Johnston whose estate "Three Hills" was only a mile away.

Mother loved the place because it was beautiful and tranquil and she found time for reading and writing her engaging notes and getting her mending done and because everyone adored her. There was much of the South in her blood and she fitted admirably into the setting. But her active mind would never have allowed her to have relaxed completely into the lazy rhythm of daily hotel routine. Her interests could never have been confined to fancywork and conversation and, thank God, no one of us ever learned to play bridge. Her creative need found a number of outlets. Every year she staged a dramatic entertainment, a sort of drama-variety-pageant show, acted by the younger element—bright, inconsequential pieces based on matters of local amusement. She took an interest in the mountaineer people who lived, or rather, barely managed to exist, in the squalid cabins on the near-by hillsides, helping the apathetic women out in a small way, encouraging any aptitude they might show for their crude native crafts, arranging for them to bring their patchwork quilts, rag rugs, and crocheted doilies to sell at the hotel, purchasing some herself, though not many. Her Missouri economy kept a restraining hand on her pocketbook, except in the case of hand-woven baskets.

She had a mania for any sort of basket. She was always buying them and there was never any place in which to pack them. Among my clearest girlhood memories are those of homecomings from all summer vacations, whether spent in Virginia, Colorado, or Europe, laden down like Mexican peddlers with wicker receptacles of every shape and size.

And I liked Warm Springs for countless reasons, the pool, the mountains, the group of young things of my own generation. I even liked the fact that for two summers I got roped into playing the organ in church, although I imagine I was the only person who did. In "piano" I had got as far as MacDowell's "Wild Rose," at which frail blossom I had stuck. It was with considerable anguish that I mastered five easy hymns, three of which, in rotation, were wheezed out every Sunday while my offertory selection varied between Chopin's Nineteenth Prelude and an old English drinking song played at funeral tempo. I used only one keyboard, ignoring the stops, which didn't work, anyway. The crude little instrument was pumped for me by an ancient mountaineer who was afflicted with deafness and an overwhelming tendency to fall asleep. He had to be kicked awake a few minutes before each hymn and that was dangerous because my foot in transit was apt to hit one of the pedal keys which gave out a deep groan as soon as the air got going. It was all very informal, but so was the little church itself. Bees droned in and out to feed from the flowers on the altar, a thoughtful cow occasionally stuck her head in at the window snuffling in mild-eyed interest, and some days my Irish terrier would trot down the aisle to flop comfortably at my feet. Quite a number of years later, I was married in that church. The old resort had gone to rack and ruin and the place had been closed up for a long time. A family of flying squirrels had nested in the wheezy organ and some hornets, infuriated at having their peace disturbed, quietly stung Father and my maid of honor. But the little house of worship still looked sweet and as I had remembered it; a few of the village people wandered in to witness the ceremony and I was met at the door by Willie, Aunt Fanny's granddaughter, who gave me a four-leaf clover to wear in my shoe.

But chiefly I loved those summers because I was in the dawning teens and boys came into my life. We called them "men," of course. Our pleasures were simple—picnics, doubles of inept tennis, a little horseback riding, and an occasional watermelon party. The fact that there was no orchestra failed to dampen our dancing enthusiasm. In the evenings someone would light the crystal wall brackets in that scene of vanished quadrilles and lancers, the red and white ballroom, someone else would go in search of the Armenian lace-merchant's son whom we paid to tread patient miles on the upright pianola and to the strains of "Row, Row, Row" and "My Hula Lou" we hurtled giddily in the foxtrot, the Maxixe, and the Florence Walton tango. Once in a while there would be an expedition over to the Hot for an evening of gaiety in the Japanese Room. But not often. Our "men" didn't have the money and the practice of going dutch was unknown.

I was nearly always in love. My first *grande passion* was for a beautiful youth from Richmond who bore the proud name of a Confederate general and was considered definitely "fast." He must have been all of the world-weary age of seventeen. I was just fourteen, trying to pass as twenty-one, but I doubt if I fooled many people. I put up my hair, which didn't stay up very long at a time, and let the hems out of my skirts, never bothering to face the rough edges and seldom taking the time to iron out the ridge of the original hem. Sallow and grotesquely thin, I knew I was not pretty, but I thought there might perhaps be something rather fascinating about me. So did the seventeen-year-old roué from Richmond, Virginia. For just about one week. The romance started on a hayride when he suddenly grabbed my hand in a tender clinch. I was startled and extremely pleased and pretended elaborately not to notice it. In my state of fluster, I didn't know how to withdraw and Casanova apparently didn't know how to let go. For the better part of an hour we sat motionless and speechless, our palms clamped together in an adhesion of love, embarrassment, and perspiration. Two nights later there was a moonlight picnic on the top of Flag Rock, the adults driving up in carriages and chugging motor cars and the juvenile element going on foot. We pedestrians were supposed to stay together, but on the way down, my seducer snatched me off onto a side path and we made the descent, with his arm around my waist and his hand firmly grasping my stomach. The next evening we sat on the steps of the church and he kissed me with a smack which, as I recall it, landed somewhere between chin and ear, but which was sufficient to keep me awake all night, my heart pounding like crazy. The following night he kissed me again, this time getting nearer the mark, and twenty-four hours later, his aim was deliciously accurate. I reeled home to our cottage in a blear of love. I, of course, took it for granted that I was engaged. I also took it for granted that I was going to have a baby. How I arrived at this biologically phenomenal conclusion, I can't imagine. But I was perfectly happy over the prospect. I was in love—wildly and rapturously in love. That it was reciprocal, I never questioned. Within two days life dealt me a blow in the solar plexus when a Richmond sub-deb, an older woman of nearly eighteen, with a "baby-blue stare," arrived, took one look at my un-intended, and vamped him away from me. I was deeply and genuinely heartbroken.

There were other summers and other romances at the Warm, but none of them as searing. My dalliances were fraught with a good deal of conflicting emotion, a combination of happy abandonment followed by sudden refined compunctions and ending in a pious remorse, which never lasted long enough to deter me from doing it all over again whenever I had the chance. Mother had, of course, delivered the maternal formula talk about boys, and how, if I let them kiss me, they would lose all respect for me. She was right, they did. But it was less for moral reasons than because I did it quite badly. The chief effect of Mother's words of warning was to cramp my style; my underlying conduct remained as loose as ever. Ours was really a very pure sort of looseness in those pre-bobby-sox days. But all things are relative, especially those which cause the heart to race, and during the course of more mature experiences, I have more than once wished for the touching seriousness, the shimmering tiptoe breathlessness, of those ludicrous teen-age loves.

The subject of sex was one around which every mother shied like a skittish horse around a piece of blowing paper. Mother for all her advanced ideas (and she was one of the first to have the courage to champion Mrs. Sanger) was no exception. The first time she volunteered any enlightenment of a biological nature was one evening at home when she came out suddenly and quite crossly with, "Cornelia, there's something you should know. Babies grow inside their mothers." And a week later she called me down into the cellar to feel the distended and heaving stomach of our cat who was about to kitten. The only unabridged information I heard was from certain of my schoolmates. I was shocked, fascinated, and disgusted with the girls who talked of such matters, but of course listened wide-eyed. Incidentally nearly everything they told me was quite incorrect. I was fully fifteen when, one wintry afternoon, Mother undertook to inform me of the facts of life. There was a room in our house which no one ever used. A day bed gave it the potentialities of an extra guest room, a desk lent it the air of a study, and it might have been called an upstairs library owing to the presence of a bookcase filled with a number of those never-looked-at volumes which families feel they can't throw away. A horrid place, dark, cheerless, and ugly, it was stuffy in summer and glacial in winter. Our interview was on a bleak afternoon in mid-January. Mother called me into the place and for some unaccountable reason locked the door. She pulled a hard, straight chair out into the centre of the floor and told me to sit on it. Then she dragged up its mate directly opposite and sat down facing me, our knees touching, like a throat specialist and patient. After that she said she had something to tell me, paused for quite a frightening space of time, and then all at once burst into tears. This unnerved me considerably. Moreover, I had an uncomfortable premonition as to the topic of the impending interview, and that unnerved me even more. I wanted desperately to bolt, and I rather think Mother did too. It was I who finally broached the awful subject.

"Mother," I gulped, "if you're going to talk to me about 'You-Know-What,' I already know."

Mother stared at me aghast. "Who told you?" she asked.

"Catherine W.," I said.

"Catherine W. is a nasty, evil-minded girl," she said. "But since she's told you, that's that." And with a sigh of relief, she rose and unlocked the door.

And yet Mother was by no means a prude. She had in her a lusty streak which was pure Rabelais. I can see her now, holding her hands over her eyes in a see-no-evil gesture and letting out an honest belly laugh over some earthy joke. Most of the time her laugh was a ripple of music, but on these rare occasions, it was a wonderful guffaw such as must have burst from the throat of the Wife of Bath. Any serious aspect of sex, however, was emotionally upsetting to her. Certainly as far as I was concerned it was, for if I ever brought up the topic, she always started to cry. I think she went on the theory that unless she implanted in me the idea that the joys of the flesh were not only wicked but, from a woman's point of view, highly unpalatable, I'd sooner or later be picked up for soliciting along the streets of Bryn Mawr. It was an attitude she maintained even after I was grown. When I was in my early twenties, I happened one day to mention the fact that a close friend of ours, an actress, had for years been the mistress of a certain actor-manager whose wife refused to grant him a divorce. Mother appeared horrified, scolded me for harboring such unworthy thoughts, and protested that of course no decent woman, certainly not one who had been on such intimate terms with our family, would have so demeaned herself. I knew better, but at the time, said nothing. After I was married, the subject again arose, and Mother with serious sweetness announced that of course L. had been So-and-So's mistress; she'd have been the fool of the world if she hadn't been.

I shall always cherish the recollection of an incident that occurred not long after I had married and was living in my own home. Mother and I had not seen one another for several days and had planned to lunch together at a midtown restaurant, meeting first at the Guaranty Trust in order to cash some checks and to accomplish that human necessity which refinement chooses to call "powdering the nose." Mother, quite unbeknownst to me, had been to see *The Front Page* and had been startled and fascinated by the language, much of which was new to her. She thought that an amusing way of informing me that she had attended this play, whose realism had so shocked the audiences of the late twenties, would be to casually quote one of the more colorful phrases. Happily she fluttered over to a strange young woman who, with back turned to her, was making out a check, put an arm across her shoulder and with a beatific smile said, "Darling, I'll meet you in the Can." The young woman who, incidentally, didn't faintly resemble me, looked up in blank amazement and Mother, blushing crimson, clapped a hand to her mouth and cried "OO! I'm so sorry! I thought you were my daughter!"

Mother was a person of lovely contradictions. The gentlest creature in the world, she could also be the stubbornest, holding onto an objective with a bulldog tenacity which defeated everyone except Father whose method of dealing with such spells was to stay away from home until they were over. Another of her contradictions was in her attitude toward her immediate family. Husband, child, sisters, brothers, nieces, and cousins, she felt for us always a great love, frequently pride, and almost never a scrap of confidence. To her we were lovable, irresponsible children, quite apt, if she didn't keep an eye on us, to spill our soup or pick our noses in public. For someone who was lavishly generous in spending of herself, she was surprisingly sparing in the spending of money. Her lamentations concerning the high cost of living and our limited income were frequent and baleful, and it used to seem to me inevitable we should wind up our days in the Edwin Forrest Home for destitute actors. If Mother purchased a new dress, she agonized over the expense and when the garment arrived, kept it put away in a chintz bag for so long, it was almost out of style by the time she could bring herself to wear it. Even in her sparingness she was inconsistent, for she would frequently fix up little impromptu presents for her neighboring friends, then save postage by sending me on my bicycle to deliver them. When we lived in Paris, it was my mortifying duty, whenever we had finished our weekly supply of honey, to trudge with the empty jar five blocks to a certain *épicier* who would grudgingly exchange it for either thirty centimes (the equivalent of about two cents then) or one scrofulous little orange. Once when visiting Emily Kimbrough she suggested they play Russian Bank, adding that it might perhaps be more fun if they played for low stakes. She was quite good at the game, but it so happened that Emily made off with the winnings, a modest total of forty-five cents. Mother, after a little moment of dismay, met the setback with: "Emily, darling, I've got a lovely idea of how we'll settle. I just remember I left a tin of bicarbonate of soda and a brand-new cake of imported French soap in your bathroom and that surely comes to even more than forty-five cents! So we'll just call it square." She was blandly shameless about such matters. She was blandly shameless, too, concerning what she cheerfully admitted to be a streak of innate dishonesty, "Only," as she pointed out with her inimitable logic, "it can't really *be* dishonesty because I'm honest *about* it." She adored to smuggle, whether it were necessary or not, and never stepped off a homecoming steamer without yards of lace swaddled about her torso and a collection of small liqueur and perfume bottles clanking in hidden portions of her clothing. Drinking meant little to her, but during Prohibition it charmed her to bootleg in from Europe or Canada as much liquor as she dared carry in toilet-water flaçons. She never managed to scald them out sufficiently and Father's cocktails, which even with good ingredients were fairly terrible, during the days of Volstead exuded bouquets of Johnny Walker, Houbigant, and Chanel.

If she came across a coin on the pavement, she was as gratified as if someone had given her a present. After she and Father were living in New York, I dropped by her apartment one afternoon for my daily visit and noticed a new little clock on her dressing table. A fantasy of pink enamel and diamond chips, it was the costly sort of bibelot one associated less with Mother than with Peggy Hopkins Joyce.

"Who on earth gave you this?" I exclaimed.

"Nobody," she answered with terse defiance.

"You surely didn't *buy* it!" I knew that only too well.

"Certainly not!" and she sounded quite cross. "I found it in a taxi."

"In a taxi!" I echoed. "Why, whoever dropped it must be frantically trying to get it back! Shouldn't you have taken the name of the driver and told him to turn it in to the Lost and Found?" Such unimaginative honesty was obviously highly irritating to Mother, who dismissed the subject with "No, indeed! These drivers are very careless. They should look in the passenger space after their fares get out. For instance, the other day, I was riding in a Yellow and I noticed on the floor a latchkey and a fifty-cent piece, so when I got out I said to the driver, 'Someone's dropped a latchkey in your cab.' "

"Where was the fifty-cent piece, darling?" I asked with elaborate innocence. Her only answer was to repeat her statement regarding the carelessness of taxi-drivers.

Winthrop Ames once said to her, "Maud, you weren't born. Barrie wrote you!" It was a happy metaphor which occurred to him after she had happened to utter one of her startling *non-sequiturs,* those mannerisms of speech peculiarly her own, as if her active mind were too rapid to be slowed down by mere words. Deems Taylor affectionately called them "Maud Skinnerisms" and claimed that beneath her occasional moonstruck statements there was always a sort of wild logic. He still refers to the time she invited him to luncheon on a Sunday when clocks went onto Daylight Saving time. "Deems, dear," Mother had burbled over the phone, "luncheon will be at one o'clock. Well, it won't be one o'clock *your* time, but you know what I mean." And

Deems said that after a moment or two, he did. He was slightly more intuitive than the pleasantly bewildered young man at a London garden party who, touched by Mother's distress over not being able to locate her friend, Mrs. J., asked if he might not go look for her, an offer Mother turned down meltingly with "No, don't bother! You wouldn't know her because, you see, she's in mourning."

During World War One I was at the callous age when Belleau Woods and Château-Thierry seemed distantly dreadful but far less real than the election of our class president or the annual visit of the Hill School Glee Club. In the glare of the more recent and ghastlier holocaust, memories of the first become blurred; bands playing "Over There," Raemaeker's posters showing the horrors of German *Kultur*, patriotic tableaux by Ben Ali Haggin with Irene Castle posing as "France Defiant." Gasless Sundays. Elsie Janis, Hooverizing, Farmerettes, Liberty Bond rallies with appeals from Douglas Fairbanks, wounded *poilus*, and the Talmadge Sisters. Everyone talked about doing his or her "bit." Mine would hardly have rated me the Congressional Medal. I knitted numberless sweaters and helmets—all, to judge by their looks, for the use of the deformed—wrote postcards in French class with messages for little war orphans in the devastated regions, stuck pins in a *National Geographic* map of the Front indicating the Hindenburg Line, and worked up on the ukulele a stirring performance of "K-K-K-Katy" and "Joan o'Varc, they are calling you." A further contribution was the cheerful submission of my body as a guinea pig for Mother's home practice in First Aid. Returning from her weekly class in that useful therapy which every woman felt she must master, although the percentage of those who were ever called upon to put it to use must have been infinitesimal, she'd try out on me every known and a few hitherto unknown tourniquets, splints, and bandages. I bore it with elaborate fortitude, thinking brave thoughts about Cardinal Mercier, the Rainbow Division, and the Rose of No Man's Land.

Mother's patriotism, like that of a lot of people, had been slow to stir. During the first months of the European conflict, she was not certain whether her sentiments were those of the militarists or the "Too Proud to Fighters." I recall her rushing into the house one day, her cheeks glowing, her eyes dancing with excitement.

"Oh, Bobsey!" she cried, "I've just joined the most wonderful organization. It's going to be so important for our country."

"What is it, Monkie?" I asked.

She paused for a brief moment, then said, "Well, I don't know whether it's the Preparedness League or the Peace at Any Price, *but* . . ." she added brightly, "Mrs. Wilfred Lewis is the president."

The *Lusitania* sank and she knew where she stood. Fired with the fever of the times, she plunged into war work, taking on night-shift duty in canteens, helping out in hospitals, staging patriotic charity benefits in the ballroom of the Bellevue-Stratford, in one of which, whose closing spectacle was a parade of the Allied Nations, she put me to effective use as "Starving Armenia." But her chief contribution was her work with Rachel Crothers in helping launch the Stage Women's War Relief, forerunner of the American Theatre Wing. This came out with a fine record. She headed the Philadelphia branch, organized the Chicago one, and started units in other cities.

Mother's enthusiasm nearly landed us all in the poorhouse during the New York run of *Humpty-Dumpty*, a leisurely and extremely British comedy by Henry Arthur Jones. During each Liberty Loan drive it was customary for the star of every show to appear before the curtain between acts and sell bonds. Father had already invested all he could afford in the current issue. Moreover, the play was a complete flop and the bottom of the family till was plainly visible. Finding he could just manage to squeeze out an additional fifteen hundred dollars, Father planned one evening to enliven his public salesmanship by offering to purchase for himself ten fifty-dollar bonds for every ten people in the audience who would match his bid. He then intended to raise the bid to one hundred dollars for the next five, then terminate the proceedings with a five-hundred-dollar climax, bringing in all, three thousand to Uncle Sam. It was an ingenious idea and the sale got off to a good start. Mother, sitting in a box that night, was filled with the mingled pride and nervousness she always felt whenever Father made any sort of speech. The sales were well under way and Father had already committed himself for a thousand dollars when a young officer, his uniform covered with ribbons, his right arm off at the shoulder, rose and said, "Mr. Skinner, I haven't the money to buy more, but I'll take a fifty-dollar bond." It was a touching and dramatic moment and Mother was carried away with emotion. She sprang to her feet and in the tones of Barbara Frietchie cried out, "I'll take a fifty-dollar bond for every uniformed man in the house!" A little stunned, Father ordered the electrician to turn on the house lights. Mother, whose patriotic impulse had not been so sudden that she had not first taken the precaution of looking about the orchestra floor where she could see only a few uniforms, now found her eyes being drawn in horror to the balcony. It was a solid blue and khaki! Business being bad, the company manager had filled all unsold seats with sailors and doughboys. Mother, at the sight, collapsed onto a chair saying faintly, "I made the bid, but my husband will have to pay for it," then cowered in the rear of the box while the ushers counted the servicemen and reported the dreadful total to Father. The house lights went off and she rushed backstage, flung open the door to Father's dressing room, and wailed out, "Otis, dear love, you may kill me!" It was Otis-dear-love who was nearly killed meeting the obligation.

Father tried his best to go overseas with some of the entertainment units, but he was turned down as being over-age. To those who recall his vigor and buoyancy, that will seem absurd. He did the best he could for the returned men this side of the water. From Winnipeg he wrote:

> Yesterday was a day of much emotion for me. I invited about 300 invalided Canadian soldiers to my matinee. They were there with stiff legs, bandaged limbs, missing members, bound heads, lost fingers and four sat in boxes in pillowed wheel chairs. One of these last looked as if he were mouldering: it must have been mustard gas. I never felt greater exaltation than I did in playing for those lads. Had it been a trial for my professional existence I couldn't have felt more the urgent call for all my art. At the end of each act, I looked through a peep-hole in the curtain to see the effect. After Act 1, they were rather immobile, but evidently interested; Act 2 left a happy smile on all their faces and after the Third Act, they looked as if they were having the time of their lives.
>
> God! I wish I could do something real, true and wonderful for those boys! All that I can do seems so small and inadequate. When I look at these men who have seen and lived through things I shall never even conceive of and who have looked into the face of the avenging Jehovah of Israel, I know I am the meanest worm that crawls. I want to go to France! I want to serve our lads. I want to bring a smile and a moment of forgetfulness to men who are holding back the floodgates of Hell. I want to know service and sacrifice. What use is a successful play when my nights are full of self-reproach?

The successful play was *Mister Antonio*, written for Father by his intimate friend, Booth Tarkington. That excellent gentleman had said to him, some years previously, "Otis, I want to write you a play. I don't know what the character will be . . . peasant, sea captain, tinker, tailor . . . but he's going to be a *beautiful* man." The result was *Mister Antonio*. It was not a great play, the plot was obvious and it bordered dangerously on the sentimental, but the part of the joyous Italian hurdy-gurdy man, "Antonio Cameradonio, padrone, that's-a me," who every spring set forth from Third Avenue to spend the summer months vagabonding about the countryside with faithful Joe, an amiable half-wit, for an assistant, and Capitano, a little donkey, to pull the music wagon, who ambles into the little Pennsylvania town of Avalonia, where he gets the better of the mayor, upsets the plans of the sour-faced parson and family, wins the heart of June, the hired girl, and at the end takes her with him as he sets off singing down the road—was certainly a "beautiful" man. Even the critics, many of whom panned the play, admitted the charm of the portrayal, and H. T. P. of the *Boston Transcript*, the peppery critic whose exacting criticisms earned him the nickname of Hell To Pay, scribbled him a note saying, "I do not care whether *Mister Antonio* is a good play or not, your sunny, lovable *padrone* is irresistible. Have you any idea how well you are acting?"

After a mild New York run, *Mister Antonio* toured for a number of seasons. When there was no other available vehicle, it was always good for a revival on the road, for it was the sort of play people came to see time and again. The character of the engaging Italian organ-grinder became a familiar figure to be welcomed whenever he showed up in town. People felt they knew him personally, as they had known Hodge's "Man from Home" and Warfield's "Music Master." And of course the Italian population of the country regarded him as their champion, if not, indeed, as a sort of patron saint. They'd wait outside the stage door, weighed down with lurid floral tributes which they presented with ecstatic speeches in native tongue shouted at the top of their lungs, and Father would listen politely, accept the wreaths and shout back "*Grazie, grazie!*" which for all his excellent Tuscan accent, was his entire vocabulary.

Capitano, the small donkey who pulled the hurdy-gurdy, was always an object of great interest to myself, particularly as he had an unfortunate way of doing a bit of realistic performing of his own on the grass mats during dramatically intense scenes. But he was a sweet little beast and much loved by the company. From Dubuque, Father wrote:

Just now I beheld one of the most charming sights imaginable. I heard the familiar hurdy-gurdy strains of "Rigoletto" and saw heads sticking out of the machine shop windows across the way. Looking out, I saw Capitano in dress parade hitched to his shafts and Flynn (the company manager) turning the handle in front of this proud new hotel! Our stage crew was grouped about, hats in hand, staring up at my window and grinning from ear to ear. Then they started off up the street, the electrician leading Capitano, Flynn carrying the barroom scene cash register, and William following, wheeling the second act baby carriage. I laughed till I wept.

The reason for this spring madness is a teamsters' strike. The ruffians won't allow our scenery to be hauled. They have agreed to allow the taxicab company to transport our trunks and that's all. Exactly what we are going to do I don't know. There is some old scenery at the theatre. The evening promises to be rich in episode.

Next Day.

It was most creditable. Dubuque gazed at some homemade scenery like Mother used to make and all went merry as a marriage bell. Tug's Third Ave. bar looked like a hot-dog counter at a country race track. The little town of Avalonia was a collection of foliage between and under which nestled a stately brick mansion where the mayor and his family lived, and an Italian albergo with a loggia built by the First Methodist Church of Avalonia for a parsonage; and you would have been surprised to know how vastly like the Tyrol was the view from this residential section . . . so much so that a large American flag which lovingly bound the two neighbors together seemed like the carrying of Old Glory across the seas.

The play went quite as well as it ever has.

And from Omaha, Father wrote—this time to me.

Revered Personal Cherub:

Poor little Cappy is no more! In his stead is a trim, smooth sandpapered beast with a little dark stripe running down his tail to the whiskbroom on the end. He hasn't even those things sticking out of his ears that look like our fireplace brush.

Such a sporty, sophisticated creature is this new Capitano, you wonder how he can associate with a Dago and a Nut, or how he could be induced to enter the gateway of so gay a town as Avalonia. I expect at any moment to see him suddenly sit up and play a cornet or turn the hurdy-gurdy handle or converse like Baalam's ass. And yet if you look in his eyes you will see he has the same expression as the old Cappy. For it *is* Capitano, only shaved!

He had bugs! Not the nimble flea. Bugs, awful ones! When the cast found out, they all commenced scratching in unison. He's like a circus horse now, and he's horribly set up and vain.

Prohibition cast its shadow across the country when they played the Pacific Coast. A letter from San Francisco:

Dearest Wife:

The Golden Land! After the grinding work and travel of this tour, I feel I've earned this.

We had just enough of the sweltering heat of the Sacramento Valley to make the refreshing breeze of the Bay thrice welcome as we boarded the ferry. I dashed to the boat café to get biscuits for the gulls whose skill at catching high flying crusts is one of the joys of the crossing.

Oh! The St. Francis after all the bum hotels of the cross continent. And Oh! The BOOZE! The hotel bar was wide open on Sunday, and though I didn't need one, I went in all by my lone, and sat down with my Sunday paper to a long Scotch high-ball. It was a *rite!* I felt religious over it. I could weep over California and July 1st! Let all other states go dry, but California should remain forever gloriously, tumultuously alcoholic.

Old Bill Crane [the actor William H. Crane, for years the star of *Business Is Business*] is here, at the St. Francis. He leads the lobby-haunting life. He's getting old in thought and habit and retrospection. He has plenty to live on and lobby friends are sufficient. In another dozen years I shall catch up to Bill, but I can't quite see myself a lounge lizard.

To think of the whole country going dry! We shall have to beat our cocktail shakers into ploughshares!

My mother once remarked that all girls between the ages of fourteen and eighteen should be chloroformed, to which drastic proposition, my father countered no, that it was their parents who should be granted such sweet oblivion. They spoke with the bitterness of first-hand experience, for I was extremely awful. I have already mentioned my attempts to look twenty-one. To that optimistic endeavor, I added the further one of turning myself into a "vamp." My aim was to be as suave as Clara Kimball Young, as "risquée" as Gaby Deslys, as lovely as Dolores, and as wicked as Theda Bara. It was an ambitious project. There were considerable stumbling blocks, not the least of which was the question of clothes. What I dreamed of wearing were the sort of things Erté drew for *Harper's Bazaar*, hobble-skirted evening gowns with rhinestone shoulder straps, kolinsky-banded capes, lamé turbans, and ostrich-feather fans. What I actually wore was the regulation school Peter Thompson uniform—middy blouse with a sailor tie and anchor-embroidered dicky, tailored skirt with a jaunty nautical lacing down the centre of the rump. I did my best to augment this firm foundation with accessories of a nature I regarded as "slinky," long black Woolworth earrings, an immense ring of imitation jade on my forefinger, and for footgear,

Cuban-heeled pumps of patent leather glorified by white spats which I laundered nightly. Mother forbade either rouge or face powder, but I got around that injunction by calcimining my nose with vanishing cream and Djer-Kiss talcum and rubbing my cheeks with a Roger and Gallet pomade stick, which triumph of *maquillage* would sometimes be enhanced by a black court-plaster "beauty spot" coquettishly concealing one of my adolescent own. My middy tie reeked of Mary Garden perfume, my posture was a willowy débutante slouch and my languid smile a dazzling glory of the innumerable bands on my teeth. One evening at home, many years later, Father, nudged by some irrelevant prompting of memory, suddenly put down his paper and, à propos of nothing, remarked: "Daughter, when you were in your 'teens you were the God-damnedest looking freak that ever was!" Having delivered himself of which bit of nostalgic information, he resumed his reading.

In those distant and trying days, however, he had stoically refrained from comment. Not so Mother, who was in a chronic state of despair over me. She protested sometimes with anger, sometimes with ridicule, and not infrequently with tears. Nearly every day she told me I looked absurd and awful, to which harsh truth I stubbornly reiterated that she just didn't understand, although deep down inside I had the uncomfortable feeling she was right. I suppose it was in part a coltish gesture of defiance. Mother, who was little, beautiful, and dainty, had hopes of molding me in the same exquisite pattern. It wouldn't work and I knew it. I had no idea what my own pattern was, but I rebelled at the idea of becoming a grotesque imitation of Mother. I would be mysteriously feline. And my activities outside of school were in exotic accord. I lolled on the cushions of my window seat reading Robert Chambers, the poetry of Laurence Hope, and *Snappy Stories*, I burned what I chose to call "temple incense" although my pals grossly dismissed it as "punk," and I wrung from the Steinway sombre renderings of "Less than the Dust" and Tosti's "Good-Bye." I also wrote verse, some of which actually made the *Delineator* and the *Literary Digest*. Mother did her best to divert me into more wholesome pursuits. She was in the pleasant throes of a feverish enthusiasm for gardening and she urged me to help her in the tending of our modest beds. But I was interested only in languidly cutting an occasional rose, crimson, of course, to pin in my hair. It's a wonder I didn't carry it Carmen-like in my teeth. When our red Japanese poppies were in bloom, I kept a single one on my bureau in a long-necked black vase, a horticultural arrangement which was, I decided, symbolic of my soul. I made the mistake of confiding this symbolism to Mother. To my wounded amazement, she burst out laughing, not in her customary musical cascade of mirth, but in a series of harsh hysterical shrieks. In regard to me, she was at her wits' end. She appealed to Father. He, although he shared her opinion as to my awfulness, took a less despairing view of me, probably because he didn't have to see so much of me. His advice was to leave me alone, I was going through a stage of desperate self-consciousness and anything which might give me a grain of confidence should be endured, no matter how painful for the rest of the world.

I was not any too happy myself. I knew that a lot was wrong with me. For one thing, I wanted terribly to have beaux. In those days a girl's popularity was gauged by whether or not she wore a frat pin. I wore two. One I had found on the edge of a sidewalk. I had no idea what fraternity it represented, but I invented some Greek letters to fit it along with a pretty fable concerning the handsome half-back who had asked me to wear it. The other was a legitimate trophy having been thrust hastily into my hand by a pimply youth who went to Penn State, belonged to the debating society, and wore rubbers. I didn't like him very much, but as no one had ever offered me a frat pin I was in no position to be choosy. Except during the Warm Springs summers, boys seldom entered my life. Winter months I boarded at school and vacations were spent at home amid the almost exclusively feminine circle of Mother's friends. Now and then some kindly Philadelphia lady, who thought it a great pity that lovely Mrs. Skinner should have such an eccentric daughter, would magnanimously extend an invitation to one of the junior dances in town—gracious gestures to which Mother responded with happy appreciation, I with a sinking heart, for those occasions were for me pure unmitigated hell. I hated them, I hated the ladies who asked me to them, and I hated the clothes I had to wear. Mother, who, when it came to my emergence into the world of the élite, refused to let me do so looking like an illustration for *Three Weeks*, stripped me of my Woolworth earrings and scrubbed the talcum off my nose. Instead of the rhinestone and kolinsky evening gown of my dreams, I was obliged to wear my one and only "party dress," a demure little garment based on a Butterick pattern and run up at home by our visiting seamstress. It was of pink flowered silk and had short puffed sleeves and a net "modesty" at the neck, and I loathed it. I went alone to these dreaded festivities. Bundled in a wool topcoat, a chiffon scarf holding down my unruly hair, carriage boots protecting my bronze slippers, I'd take the suburban local into Philadelphia and walk with leaden steps to the respectable hall where Miss Somebody's Saturday Evenings met. I knew nobody and nobody made any effort to know me. The Philadelphia lads were interested only in the Philadelphia girls they had grown up with, smart little fluffs and past mistresses at that special form of siren technique known as a "line." I had no line. I tried desperately to copy those of the charmers around me.

I even jotted down phrases in a comp book at home and studied up on such spellbinders as "My! But you're big and strong!" the male comeback to which was, according to formula, "But oh, so gentle!" Only I never received the comeback. I did my best. I thought of my amorous triumphs behind the pool house at Warm Springs and tried to look fatal. I dropped hints implying that given an opportunity I could be pretty fast. I voiced the opinion that the girls with the snappy lines were just so many scalp collectors, and who wanted to be a prom trotter, anyway, when, after all, still waters ran deep. Such blandishments merely scared the wits out of my partner who would steer me up and down the stag line, distress-signaling his pals who carefully avoided his eye. Conversation would dwindle to remarks about the dance floor, or what a "delish" tune "Poor Butterfly" was, and finally peter out with my admission, spoken in bantering tone to hide the inner despair, "I'm afraid you're stuck with me." Sometimes a compassionate chaperon would ease the situation by bringing up another victim, and sometimes I myself would break it off by inventing a pretext for dashing away to the ladies' coatroom, where, under the appraising eye of the check girl and a few awesome personal maids sent to escort certain golden-spoon-fed heiresses, I'd stall for as long as I dared, fussing with my dress and roughing those ear-concealing hair arrangements which were graphically known as "cootie nests." Cowering there amid the rabbit-lined mandarin coats and Liberty capes, my cheeks less bright from Roger and Gallet pomade than from deep humiliation, I'd try to pull myself up by my slipper straps. Just wait, I'd tell myself, some day they'd see, just wait—some day I'd be an actress, and then, oh, boy! the way I'd break the hearts of these proud Philadelphians! I became an actress. The breaking of the heart of a Philadelphian, proud or otherwise, is yet ahead of me.

Once in a long while, I'd actually land a beau. None of

them was the Arrow Collar lounge lizard of my dreams, but they helped build a little morale. I learned upon their asking when they might call, not to bowl them over with an eager "Any old time!" I also learned to arrange for them to come on days when Mother was away. For if she were home, she had a way of drifting into the living room to see how I was getting along. It might have been swimmingly. I might even have begun to feel a dead ringer for Clara Kimball Young, but the moment Mother appeared, Miss Young turned into an absurd gawk with bands on her teeth. The fact that Mother usually addressed me as Baby didn't help maintain the siren atmosphere either. Thinking she was helping me out, she'd chat pleasantly with the youth who, in no time at all, would be completely bewitched by her, while I looked on silent and sunk in spirit. What chance had my carefully rehearsed line against Mother's outwelling loveliness? Adorable, tender, complicated, difficult Mother! I find it next to impossible to express in words what she was like. Maybe I never really knew. Maybe she didn't either.

By now, as far as Philadelphia was concerned, she was established. Local favors were showered upon her and she was in demand, not only in a social capacity, but as a speaker, as a member of committees, as adviser for civic enterprises. With her innate modesty she regarded this success with happy incredulity, tremulously surprised to find herself on a basis of friendship with such luminous citizens as Owen Wister, Langdon Mitchell, Felix Schelling, and Doctor Morris Jastrow. And yet Mother never felt completely assured. That surprising lack of confidence which she never outgrew drove her to approach with apprehension and an overzealous attention to detail every undertaking whether it were the staging of a charity pageant or a tea for a group of her lady friends. Now and then she would be called upon to put up for the night some one of the Bryn Mawr visiting lecturers—Ian Hay, Amy Lowell, Lord Dunsany—an honor that sent her into a happy dither in which she would dash to the library and attempt—although she, like all of us, was a slow reader—to absorb in a couple of hours the complete works of the impending celebrity. She entertained simply and with an apparent ease which completely disguised her underlying nervous misgivings. Quoting the words of Joyce Kilmer, someone once said of her, "She who always knew that being lovely was a duty." And she gave of her loveliness. Gave too freely, one felt, for she could never be casual with anyone. In her relationships with no matter whom, there must always be some little extra effort of attention, a note to be penned, an article or poem cut from a magazine, a bouquet picked from her tiny garden to be sent with a message that made the recipient feel the world to be a more gracious place. Her conversation was never commonplace, or even relaxed. She was on tiptoe with eagerness and a contagious magnetism which at times seemed a needless drain on her vitality.

Looking back over my girlhood, the bright picture of my mother stands out as the embodiment of all loveliness. I used to pity my school friends whose mothers, though nice enough, had allowed themselves to go physically and mentally to seed, and who could not glow with the particular pride of having a mother whom everyone adored. She belonged to a generation of women who, after a certain age, fail to bother about coquetry; not that she had ever bothered about it much, she'd never had to. Fashion meant little to her, although she dressed with taste and knew the importance of wearing clothes that were becoming rather than *chic*. Her long brown hair, of which she had a luxurious amount, she arranged parted madonna-like in the middle, pulled back softly over the upper portion of her ears, and caught in a large knot at the nape of her neck. When dressed for the evening, she was something to gasp at, and as a small girl I used to crouch at the head of the stairs when she floated into the living room to hear the echo of those gasps from worshiping guests. But with all her success, the incense of admiration never went to her head. It pleased her, of course, but she never sought it, and flattery only made her uncomfortable. Her own beauty, of which she must have been aware, she considered unimportant in her scheme of things which were important. She thought seldom of herself. But in regard to Father and me, she was as savage as a she-bear with cubs. It was as if the jealousy she had had as a girl had been transformed into a passionate desire to guard her family's interests. The only times I ever heard her talk unpleasantly of anyone was in regard to such persons as she thought might hurt or even be competitive to us. When George Arliss was engaged for a film she had always wanted Father to do, she was livid with indignation and when the picture was released fairly boycotted it. And yet even in her love and ambitions for us she was contradictory. In later years, after I had gone on the stage, she gave me plenty of criticism, but scarcely ever a word of praise. She would have gladly poisoned any rival actress and, at the same time, she would have sent me that same actress's rave notices. I welcomed her criticism, for it was invariably just, and yet I could never act if Mother were in the audience and, strangely enough, Father once confessed to me that he couldn't either. We both had the feeling that she was expecting us to commit some frightful error, and I am sure she was.

Her attitude toward the theatre was almost one of defiance. Sometimes when she and I were alone she would, all at once, come out with vehement little speeches telling me how much more worth while than the stage was her present life, how, in comparison with actors, these wonderful people she now knew were so far more distinguished—her favorite word. She would never have admitted, even to herself, that there remained latent in her a vague hankering for the career she had given up. But I believe it goaded her with recurrent restlessness. She busied herself with those activities which are the sops of the theatre-hungry, activities in the half-world of amateur groups, drama study classes and professors who write books about acting which actors never read. To all such interests she brought a touch of professionalism which was an invaluable contribution. She was the first president of the Plays and Players, Philadelphia's "Little Theatre," directing many of their plays. She worked with Mrs. Christine Wetherill Stevenson putting on large-scale pageants and outdoor musical festivals, for that was the era of folk dancing, masques, and Percy MacKaye. When Shakespeare had his three hundredth birthday, she headed committees of culture-conscious citizens who felt that America must do something about it, arranging for local appearances of Ben-Greet and Marlowe and Sothern, corraling appropriate wreath layers for statue-in-the-park ceremonies, taking part herself in the celebration at the Academy of Music when with great grace she recited the Ben Jonson ode. She even became an active member of the Drama League, a source of considerable woe to Father to whom that celebrity-stalking organization of club women and academic hangers-on was as a red rag to a bull. A letter from Cleveland voices a little of his sentiment on that score:

> I've just had a contentious 15 minutes with the Secretary of the local Drama League. She arrived with a grievance. Why had I accepted an invitation from the University Club and refused to address the D. L. of Cleveland? I told her the University Club was purely a social and enjoyable affair . . . that the D. L. had pumping stations all over the U. S. map and at all points, hooks were hurled out to catch the legs of actors

and that I spent a no inconsiderable part of my time in avoiding the local ambushes. She seemed subdued but not convinced and departed to set traps for the next star. I understand the prize vegetable is Beerbohm Tree. He loves the stunt! A newspaper reviewer here said Tree told him he'd get up in the middle of the night to make a speech.

I think the thing is all wrong and that the actor gains nothing by his attempt to advertise, or at any rate, loses more than he gains.

Why should I be asked to be bright and merry for a bunch of old fluffs who are hunting for bargain sensations? Oh, not for me shall the Drama League call again, or calling, it will call in vain.

There! Having delivered myself of that, I feel better! It is snowing and the skies are leaden. Had Villon lived in Cleveland he wouldn't have thought of his celestial similes for snow flakes, or else his Jove would have been plucking black swans and his moulting angels were from the Congo.

Whenever Father played Philadelphia, he appeared, of course, at the Broad Street Theatre. In that city of unquestioned conventions the Broad Street was The Theatre. I used to wonder if Philadelphians even knew of the existence of any other playhouses. A Main Line hostess once asked Mother to dinner and the theatre and Mother, after accepting with thanks, asked what the play would be: "Oh," said the lady, "I have no idea—but it's at the Broad Street." I used to go in town for as many of Father's matinées as school and the suburban train service would permit, striding in through the lobby with the grand manner of the star's daughter who is certain of free admittance and taking any available seat or, if there were none, standing at the back. I remember once during the *Mister Antonio* engagement hovering near the right-hand box, entranced, because an usher had informed me Caruso was sitting in it. In one scene Father had business of mixing a salad dressing as he perched on the shaft of the hurdy-gurdy. It was rather a long process during which he used to hum a snatch of tune. That afternoon I was shocked to hear him burst forth in a loud and quite incorrect rendition of "Santa Lucia." To my further shame he sang it through twice. At the end of the act, I rushed backstage to ask him why on earth he had done it; didn't he know Caruso was out front. To which he serenely replied that certainly he knew; it wasn't every actor who had a chance to sing for the world's greatest tenor and he for one was not going to miss the opportunity.

I was always allowed one theatre party to which to take a few of my buddies. We would go five or ten strong (in inverse ratio according to box-office receipts) and after the performance would troop behind onto the stage where Mother had arranged a "treat" of ice cream and cake. It was served on the set and always came in the nature of a great surprise. My long-suffering father would come out in his dressing gown and politely shake the grubby hand of each giggling girl, and the leading lady and juvenile would feel they had to stop by to meet the star's daughter and say, "Isn't she just like her father!"—which I wasn't. These occasions filled me with a sense of bland magnanimity. I acted as if I had written the play, produced and directed it, and had invented Father. My smugness was badly jolted one of these times when Father, who was in the throes of a bad head cold, had played the entire first act with an unmistakable drop gleaming brightly on the end of his nose. I was profoundly mortified, and later, when I told him in a horrified whisper how he had done something "awful," he laughed and said it was quite in keeping with the part and he thought he'd use it right along for characterization.

CHAPTER TWELVE

The Family Trade

It is part of the autobiographical formula for an author to tell of the particular incident which gave him a clairvoyant vista of his future career—the politician and his class-day oration, the sculptor whose childish mud pie suddenly turned into a likeness of his mother, the physician as a barefoot lad spearing a worm with a fishhook and realizing his calling would be abdominal surgery. In regard to acting, I had no such moment of revelation. In spite of Mother's often repeated refrain of no, indeed, her daughter was never going on the stage, I always knew, privately and simply, that I was. I was neither stage-struck nor dazzled by any delusions of what theatrical life never turns out to be, and certainly I did not experience (and never have) that happy sense of dedication to ART which press agents like to convey to be the chronic emotional state of actresses. No supernatural voices bade me come save the spoken drama and I entertained no belief that my emergence into the theatrical arena would cause Ethel Barrymore or Mrs. Fiske any great uneasiness. I merely knew that I wanted to act.

My only chance for venting the urge was with the Baldwin

School Dramatic Club which proved its earnest worth by giving one Shakespearean play a year. Mother, a good friend of the school and the adored of the faculty, was always asked to stage the annual production. She did it, of course, beautifully, cutting the text, designing the costumes, directing the performance, and generally reducing herself to a bundle of nerves. What nearly defeated her was correcting the heterogeneous accents of the cast which hailed from all over the U.S.A., gently informing the girl from Chattanooga that *can't* does not rhyme with *paint* and the girl from Philadelphia that a *garden* is much prettier when it's not called a *gorrrden.* She must have written Father of her trials, for in one of his letters he indulgently chides her for wasting her time "plugging away at those little nasal Baldwin dubs—the daughters of the Great American *R* which gathers force as it rolls across the midwestern plains." Because I was tall and angularly shapeless and had access to Father's costume trunks, I was usually the leading man. As Petruchio I strutted in Father's boots, periodically walking out of them. As Orlando, a leather jerkin which had once belonged to Booth was apprehensively placed upon me with strict instructions I was to take it off during the ice-cream party after the show. In that *As You Like It* production, the part of Charles the Wrestler was in the untried hands of my roommate, a big and genial Irish girl by the name of Lib Donohue. Choosing her to play the Elizabethan Strangler Lewis was a case of type-casting only as far as her bulk was concerned, for her personality was anything but menacing. Her voice was extremely soft and high-pitched and she had an engaging grin which turned into an uncontrollable giggle whenever she started rehearsing her scene. Mother did her best with her, cut her speeches down to a single line, and the night of the performance achieved on her a triumph of costuming and make-up. Her amiable face was disguised with rustic tan greasepaint, beetling eyebrows, and a bushy beard. A shaggy wig, many sizes too large for her, was fitted to her head with a tuck and a safety pin. Her legs were painted brown and she wore a tunic of burlap. A leopard skin swinging fiercely from her shoulders put the finishing Herculean touch to her savage aspect. She took one look at herself in the mirror and froze with fright. Her already gentle voice weakened into inaudibility. Lib's mother, sister, and aunt had journeyed over from Bound Brook, New Jersey, and were sitting in the front row awaiting her dramatic début with happy anticipation. The play went on. Lib made her entrance and none of the Donohue clan knew her. Nor did they recognize her when she spoke her one line, for although they were only a few feet away, not one of them could hear her. The wrestling match started and Lib, realizing she had not come through vocally, began to retrieve herself physically. Under the dubiously authoritative instruction of the gym teacher, we had practiced a few wrestling holds which Lib, now in a revolt of brave independence, completely disregarded. Seizing me by waist and shoulder, she flung me to one side, grabbed my wrist as I shot past as in a movement of a wild Virginia Reel, and hurtled me to the other. I struggled frantically to remain upright. I pushed, I pinched, I tried to trip her, to tickle her—anything to make her let go. Finally, when she had got me clamped in a sort of bear hold, I managed to pant in her ear that she must let me pretend to throw her—the plot of the play hinged on it!—the reputation of the Dramatic Club!—the honor of Baldwin! This last appeal to her inner integrity worked, and with a certain amount of reluctance she disintegrated in a swift, backward collapse. At that moment, her wig flew off, soared over the footlights, and landed at the feet of Mrs. Donohue, who during the space of the audience's gasp of astonishment came out with a loud "Mercy! That man's Elizabeth!"

The selection of the play each year was made at the close of spring term by the forthcoming president. When I had been elected to that position of distinction, I settled on *Macbeth.* It seemed a quaint project for a girl's school, what with Lady Macbeth the only woman in the piece, Lady Macduff being usually cut, and the sex of the three witches being doubtful. But such obstacles in no way daunted me. I had a burning desire to play Lady Macbeth and I silenced any question as to the incongruity of a cast of primitive Scot warriors being impersonated by a bunch of Junior Misses, bands on their teeth and plumpness on their fannies, with the smugly cultural observation that in Shakespeare's time Ophelia and Juliet had been played by boys. The rôle of tragedy's most sinister heroine fitted in with my exotic picture of myself. I would, I planned, dedicate the vacation months to a profound study of the part.

We spent that summer in Colorado at Enos Mills's Long's Peak Inn. In those days, Estes Park was a delightfully simple resort with few hotels, no neon signs, and but one shop specializing in Rocky Mountain souvenirs. Concrete roads had yet to violate the majesty of the Range and the only motor vehicles able to make the tortuous climb from Denver without boiling over every two miles were Model-T Fords and Stanley Steamer char-à-bancs which lumbered up daily, whistling like mammoth peanut wagons and scaring your horse just enough to make you feel proud of being able to handle a spirited mount.

The Skinners went Western in a manner all their own, riding daily and with an enthusiasm as boundless as their knowledge of horsemanship was limited. Father was allotted a horse named Midnight who jogged along most of the time in a docile, apathetic fashion. Mother, on a little beast named Carrie Nation, trailed behind at an ever-widening distance, due to a tenderness of heart which prevented her from pulling on the reins whenever the animal took a notion to stop and graze. I rode a pinto named Pet who sweated a lot. When his lather had reached a fly-attracting stage, I'd hitch him to our cabin porch and humanely wash him down with warm water, a rubber sponge, and Maxine Elliott soap, a process which convulsed the cowboys and mildly astonished Pet.

That was the era before the smart Eastern visitor went in for blue jeans and plaid shirts, and my riding attire was a symphony of my own devising. Feeling that a regulation tailored habit would jar with my sultry personality, I wore a divided linen skirt, low black shoes which distantly adjoined brown puttees, and shirtwaists of sheer batiste with hemstitched collars and cuffs edged with filet lace. Fired by the vampire motif, I encouraged my nails to grow into long tapering claws which were always breaking off at the quick, while that Theda Bara seal ring on my index finger added considerable impediment to handling the reins. I imagine the only reason I didn't also wear my long earrings was that I was afraid Pet's clopping gait would jolt them off. Days I was not riding, I studied Lady Macbeth, still clad in my exotic equestrian costume. Father, with patient indulgence, and, I suspect, a fair amount of carefully concealed amusement, helped coach me. For purposes of privacy we'd go a short distance from the Inn to a small steep hill on the summit of which was an ideal hide-out, a flat space, boulder-encircled, where there was no one to see or hear us except bluejays and chipmunks and one beady-eyed old marmot. Sometimes I worked alone. Father had told me that a part must always be studied aloud, at full tone. His specific instructions were, "Take the pins out of your diaphragm, Kiddie, and let 'er rip!" And I obeyed him to the best of my vocal capacity, feeling very inspired indeed. One afternoon, the divine fire was, it seemed to me, unusually well kindled and I was tackling full tilt the scene in which Lady Macbeth urges her vacillating husband on to the murder. A party of Iowa tourists, the men in seersucker overalls and Stetson hats, the women in Mother Hubbards and boudoir caps, and all of them, including two small children, wearing spectacles, had parked their open Model-T a short distance away, and after picnicking amid the familiar dust of the roadside had decided to explore the beauties of Nature's near-by wonderland. Led on by the sound of my voice, like Siegfried by the song of the bird, over rock and fallen tree, they toiled up the little hill and peered over into my private sanctuary. The apparition which must have met their eyes was that of a gangly sixteen-year-old girl in dazzlingly unorthodox riding clothes, clutching at a skinny chest which flatly denied the words she was in the process of shouting, which were, "I have given suck and know how tender 'tis to love the babe that milks me." After whooping forth this bit of gratuitous information, I became slowly aware of the presence of the line of heads above the encircling rocks. For a moment we all froze into stunned immobility, the Iowans staring goggle-eyed through their specs, I staring back through a blush which deepened into the rich tones of the Harvard banner. Then, as at a word of command, they ducked and fled down the steep slope in full rout, scrambled into their battered jitney, and raced down the highway, probably back to Iowa.

Macbeth was the big event of the following school year. It looked at one time as though the performance would have to be called off owing to the fact that twenty-four hours beforehand, the girl playing Macduff, a lass from Savannah, Georgia, who sounded less like the Thane of Fife than the Little Colonel, came down with mumps. But the day was saved by the young thing cast as the Bleeding Sergeant who rushed forth with the news that she knew the lines of Macduff and if anyone could take her place on the gory army cot, she'd go on in the part. The girl was short, plump, and pretty. Her eyes were a clear blue and her hair a shimmering mane of genuine platinum blonde. She was hardly the ideal of a Highland war lord, but we camouflaged her as best we could with a horn-trimmed helmet, a bearskin hearth rug, and a Viking mustache. She was not only letter-perfect in the lines, but she gave evidence of great talent. One extraordinary thing about her was her voice, which she could turn from a tone soft, gentle, and low into a basso profundo bellow. That night she unleashed its full diapason, her impersonation was remarkable, and she saved the situation for everyone. But in doing so she strained a vocal cord and claims it was the cause of a certain throatiness which is still one of her most attractive characteristics. The name of that girl is Ann Harding.

Those happy amateur days! And that delirious amateur confidence! My Lady Macbeth must have been terrible, but at the time I was completely charmed with it. Long after the actual performance, I continued to recite the Sleepwalking Scene at the drop of a hat, or even without that much encouragement. Julia Marlowe, I felt, had better start looking to her laurels and I had better start preparing for the stage. I had yet to broach the family about it, but a performance of *Within the Law* with Helen Ware gave me the impulse to write Father about my ambitions. This was his reply:

Maiden Mine:

I rejoice that your week-end brought you such joys as marshmallow breakfasts and *Within the Law*. Your question regarding Helen Ware startled me a little. Are you going to be an actress? I was hoping you *wouldn't*. But if you *are* there is a long time yet; and the one thing that will put you ahead of others on the stage will be the soundness of a good education, and the mental training your studies will give you. I have often regretted deeply that my own schooling was not more thorough: it would have made things much easier for me.

You speak of Helen Ware—she was a school teacher before she became an actress. The road from the bottom where she started up to her stellar position in *Within the Law* was a long and hard one.

If that is the road you are thinking to take, you must prepare yourself for it in these present years. Every bit of good work you do now will be of inestimable help. Your knowledge of languages will refine and render beautiful your use of English. Your history will enable you to estimate the subtleties of characters that have been transferred to the literature of the drama; even your abhorred algebra will give you a grip and a poise in your mental ability to meet the tough situations of character portrayal. It all *helps beyond words.*

Above everything, don't neglect your voice. Start in just as soon as you read this and listen to every word you speak. Let your vocal teacher tell you where your voice comes from and how your tones are produced. If I had known these things in the beginning of my career it would have saved me thousands of dollars in doctor's bills. I have had to find out through the years, alone and unaided. I know *now,* but think what I could have saved by an early knowledge of vocalization.

And *sing!* Sing your little head off!!! You cannot realize, daughter mine, what wealth will be added to your speaking voice by a complete knowledge of singing even though your profession doesn't require you to sing a note. And know the *best* in music. Not the cheapest—know the best in literature. That is the sort of training the great ones of the French stage have gone through and the French are the greatest actors in the world to-day.

It was the *voix d'or* of Sarah Bernhardt that gave her the mightiest asset of her career.

Your voice, first, last and always. YOUR VOICE!!

Your Daddy's love, dearest Daughter.

So, reluctantly, I resigned myself to trying a year of college, God willing and pushing me through the entrance exams. It would be pleasant to be able to say that I sailed into Bryn Mawr with flying colors. But when I finally managed to squeeze in, the only color I exhibited was a red failure mark in algebra, a subject which remained a condition throughout my brief academic career and got to be known among my friends as "Cornelia's interesting condition."

I am glad that I went to college, and glad that I stayed for only two years. It gave me much to be thankful for and quite a good deal which it took some time to get over. It would be untrue to say that the Bryn Mawr atmosphere in those days was one of intellectual snobbishness. But there was, among the Big Shots, a youthful assurance, a bland acceptance of the fact that they were the elect—of what, they themselves couldn't have said. We ourselves were somewhat aware of this attitude, and one of our own popular campus songs satirically sung to a Gregorian chant expressed it to a nicety in its solemn refrain of "We are the Leaders." The standard ideal was to be athletic, studious (to a temperate degree), and splendidly clear-eyed. The improvement of our minds was no more important than that of our bodies or our souls, and scholarship went hand in hand with hockey and chapel. Miss Bryn Mawr was the wholesome American peach, good at studies and sports, determinedly fair-minded, and bravely guiltless of make-up. She was typified by the girl who, selected as the best all-round jolly-good person of the year was awarded a prize known, I regret to say, as the "Sunny Jim," a distinction rating as much local publicity as the European Fellowship given for academic excellence. Youth and what we chose to consider serious-mindedness made for a mixture of pleasant contradictions. The precious blended agreeably with the immature; permanent waves frizzed prettily beneath mortarboards, and sweat-shirts were worn over hand-made lingerie blouses. It was *chic* to postulate to a fine indifference to the male sex and at the same time, most of us had crushes on the younger men professors.

Social equality and the abolishing of ranks in the army was fiercely championed, yet freshmen were obliged to step off pavements and stand at attention when upper classmen went by. The intelligentsia would gather for evenings of discussion in one another's sitting rooms, hung with Princeton banners and reproductions of Marie Laurencin, and delicately sipping endless cups of "muggle," a frightening concoction of Whitman's instantaneous chocolate, marshmallow whip, and hot tap water, would talk late into the night about H. G. Wells, the French debt, syphilis, Freud, Stanislawski, and Marilyn Miller. We adhered valiantly to the humanities. Each class had both a Greek and a Latin cheer and the one for Varsity athletics was an adaptation of Aristophanes. And a good deal of emphasis was placed on the sort of hearty religion which espoused settlement work, attendance at Theological sessions in summer camps, and carol-singing in snow-drifts.

My brief college career was not brilliant. I was not the splendid all-round type. I avoided most rah-rah activities and I attended chapel only because I sang in the choir, a duty I found not only agreeable but remunerative, as it paid a salary of fourteen dollars a semester. I savagely loathed all organized exercise, a certain amount of which was compulsory, and wasted a lot of valuable hours trying resentfully and vainly to find my athletic niche. But Bryn Mawr offered plenty of other advantages far more agreeable than those of an Atalantean nature. I found a number of amusing and stimulating acquaintances and made a few warm friendships which have lasted a lifetime. And best of all, there was, for me, a gradual coming to life in regard to matters of the mind. The dark clouds of adolescent mental apathy slowly began to disperse and there started to dawn the revelation of intellectual adventure. Not, God knows, that I ever became any sort of scholar, but I discovered that a world I had hitherto dismissed as pedantic and dull could be rich and exciting. Browsing amid the stacks in the library, or sitting comfortably in the great dim Gothic reading room, with a pile of books beside me, I realized the amenities of research. Having no intentions of graduating, I had postponed all required courses I considered unsympathetic until a junior year which I knew would never materialize, and went in solely for the studies I liked. What specifically I learned, I couldn't say, but I recall with grateful warmth my instructors and the subjects they imbued with such vitality. Miss Lucy Donnelly's entertaining lectures on English literature, Eunice Schenck communicating in the most perfect French diction the charms of *La Civilisation Française,* and Doctor Tenney Frank through whose affectionate interpretation Horace once more sang and Plautus acted. Then there was the stimulating class in English composition given by Esther Cloudman Dunn whose book, *Pursuit of Understanding,* is a happy reflection of her own keen and graceful mind.

And college offered opportunity for venting my yearning to act. There were class shows and Varsity dramatics, and one spring the May Day Fête was held. The big festival that year was staged by my mother and I believe it was the loveliest and most imaginative production ever seen at Bryn Mawr.

I spent my sophomore year on bounds as punishment for having cut all classes the last few weeks of freshman term. It was a penance in which I rather gloried, for I had taken the cuts in order to fill my first theatrical engagement. It was only a four-week engagement (two of which were taken up by rehearsals), but it gave me an excuse for calling myself an actress, although it is doubtful if anyone else would have done so. George Tyler had taken the National Theatre in Washington in an experimental stock venture for trying out a number of new plays. As it was his intention to bring them into New York the following season, they were all pretty well finished productions with top-notch casts. A nucleus of competent actors was kept as a permanent company for supporting parts while the leads were played by a series of visiting stars—Helen Hayes, Emily Stevens, and others. The Lunts came there, too. Only they weren't the Lunts then. It was at this engagement that Miss Fontanne and Mr. Lunt met and soon afterward started that partnership which has proved so felicitous for the English-speaking world. They appeared in two of the try-outs in which I too was to be seen; that is, if one looked quickly enough. In Richard Washburn Child's *Made of Money,* I was discovered at the rise of the first-act curtain, arranging some roses in a vase. A comedy butler, excellently done by Sidney Toller, entered, looking glum, and I spoke my only line which was "What's the matter now?" He made some sort of reply after which I said "Oh," turned, and exited up-back-left. The "Oh" was my own gratuitous padding of the part. This opening bit, of course, was over before half the audience had settled into their seats, but to judge by the earnestness with which I approached it, it might have been the big scene from *Za-Za.* I put my all into that single speech, elaborating it by preceding it with a humorous "Ho-hum!" and winding it up with a curious sound I endeavored to make into a ripple of laughter. I worked up fancy bits of business such as burying my nose in one of the roses and sniffing ecstatically. The dye in the cloth petals gave forth a vile smell and a deposit of property-room dust made me have to struggle not to sneeze, but in the service of Art such slight discomforts were to be ignored. In an ensuing act laid in a beauty parlor, I came on as a manicurist and worked industriously on Lynn Fontanne's fingernails, while a hairdresser, a real one, gave her a genuine marcel. The only person to be impressed with my characterization was the hairdresser who offered me a job in his salon across the street.

The next play, *A Young Man's Fancy,* in which Jeanne Eagles later starred, was a rather nice whimsy about a youth who falls in love with a dummy in a shop window. The curtain rose on a shallow set representing a pavement outside a store front which had a window display of sports clothes modeled by a number of wax ladies and gentlemen foregathered in what appeared to be a portion of a Country Club. Lynn was a wax lady and Alfred was the flesh-and-blood young man who, observing her through a transparency plate glass, fell in love with her. I too was a wax lady. Only no one fell in love with me. Not even a wax gentleman. I was one of the small group at the back standing about an undersized tea table. There was a short but uncomfortable scene during which Alfred, out on the pavement, confided his infatuation to a friend, while we dummies stood frozen in attitudes of quaking immobility; then the transparency lifted, the set widened out into a realistic lawn and porch, and we all, mercifully, came to life. I had some three or four lines. What they were, I have no recollection, but I still cherish the memory of the ad lib remark of an actor named Cushman who played one of the wax society men and who, having been directed at one point to stroll over to me, turn upstage, and engage me in polite sotto-voce chitchat, always at each and every performance came out with the elegant observation, "About this time of the afternoon I always prefer a nut sundae."

My salary was thirty-five dollars a week. I was barely eighteen and Mother considered it necessary to go along with me. We took a minimum-rate room at the old Shoreham and ate our meals at a dairy-lunch counter, but my pay hardly sufficed, and Father, who was in California at the time, sent Mother a check "to defray the expense of our daughter earning her own living." "Never fear," he goes on, "Father will stand the gaff! It is all very funny and too good to keep, so to the dozens of enquirers out here who daily ask me 'How is Mrs. Skinner and what is the Daughter doing?' I reply 'Doing? Why, doing Father of course!' "

The silent screen version of *Kismet* was produced the following summer in Hollywood, and my next professional disappearance was in that. Father had asked the producer if he could manage to find a part for me, and he did, at the heady salary of seventy-five dollars a week. The producer must have been prompted more by motives of courtesy to the star than because he was struck with my camera potentialities. Hollow-cheeked and still wearing a partial band on my upper teeth, I was hardly a coming rival for Clara Bow. But they got around the problem by costuming me in voluminous veils and a thick yashmak. I was down in the cast list as "A Hand-maiden." The part was really that of general messenger and door-opener. Whenever the Wazir paid his harem a visit of the utmost censor-conscious decorum, it was I who saw him in and out; when the Wife of Wives took a fancy to send a note to her lover, it was I who delivered it. Whenever an official came to the palace, it was I who salaamed him through the portals. I was always coming and going. In the finished picture, any superfluous action of mine was cut, and my friends who loyally went to see the film had to sit through it twice in order to make certain that the shrouded figure occasionally flashing across the screen was really me.

The day of my début before the camera was one of considerable nervousness for the whole family. I arrived at the studio hours too early, got into my costume before anyone else was dressed, and perspired off most of my make-up by the time they were ready to shoot my scene. Father, who was not in the shot, sat beside the director looking patient and not over-happy. Mother, along with two friends from Philadelphia to whom she was revealing incorrectly but beautifully the mysteries of motion-picture-making, was somewhere off in the dark background. I couldn't see where, but I could hear the little coo of maternal misgiving. The scene was set in the Wazir's palace. I was to stand in the shadow of a pillar while a half-naked eunuch came down a corridor. When he had reached a certain point, I was to step forth, stop him, and ask him the identity of a man outside the gate. The eunuch was acted by a gigantic Negro whose brawny chest and basso voice proclaimed him as anything else but. We were given no preliminary run-through. In fact, in those non-talking days, as I recall it, only the scenes with the star were rehearsed. The director, an amusing Frenchman named Gasnier who had a gay way of calling Father "Mr. Kismet," megaphoned that they were set to shoot and was "Mees Keesmet" ready to register. I answered with a tentative yes and asked if during the action one were expected to say any sort of lines. Gasnier replied that speech was optional, some actors preferring to keep silent, others finding it easier to murmur a few words appropriate to the pantomime. I decided I would murmur. The kliegs glared on, the camera men stood prepared to crank, and Mac the accordion player, who during every take wrung mood music from his gem-studded instrument, started a soft introduction to "April Showers." As the eunuch reached the indicated position, I strode forth like Womanhood Triumphant and in a voice that would have filled the Metropolitan Opera House cried, "Stay, Slave!" The slave regarded me with astonishment and stayed. I continued, still at the top of my lungs, "Who is yon fair stranger without the palace gate? Speak, else thy life be forfeit!" The slave's eyes grew to the dimensions of saucers, his jaw dropped, and, in a voice of genuine earnestness, he said, "You kin search me, lady!"

My second appearance before the camera was on a day when the company had been taken on location fifteen miles from Los Angeles to an abandoned reservoir which had been reflooded and converted into a section of the Tigris River. From the midst of the waters arose a beaverboard and stucco palace, a profile construction with nothing behind the façade but a small platform onto which opened an immense nail-studded door, representing an ancient watergate. Through this the beggar Hajj was to make his clandestine way into the harem, being stealthily admitted by a conniving emissary. I was the conniving emissary. Father, after putting forth in a small Oriental craft, was to scull himself across to the watergate which I was to open, beckon him through, then close. The reservoir being wide and the palace a good distance from shore, the scene was to be a single long shot. Soon after we had arrived at the site, the assistant director rowed me across to my post, helped me through the door and onto the platform, told me I'd not have to wait long, and rowed away, leaving me entirely surrounded by water. The platform was small and wobbly and had no railing or wall other than a canvas backing which offered about as much support as a slack sail.

Father meanwhile was being introduced to his small Oriental craft. This was a curious barrel-like contrivance bearing more semblance to a large oil jar than to a boat. It held only one person, who had to stand up, in the manner of a missionary in a cannibal pot, and propel it by means of a single oar held in a wooden lock. The studio set designer swore that it was authentic and that it was called a "go-far," which proved to be the last name in the world one would have picked out for it. Father stepped from the stone reservoir parapet into the thing and someone gave him a shove that got him and the go-far a slight distance out to sea. He looked like a wise man from Gotham in a single-seater. The grips trained the reflector glare on him, the director called for action, and the camera men started cranking. Father, out on the waters, struck a pose slightly reminiscent of Washington halfway across the Delaware, grabbed the propelling oar, and gave it a forceful yank to starboard. The go-far, which was light as cardboard, round as a teacup, and guiltless of any keel, went into a dervish spin. Father, in an attempt to counteract the motion, yanked to port and the little vessel responded with a reverse pirouette. He tried again and with more temperate strokes, but with the same dizzy results. It was clear the thing would go in any direction other than forward. The director called "Cut" and went into consultation with some technicians. Father whirled himself back to shore.

I waited on the water-encircled platform while on shore people had assumed attitudes of relaxation except for the assistant director and three grips who got into a car and sped off along the Los Angeles highway.

After an hour the group in the car returned bearing a great many yards of wire. The property man attached one end to the go-far, jumped with the rest of the coil into a rowboat, and unwinding it in the manner of laying the Atlantic cable, made it out to my platform and, still holding the wire, scrambled out onto the shaky structure which, under our combined weights, gave considerably. He reassured me by saying, "Sister, if you gotta swim, don't swallow none of this-here water. It's po-luted." Then he yelled that he was ready, Gasnier megaphoned back to take it away, and pulling the wire hand over hand, the propman began hauling in the go-far while Father made appropriate paddling gestures. When this line ferry was halfway across, a camera man bellowed out to stop, the shot was n.g. The wire being copper, the lens picked it up. The property man emitted a fascinating oath I had never heard before, pulled shut the great door with a slam that jammed it, jumped in his boat, and rowed away, leaving me again solitary and marooned. Again the car departed for Los Angeles. After an interminable wait with nothing to do but stand with aching feet (the freshly painted platform would have ruined my costume had I sat on it), wounded pride, and rumbling stomach, the technicians returned at last with a new load of wire. This time it was piano wire of a dull shade the cameras would not pick up. This was attached to the go-far, Father was summoned from his dressing room, and the shot was again well under way when again someone yelled "Cut." An accumulation of wood shavings and débris from the construction of the palace had floated out within range of the camera, and an individual had to go out in a boat and clear it away with a garden rake. About four P.M. they made the shot. Father in the by now rapidly dissolving go-far sculled gracefully while the prop man hauled him across the troubled waters. I managed to open the door with a grunt that would have shattered a sound track and beckon him in through the portal. There being room on the platform for only myself and the property man, the latter, upon Father's emergence through the doorway, courteously backed off into the "poluted" water, the go-far went softly to pieces like a biscuit in hot soup, and the director triumphantly cried, "Print it!" In the finished picture, the scene was completely cut out.

CHAPTER THIRTEEN

Curtain Going Up

My thespian initiations, instead of getting the theatrical bee out of my bonnet, merely whetted my ambitions to become an actress, and my family, while dubious as to whether or not that would be the ultimate outcome, was at least reconciled to the prospect of my going on the stage. But not immediately. Nineteen they considered too tender an age and Mother felt I needed more educating. Agreeable as college had been, I balked at the prospect of another term and any suggestion of dramatic school was loudly vetoed by Father, who considered such establishments a waste of time and money. We compromised–felicitously so–on a year abroad. I was to spend the winter studying–just what, I was not quite sure and, when asked specifically, would answer with a vague gesture and an exalted expression, "Oh, you know. Drama. The Theatre. Things."

I wanted, of course, to go over alone. I had ideas about student life, emancipation, and the post-war generation which in those early twenties had yet to consider itself lost. Mother had her own ideas about the same things. Moreover, she had read F. Scott Fitzgerald and she wouldn't hear of my going abroad alone. What if I were to start running around with those people? With offended dignity I pointed out the fact that I would not be wasting my time on "those people." They were riffraff, the "flaming youth" set, composed of the idle rich who were in Paris purely in pursuit of pleasure, whereas I was of modest circumstances and would be in Paris purely in pursuit of Art. They all stopped at such vulgar places as the Crillon and the Meurice and I rattled off the names with a gargling *r*—whereas I would be living in some serious-minded pension. I would have preferred making it a garret on the Left Bank, but I knew she would never cotton to that. Mother, for all my logical eloquence, was not to be persuaded. She raised a number of fanciful objections which wound up with "You can never tell about Frenchmen, and then, Baby, there's always your appendix." Mother had a lifelong obsession in regard to my appendix which, for some reason, she decided was in a chronic state of disintegration and would eventually "kick up" in some inconvenient environment such as the high seas or halfway down the Grand Canyon. Maybe it will. I still have it and to my knowledge it has never kicked or even gently shoved.

We sailed in the fall and went direct to Paris. Be it to Mother's credit that she tried valiantly to let me go on my own. She stopped at the France-et-Choiseul, that pleasant and inevitable little caravansarie which, because it was so exclusively French, was patronized exclusively by Americans, while I stayed, not in the romantic garret of my Murgeresque dreams, but with a highly respectable family who lived in the most banal section of Passy and took in an occasional paying guest. It was an agreeable enough *ménage*, albeit I never felt completely at home in it. But then it was not the intention that I should. The French family does not take an outsider to its self-sufficient and politely calculating bosom. These people quite plainly regarded me as a necessary inconvenience, a somewhat regrettable means of augmenting their modest income. They dismissed me, along with all other Americans, as a peculiar but harmless barbarian whose point of view they made absolutely no effort to understand.

Madame was the traditional bourgeois head of the family —fat, jolly, shrewd, devoid of sentiment, and, when it came to money matters, as hard as nails. She was good-humored and had a salty wit and at times could even show affection. If I came down with a cold, which I did fairly frequently as a result of their *chauffage centrale* which *chauffed* only a small middle point of the *centrale,* leaving the remainder of its supposed area of radiation, and my room in particular, in a Nordic chill, Madame would mother me in her brusque fashion, bustling me into bed, bringing me a bowl of hot mulled wine, and placing at my reluctant feet one of those frightening china "pigs" which retain their heat and consequently their searing properties all night. And at the same time, she would add onto my weekly bill mysterious petty extras—a franc here, seventy-five centimes there—too paltry to quibble about, although, by the end of the winter, they added up to quite a tidy sum for someone who was trying to live on a shoestring. Monsieur, her husband, was an elegant little gentleman, a *professeur* at a boys' *Lycée,* formal, pedantic, fond of classical music, the *Causeries* of Sainte-Beuve, and of giving one's fanny an occasional well-mannered tweak. There were two husky daughters who did all the housework. They must both have been in their mid-twenties, but they were still treated as carefully cloistered *jeunes filles.* The fact that I used to go about Paris by myself in buses and the Metro and even now and then return home at night alone in a taxi, on which last daring act, had they but known it, I ventured only after Mother had made a note of the license number and had satisfied herself that the driver looked like a family man—all this they regarded as shocking emancipation. The *jeunes filles* were aware that I was studying something, but their *Maman* asked me please not to let on to them that it was for the stage—"Parce-qu'en France, les actrices—vous savez!" and she looked knowing. I looked knowing too and made some concurring remark which I hoped implied that *en Amérique* too it was the same story, but that *nous autres,* we women of the world, understood such matters. I doubt if I was very convincing. When later, at the instructions of my teacher, I began working on parts aloud, she told her modest violets that it was for my "leçons de diction."

True to formula, the family kept itself a private unit, apart, uncommunicative. Their comings and goings seemed to be of an almost secretive nature. They never discussed any plan in my presence and if they went on an outing *en famille,* they slipped away from the flat in the manner of conspirators. Any guests who came to see them were whisked off amid vociferous *chuchotements* into the tiny salon, the door was discreetly shut, and conversation was carried on in undertones. At my present less convivial age, I should welcome such an arrangement, but in those days this arm's-length behavior bewildered and offended me. Then gradually I came to understand the nature of the Gallic *foyer,* close-knit, self-sufficient, and jealously set apart. The individualist family in the capital of that country of individualists where the foreigner is to be tolerated only by being at once dismissed with a shrug of the shoulders.

However, the personal attitude of my landlady and her household did not bother me greatly. There was all of Paris around me and I was desperately aware of being abroad and young and on the threshold of something I chose to think of as "LIFE." I attacked everything—study, sightseeing, even amusements with conscientious enthusiasm. If Mother in the past had goaded me into "getting things out of things," I was by now way ahead of her, at least in eagerness. Twice a week I reverently entered an amphitheatre at the Sorbonne to listen to a lecture on *La Civilisation Française,* part of a popular course open to the public, intended to please rather than mentally overtax the attending student body which was made up of persons of all ages and all nationalities. The *discours* were easy rambling talks on a variety of subjects—the significance of Proust, the policies of Mazarin, George Sand *et ses amours,* and the exploits of that Charles known for some reason as the Hammer, or maybe it was the Pippin. One heard nothing very new or startling, but I enjoyed it avidly, partly because I was determined to, partly because I could in future bring into casual conversation the dazzling phrase "when I was at the Sorbonne," and partly because I had a case on a young Norwegian who had a reciprocal case on me. He spoke no English and his French was limited to about ten words, but we communicated in an exchange of shy and rather peculiar glances which I chose to consider the language of the heart, and once in a while we'd lunch at a little bistro in the Boul' Mich' where, under the encouraging influence of gamy horsemeat and a glass of sour wine, my Viking would reach across the spotty tablecloth to take my hand which, after an intoxicating brief moment, I would slowly withdraw, smiling a little sadly and heaving a catching sigh meant to imply that, alas, nothing could ever come of it. I took some other courses at a sort of University extension place called L'Université des Annales, which I rather looked down upon, as it was patronized largely by culture-seeking Americans very much like myself; all of whom I considered bourgeois contamination.

But my chief study was acting. I took private lessons from one of the *Sociétaires* of the Comédie Française, a cheery little man named Dehelly who for immemorial years had specialized in the Molière and Marivaux comedies, playing always *jeunes amants,* those curly young men with names like Dorante and Sylvestre who are constantly sweeping the floor with the plumes of their hats, taking more snuff than any snuffbox could begin to hold, and are ever in the highest of spirits, over what, it's hard to say, for they never seem to have much connection with the plot. As a person, Dehelly was a darling—as an actor, I have an idea he was pretty terrible, but at the time, I thought every member of the French theatre was wonderful and I considered Dehelly a second Coquelin. For years he had been augmenting the stipend the Français paid him by giving diction lessons to rich American schoolgirls. I was neither rich nor a schoolgirl and I wanted to study more than just diction, but I made an appointment to go see him at his apartment. Mother was a trifle apprehensive and muttered a few little incoherencies about Frenchmen, but consoled herself with the thought that Monsieur Dehelly had been highly recommended by that nice woman at the Guaranty Trust and she *had* gone to Vassar and after all he must surely understand about American girls by now. With palpitating heart I went to the rue Lauriston, *numéro 16 bis,* where he lived in a small but attractive apartment surrounded by some magnificent examples of Gothic carvings and *objets d'art.* He had collected them on holiday trips he had made about the provinces in company with Jean Richepin, and that gave me a break because I could tell him that my father knew Richepin and had produced his *Le Chemineau* in America. Timidly I asked if he would consider giving me lessons in action—I could not afford more than one a week, but I was *une personne sérieuse,* I would work with diligence if he would have the *bonté* to accept me as his *élève.* It was a speech I had been repeating to myself all the way from the rue St. Honoré. He answered with a noncommittal "Ah?" then questioned me about the New York theatre and inquired if I knew personally Norma Talmadge. I had to admit that I didn't, but would he take me as a pupil, nevertheless? In my earnestness I called him *cher maître,* which must have amused him, for he laughed and told me to recite something for him. In my confusion I could think of nothing but Alfred Noyes's "Highwayman." It would have been interesting to know what he made out of the recitation, understanding as he did not one word of English. At the finish he merely again said "Ah?", eyed me for an upsettingly long pause, then, with something that sounded suspiciously like a sigh, said *eh bien,* yes, he'd take me—only one lesson per week would not be sufficing, there must be two. I repeated the fact that I could not afford two, and with disarming grace he came down in his rate. He would give me three lessons for the price of two. Being unable to make any mathematical calculations in my head—or out of it, for that matter—I had no idea how much this would set me back, but I didn't care. I'd go without that one Chanel evening dress I had figured on in my budget. I uttered the French equivalent of "It's a deal" and Monsieur settled on the hours. My first lesson, he said, would be Thursday and my assignment would be the part of Célimène in *Le Misanthrope*. I could hardly wait to begin.

"You mean read it over and get familiar with it?" I asked.

"I mean have it by heart."

"Oh." I had never memorized anything in French except *Frère Jacques* and the chorus of *Madelon.* "How many lines?"

"How many lines?" he looked amazed. *"Mais comment donc! Le rôle entier!"*

Weakly I croaked, *"C'est entendu, Monsieur,"* and staggered out onto the street. That was Monday afternoon and I had three and a half days in which to memorize the leading feminine rôle in a five-act classical comedy. I plunged into the Métro, tore into Hachette's, and purchased the works of

Jean-Baptiste Poquelin Molière, complete in four volumes, then hurried back to my room in Passy. I had never read *Le Misanthrope,* never for that matter read any plays of Molière. There were innumerable words to look up and the rhymed couplet form to get accustomed to. How I ever learned the part in that short time God, who must have been prompting, knows. I couldn't begin to do it now. But by some miracle I was able at my first lesson to babble out every speech without missing a word. Dehelly's assignments after that were less Herculean—that first one it seems had been a test to prove whether or not I was really *sérieuse.* Dehelly was an exacting taskmaster and I knew that unless I came up to scratch he would lose the interest he seemed to have in me. All winter I worked like crazy, practicing diction exercises, memorizing the interminable speeches at the top of my lungs to the shoulder-shrugging amusement of Madame and her two daughters, muttering them to myself on bus or Métro, even saying them over in my sleep. The repertory crammed into my head included *Phèdre, Andromache, L'Aiglon, Théodora, Juliette* (in the translation of that classic in which the French express their innate gallantry by conceding feminine precedence in the title of *Juliette et Roméo*)—any number of Molière, Marivaux, and De Musset heroines and a few of Dumas *fils,* and Emile Augier. Occasionally, by way of change, I'd be assigned poetry or a few La Fontaine fables. It was an exciting experience and I am endlessly grateful for it. Dehelly may have been an indifferent actor, but he was a brilliant teacher. To be sure, he belonged to the mock-heroic overstilted school, but he had an inspiriting gift of imparting the grand old manner and making it believable. At first I rebelled. Why, I protested, must Hermione raise her hand above her head on such-and-such a line—and I'm afraid I added the inevitable actor's "I don't feel it that way."

"Hermione has always raised her hand, Mademoiselle,

not only on that line, but on this particular word. Madeleine Roche does it, Bernhardt did it, and Bartet before her. It's tradition." And he went on to explain that at the Français they still went by the stage directions set forth in the prompt books of Molière, and when they wanted to introduce an innovation so modern they were likely to be booed by the public, they had someone enter from the left instead of the right. I considered it stultifying and wrote to Father in New York an arty letter which must have amused him, complaining about the old-fashioned fetters which I felt were tying down my ample cabin'd spirit. He wrote back soothingly:

> Take it easy, Kiddie. That's all fine training, exaggerated as you think it is—it's a loosening up process, like a pianist stretching two notes above the octave. Don't make fun of it. It's a grand old school to learn—*and then forget!* Rather like the experience your sire had with Lawrence Barrett.

To offset this heavy dose of classicism, I decided I needed some grounding in modern methods. Jacques Copeau was running the Théâtre du Vieux Colombier, a Left Bank playhouse, a bit on the Art order, but interesting, and he had a few excellent productions to his credit. As part of his theatre project, Copeau was starting a dramatic school and I signed up for it—full payment, of course, in advance. I was the only American in a group of aesthetic French adolescents who didn't bathe very much. The girls were emaciated and had greasy hair and the boys wore flowing black ties and suffered from acne. Mother, when I told her about them, was uneasy. She was sure the former were all phthisic and the latter all had "a disease we don't talk about."

The classes were held in a barren atelier up four flights of rickety stairs above the Vieux Colombier Theatre. The place had no heat of any sort, no vestige of ventilation, and the only illumination came wanly through a dirty skylight. We students would assemble at ten A.M. shivering with cold, for the temperature in the room was usually several degrees lower than it was outdoors. After a time, a brisk young woman wearing what looked like a homemade skating outfit would breeze in with a curt "Bonjour, Messieurs—Dames." She was an *institutrice de gymnase* whose job it was to put us through twenty minutes of limbering-up exercises. Her Gallic brand of calisthenics, mild exertions interspersed with deep breathing done to the count of "*In*spiration! Un! Deux! *Ex*piration! Trois! Quatre!" were anything but limbering, especially as for some unaccountable reason we had to perform them in our bare feet. By the finish of the routine, they would be quite blue and numb.

As soon as our limbering exercises had completely congealed us, we were permitted to resume our shoes, after which with chattering teeth we took our places on campstools lined up in crescent formation to face a large thronelike chair. After an impressive pause, Copeau, swathed in muffler, galoshes, furlined coat, and sealskin cap, would make an entrance, bid us good day, and take his place on the throne from which eminence he would deliver a brief discourse on some phase of the art of acting, the students dutifully hanging onto his every word with incense-burning receptivity. Then he would rise, bid us another good day, and make an effective exit, and that would be that. Sometimes, though not often, he called upon us to go through certain antics which he designated as elementary steps in acting. I thought, at that time, they were just wonderful—now, I don't know. One day he told us to get out onto the floor, all at the same time, and imitate animals—whatever animals we liked, while he sat watching us with inscrutable speculation, saying nothing. It distresses me to admit that I chose to impersonate a swan and the only comment upon my performance was passed by a pasty-faced youth who paused in his own interpretation of a bulldog long enough to whisper admiringly in my ear, "*Mais c'est parfait, Mademoiselle! Vous êtes absolument une giraffe!*"

Copeau's school was highly entertaining and in certain ways rewarding. I can't say that I learned very much about acting, but I came away with a greatly augmented vocabulary of Parisian *argot.* The curriculum was of short duration. Copeau succumbed to an offer to go on a tour through Belgium and during his absence, he left the classes in the unpredictable hands of two of his actresses, temperamental individuals who, on the first day after the master's departure, got into a free-for-all fight. The fracas started with a polite argument as to which one had superior authority. It grew more and more heated in tone and more and more unmincing in language, although they retained the formality of addressing each other as Madame and Mademoiselle—"You are a kind of a cucumber, Madame!" "Ah! I assure you that you lie like a dirty pig, Mademoiselle!" etc., etc. As the discussion gained momentum, they both rose and started walking around each other like newly met gamecocks, the students rose too, and lined themselves up in a surrounding circle in order not to miss a move of what promised to be a good show. All at once one of the ladies with a shrill invective flung herself upon her snarling adversary and there followed six or eight minutes of kicking, scratching, squalling, and pandemonium. They gouged holes in each other's cheeks, yanked out chunks of each other's hair, and tore each other's blouses into ribbons, all the time continuing to observe the Madame-Mademoiselle formalities. The students, far from offering to separate the two, watched with delight, spurring them on with shouts of encouragement while I thought it wise to maintain a policy of American neutrality. Copeau's business manager eventually rushed in, separated the two termagants, and restored law and order. He wrote an account of the battle to the boss who sent back an indignant announcement saying that such behavior was disgraceful, it was an insult to him, to his theatre, to the acting profession—possibly he even added to the Glory of France, I don't recall—and he peremptorily closed up the school. My tuition was never refunded. Ah, well, the rate of exchange was in my favor.

It was a fine year in the Paris theatre and I went to everything. For about forty cents one could get a good balcony seat for Marthe Regnier, Victor Boucher, Max Dearly in his delicious absurdities at the Palais Royale, and the grand old reliables at the Odéon. The Guitrys were at the Edouard VII that season and whatever may have been Sacha's subsequent behavior under Nazi influence, his plays—*Debureau, Le Grand Duc, Mozart,* etc.—were a joy; Yvonne Printemps was enchantment itself and to have seen the acting of old Lucien was, in my opinion, to have seen the greatest acting of our time. In my tireless pursuit of culture, I bought a subscription *abonnement* to the weekly *Matinées Classiques* at the Comédie Française. That was theatre-going with a vengeance. Performances started at one-forty-five or, as the posters announced it, at fourteen hours less fifteen, and lasted till well after dark. The bill was a classical double feature, a traditional five-act tragedy and an equally traditional comedy, also of five acts. Things like *Hernani* serving as a two-hour curtain-raiser to *Le Mariage de Figaro*. It was an aesthetic ordeal and a dorsal and posterior one as well, for my subscription ticket was for a *strapontin,* one of those hard little folding seats that let down into the aisle making escape in case of fire completely impossible.

Sometimes I went alone, sometimes Mother went with me. Theatre-going for Mother must have been considerably strenuous, for, try as she did to master French, and she had tried for years, it was a losing struggle. She could never get the knack of thinking in the language and had to translate everything into English before she understood it, which slowed things up for her quite a lot. At a play, she would sit on the edge of her *fauteuil,* tense and keen, her eyes shining, her ear cocked, her lips moving in a frantic effort to keep her English translation up in pace to the speed of the dialogue. Chevalier was singing then at a Boulevard theatre and we went together to hear him. Mother, of course, fell completely captive to the bland wiles of that ingratiating charmer and with enraptured concentration turned his every word into the nearest English equivalent she could hit upon. By the time he sang *Valentine,* she was murmuring some of them aloud, and when he came out with the engagingly realistic portion about the *pétons* and the *tétons* and the lady being *toute frisée comme un mouton,* she swung happily along with him, then stopped short, emitted a sharp gasp, and exclaimed quite loudly, "Oh, I don't think he meant that! He's such a nice chap!"

Mother's French, like everything about her, had a distinction of its own—one of her most felicitous phrases was uttered to the concierge of the France et Choiseul, whom she wanted to have send up her steamer trunk and whom she sweetly requested to please *fair monter* her *malle de mer.*

A letter from Father informed us that he had signed up with Gilbert Miller for the oncoming season to play in Tom Cushing's dramatization of Blasco Ibáñez's novel of the bull-ring, *Blood and Sand.* He would come to Paris in the spring and we'd all go to Spain where he could soak in atmosphere.

> You and Bobs have got to personally conduct me. San Sebastian sounds good to me. We will get the wealthy classes there, I presume, and can watch the bathing of the aristocracy. I want to see the people who represent Spanish "society"—not necessarily *refined* society, but you know what I mean. I want to get in touch with the bull-ring and what it means.

> I want to see the *toreros* in and out of dress uniform. I want to see bulls. I want to attend the *corridas.* I want to wander and mix with people, to *idle* among them. I want to see them marketing and at their devotions. I want to know the country districts and the peasantry. I want to find little unfrequented chapels, and I want to get off the highway of Mr. Cook! All the palaces, cathedrals, Velasquezs, El Grecos and the cabbages and kings may go hang if I can't get what I'm going for. Spain's historical monuments are purely secondary affairs. I want an idle month in the Peninsula with no necessity of a daily consultation with railway guides. I want to be the human blotting pad, carelessly laid upon the ink of national life—and I don't want to go as a student of art or history. Whatever comes I shall drink in at the pores. Also I can collect a few costumes, shawls and other appurtenances for the production.

It was a good excuse for a trip—not that Father ever needed an excuse for any trip. But it salved Mother's cultural conscience to think that while he was absorbing atmosphere for his rôle, she and I might get in a little aesthetic absorption, while her economic one was mollified by the comforting knowledge that the "costumes, shawls, and appurtenances" could all be charged off to Gilbert Miller.

Father joined us in June and we went through Spain more or less according to the itinerary he had mapped out, avidly exposing ourselves to all that seemed characteristic even to the extent of submitting our insides to a diet of oily meat, dry Amontillado, bitter cheese, and Cascara pills.

We met up with Ibáñez in Madrid. He proved to be a rough, affable creature with a paunch equaled in enormity only by his ego which at the time was being fed by an orgy of national adulation. He had recently been recalled from serving a term of exile as punishment for some revolutionary ideas expressed in his *Shadow of the Cathedral* and the forgiven prodigal was being welcomed back by each of the provinces, his native Valencia in particular, with rounds of celebrations. Testimonials were being proffered him, holidays declared, and fiestas held. He was the national hero of the moment. From such heady adulation, however, he took time out to pay us a generous amount of attention. He proved to be extremely kind and rather endearing in a Gargantuan sort of way. Childishly pleased over the success his books were currently enjoying in America, he was especially enchanted by the fact that he had reached such popular eminence as to have his *Four Horsemen of the Apocalypse* produced as a picture with Rudolph Valentino as the star. His greatest remaining ambition, now that he had regained his citizenship in his beloved country, was to go to Hollywood and meet Mae Murray.

Mother thought this somewhat lamentable, but she refrained from comment. She also refrained from comment upon the fact that traveling along with the author was a large blonde Chilean lady with whom he was obviously sharing his board and, one presumes, the other thing that goes with it. Mother, on first meeting her, committed the laudable error of addressing her as Señora Ibáñez and was blandly informed that the gentlewoman's name was something quite different, and after the communication of that bit of intelligence, Mother decorously referred to her merely as "The Señora."

The Señora was a sweet amiable soul of middle years with dyed hair and an emotionally sentimental nature. She looked a little like Sophie Tucker and we all liked her enormously. She and Mother struck up a cozy friendship, Mother, with her quick understanding and tact, becoming the confidante of the lady who gave her shopping addresses, sobbed onto her sympathetic shoulder her indignation over Spanish cruelty to animals, and told her of her ups and downs with her eminent protector. At first her presence was a little upsetting to Mother, who, trusting that in my natural innocence I was unaware of the nature of Ibáñez's amicable liaison, pretended for a time that the Señora was a social secretary. Then, after I had made some remarks which led her to believe that my innocence might not be so natural after all, she gave up, settling the problem with "You see, Baby, things are different in Latin countries."

We were never quite clear as to the Señora's actual name. Ibáñez, on the other hand, was vociferously clear as to his. When we first met him he stated emphatically that he wished to be called the whole thing, Blasco Ibáñez—as though it were hyphenated—like Burne-Jones, though not very. This was rather a mouthful and it slowed things up considerably having to say, "Good morning, Señor Blasco Ibáñez," "Yes, Señor Blasco Ibáñez," "Pardon *me*, Señor Blasco Ibáñez"—especially for Mother who politely addressed him by a variety of Spanish Spoonerisms of her own devising —Blanzo Ibasneth, Blisco Ignatius, and occasionally Blanco Posnet.

We saw a great deal of him. Intensely interested in the forthcoming production of *Blood and Sand*, he turned his large self inside out to take Father around to every place of authentic local color. I went along as interpreter. We conversed in a curious jargon, partly what Ibáñez chose to consider French and partly what I hoped was Spanish. The constant presence of a gangly nineteen-year-old female interlocutor was, I suspect, fairly irksome to the illustrious journalist, but he was always kind, bombastic, and affable. He took us to curious little shops, sort of select pawn establishments, where star bullfighters, the vainest of prima donnas, turned in their dazzling thousand-*duro* suits which lesser toreros might purchase second-hand, and where aristocratic ladies sold their shawls and tortoise-shell combs. Father would indicate what he wanted to buy and Ibáñez would do the bargaining in a voice of thunder accompanied with threatening gestures of extreme violence, while Father snorted with amusement and I cowered, filled with adolescent embarrassment and the extreme discomfort I have always felt in the presence of any haggling.

Under his flamboyant aegis we went to gypsy cabarets, to the cafés patronized by the leading toreros and their crowds of worshiping satellites, to the *chic* restaurants of the social world. The morning of a big *corrida* he took us on a backstage inspection of the arena, the fighters' quarters, the stable for the miserable horses, and the darkened death-cell pens which were being filled each with a beautiful little Miura bull, his black coat quivering, his hoofs pawing the ground in savage terror. We met bullring managers and experts who explained the cape passes and sword thrusts and he introduced us to a few star *espadas*. One in particular, Granero, was a shy, quiet youth who, when he was not slaughtering bulls, was playing *Palestrina* on the violin. He had a delicately sensitive face and his expression in moments of repose was one of quiet resignation. It was as if he had a foreboding of the ghastly destiny he was to meet only two months later in a provincial *corrida* when, as he tried to help out a novice fighter, a bull was to catch him on his horns, toss him into the air, and gore him to death through the eye. The only time I didn't go along was on the occasion when Granero invited Ibáñez and Father to join the masculine audience of admirers and hero-worshipers who were allowed to sit in his apartment while his valet squeezed him into his dazzling regalia for the fight.

And the only time Ibáñez didn't come along with us was when we went to the fight itself. He had seen his last one, he said. And so, a few hours later, I could say, had I. The one we attended was a gala affair held, quaintly enough, for the benefit of the Spanish Red Cross and patronized by the beau monde of Madrid including the Queen herself. I stood it through the slaughter of six horses and two bulls. Then, when they started taking out the gored horses that were still alive, stuffing them with straw, and sending them back into the ring to be eviscerated all over again, I went to pieces. I covered my eyes with my hands, I cried, I sobbed, I bawled out loudly, "These are barbaric people! I wish they'd throw *them* to the bulls!"

Mother, who was anguished too, but more controlled, patted my knee and said, "Hush, Baby! Someone may hear you."

"I hope they do hear me!" I wailed back. "I hope the Queen hears me!"

Mother, fearful that this might develop into an international incident, decided it was time for herself and me to go. Father, of course, must stick it out for the sake of his play—although at the moment he was not any too happy himself; he was shaky and very green and looked as if he were about to throw up all over the mantilla of the lady directly in front of him. I hoped he would. We made our way out through the row of yelling enthusiasts who clearly thought us demented for leaving at this point when a special thrust was being made by El Gallo. Once outside the stadium, Mother and I looked about for a means of conveyance back to town. A number of taxis were drawn up in line. None of them was of much use, as their drivers were all inside watching the *corrida.* A few private limousines were parked near one of the entrances. Their chauffeurs too were absent, with the exception of one, a handsome creature who lolled against the mudguard of an especially swank vehicle. His cap at a jaunty angle, a cigarette in the corner of his mouth, he eyed us with disinterested amusement. I was still weeping bitterly. An old gatekeeper whom we passed on our way out, seeing my tear-stained face, had muttered softly, "You don't like it, Señorita? Neither do I.

They bought my neighbor's old horse for the fight today," and that had opened the dam for a fresh flood of humanitarian woe.

The chauffeur watched us for a time, then, prompted less by my hysteria than by Mother's gestures of distress, ambled over to us and inquired in impeccable English if there were anything he might do for us. Mother thanked him and said she was awfully sorry, but that we were Americans and we knew we shouldn't leave so early, but we did want to get back to our hotel because you see her daughter was so fond of animals—she was too, of course, but then her daughter was young and had been working so hard all winter in Paris and did he know where we might get a taxi. The chauffeur thought for a second or two, then he dropped his cigarette, ground it out with his heel, flashed a smile, strode back to his Hispano-Suiza, opened the door and said, "I shall take you to the tram line. Jump in. But quickly!" Obediently we clambered into the car which we found to be one of frightening elegance—the upholstery was of a delicate dove color, crystal vases attached to the walls with silver brackets contained live orchids, and the speaking tube had a carved ivory mouthpiece. Mother and I perched gingerly on the edge of the seat feeling that our mere presence was a contamination. Our unknown knight errant drove us a short distance to a streetcar terminal, where he let us out and told us the number of the tram we should take. Mother, profuse in thanks, started to fumble in her purse for a tip, but could find nothing smaller than a five-duro bill. The chauffeur, drawing himself up, made a gesture of haughty refusal. "Madame," he said, "I have the honor of being the Queen's chauffeur. That is Her Majesty's car you have just ridden in." Mother gasped "Goodness!" and froze into immobility, the five-duro bill clutched in her hand. The man bowed, assured us it had been a pleasure, got back in the limousine, and drove away. Open-jawed we stared after the retreating cloud of dust. Then gradually we returned to earth, Mother looked down to close her purse and uttered a small cry, half rueful, half amused. The five-duro bill was gone.

During our weeks in Spain, Mother went a little mad. Her tendency to lose control over her words seemed to be heightened under the hot Spanish sun. Of the countless "Maud Skinnerisms" she committed that summer, my favorite was the one she uttered in Seville. From Madrid we had traveled southward, armed with a stack of letters of introduction from Ibáñez to persons he thought would be of interest to Father. One was an entrée to a certain Don Diego Gomez who, from what we could gather, was an Old World aristocrat and all sorts of a personage. He lived in private quarters in the Alcazar of which historic monument he was curator. Ibáñez's note was sent off and within a few hours a ceremonious reply inviting us to tea was brought by a liveried servant who might have gone right on as an extra in *The Marriage of Figaro*. We accepted with nervous pleasure and alacrity. Mother found herself in a good deal of bewilderment over the nobleman's name. The servant had pronounced it "Gometh" which I said was pure Castilian, but which Mother somewhat crossly said was a pure lisp. "Anyway, you shouldn't call him Señor Gomez," I went on. I spoke with the authority of having taken five Spanish lessons at the Berlitz School. "You're supposed to call him Don and his first name—Diego. Don Diego." Mother said "Oh," but it was apparent she was not convinced.

Don Diego Gomez was standing in the arched doorway of his house waiting for us as, feeling very American, we walked up the ancient cobbled pathway. He was a picturesque rapier-like old man who looked the embodiment of one's idea of a grandee, which in fact is precisely what he was. Stiff, unsmiling, an exquisite of the *ancien régime*, he was obviously full of whatever constitutes Spanish Pride and obviously totally lacking in humor. He greeted us with rigid courtesy and volunteered, before taking us into his living quarters, to conduct us first through the buildings and grounds of the Alcazar on a formal tour complete with appropriate bits of historical information. After which we repaired to his great gloomy salon for refreshments of bitter tea and dreadful cakes with cloyingly sweet icing, which last the old gentleman kept pressing upon us and which, in our terror of offending that highly inflammable Hispanic pride, we meekly choked down. Mother, of course, got on beautifully with Don Diego. She hung on his every word, was duly ecstatic over the Torre del Oro, the flowers, the Moorish fountains, and even made noises of delight over the cakes, although she spent the remainder of the day chewing soda-mint tablets. She was still mixed up as to the old gentleman's name. At one moment when his back was turned she asked me in a frantic hiss, "What is it I call him?"

"Don Diego!" I hissed back.

The last of the pink cakes was gagged down and we rose to go. Mother tripped across the room, held out a hand, and as the elderly courtier bent to kiss it, said in her most bell-like tones, "We've had *such* a lovely time, San Diego!"

In Granada we "did" the Alhambra, where Mother, with her weakness for souvenirs, was guilty of falling for an old Moorish tile which a workman repairing a balustrade in a thirteenth-century courtyard had surreptitiously rifled for purposes of sale to the tourist trade. This bit of vandalism she excused on the grounds that had she not taken it some other awful Americans would have and, besides, it would be so nice for the coffeepot when we had breakfast out in the pergola. Reverently she wrapped it up in one of Father's undershirts and stowed it amid her collection of characteristic treasures which she kept in a great wicker hamper she'd bought from a beggar in Toledo because it was such lovely weaving and the man did look so like one of Velasquez's dwarfs. The hamper contained a number of fragile articles, and as Mother would never entrust it to porters, Father or I carried it. Father patiently, I protesting. It was only one of the additional native impedimenta Mother would acquire during the course of foreign travel to eke out the Skinner luggage which was always quite frightful to begin with. Mother's policy was to use up whatever one had on hand and what we had on hand was an ill-assorted collection made up of battered valises, theatrical cases, automobile trunks, hatboxes of peeling patent leather, and the sort of straw "telescopes" Armenian peddlers carry their lace luncheon sets in. Handles were frequently coming loose and as no one ever got around to having them repaired, the pieces would be secured with shawl straps and sometimes a few feet of clothesline. Viewing our steeragelike pile-up on the New York dock, we at least had the satisfaction of feeling assured that it would never occur to any customs inspector that we would be bringing in anything worth looking for unless possibly a Chinaman or two.

In August, we loaded our paraphernalia onto the *Paris* and sailed for home. Father started in mapping out his preparations for *Blood and Sand* and I started in earnestly working on the part which parental indulgence had vouchsafed me in the production. I was to have in all three speeches to say. I blush to recall the fact that I referred to it as "my rôle."

Mother, meanwhile, was busy with another task and, for her, it must have been a sad one; for after a lot of deliberation, she and Father had made the decision to sell the Bryn Mawr house and move to New York. It was a decision that must have cost her many pangs. But now that I was going on the stage, my interests would be in New York where

Father's had always been and she willingly pulled up the roots she had taken such pains to plant. It was characteristic of Mother that she never dream of allowing her own preferences to interfere with Father's and mine. And it was characteristic, too, that she never so much as hinted what a sacrifice it was for her to leave Philadelphia and the Main Line way of life. Her friendships there were deep-rooted and numerous and in that civilized and conventional community she had become a personage not only well loved, but—oh, ultimate reward!—undeniably *distinguished.* After a few years she was to become a well-loved and distinguished person in New York, too. Her life was never idle. She busied herself with following the arts, with knowing interesting people, with decorating our old studio apartment at Sixty-Sixth and Lexington with the tasteful loot she acquired at auction sales and out-of-the-way antique shops, making of it a place of dignity and beauty, a home rather than an apartment. The simple, gracious dinner parties she gave there had the quality of an intimate salon, alive with good talk, mellow and never formal. She seemed the easiest hostess in the world. Only her family knew of the nervous misgivings, the meticulous attention to details, the splitting headaches that preceded these evenings. She was always certain they would be dismal failures and they were always brilliant successes. She took to writing and her style was graceful and entertaining. A first-rate one-act play, *The Ne'er-to-Return Road,* was produced in Little Theatres all over the country and her collaboration with Jules Eckert Goodman on *Pietro* supplied Father with an effective vehicle throughout an entire season. The short articles she sent off to magazines never elicited a rejection slip. With Father she edited the diary of an early American actor, a colorful chronicle of the struggling theater during the days of the Spanish War. They called it *One Man in His Time,* and the

University of Pennsylvania Press published it. Mother was a woman's woman. She liked the company of intelligent women and found their interests stimulating. She liked the activities of women's clubs, although Heaven knows there was nothing of the Hokinson committee lady about her. For several years she was president of the Cosmopolitan Club which, she would point out with disarming pride, was "the club of Women Who Do Things." She continued to be a delight and incentive to everyone she met and the stray cats continued to flock to her with their woes. I believe her life might not have been cut off so early had not such countless people made so many demands upon her and had she not so generously given of herself.

Rehearsals for *Blood and Sand* started at the end of August in New York. I was very ardent and earnest about them and about beginning what I'm afraid I reverently called "my life's work." Every morning I'd arrive a good half-hour ahead of time and, after the run-through of my brief scene, when those of us who were in it had been dismissed for the day, I'd stay on avidly watching the director B. Iden Payne putting the rest of the performance into shape. I thought everything, the play, the cast, was wonderful. They weren't especially, but it was a good way to feel. The play was highly effective, but it was indifferent drama and the cast, with the exception of Father and that excellent old artist Louis Calvert, was routine run-of-the-mill. The part of the siren, Doña Sol, was played by Catherine Calvert, star of the silent films. She was no relation to Louis Calvert in either consanguinity or talent. But she was extremely beautiful, and when she turned to the audience her magnificent back exposed to the waist in a black satin Callot creation, it brought forth an occasional appreciative whistle. Father's impersonation of the torero hero, Juan Gallardo, was undoubtedly fine, although it was never one of his greatest performances. He used to refer to it as "the last lover I ever played, thank God!" and when one considers the fact that he was sixty-six years old at the time, that in itself is no unremarkable feat. "My rôle" was that of a lady named Doña Sarasate, a sentimental aristocrat interested in poetry and medieval music—purely a side issue for the sake of atmosphere, as the character had no remote connection with the plot. I was "discovered" at the rise of the second-act curtain along with a few other select guests of Doña Sol's at a party which was giving every indication of being about to break up. I wore a Paul Poiret *robe-de-style*, waved an enormous blue quill fan, strummed softly on a piano situated well upstage, and sang a fifteenth-century canticle to which nobody paid the slightest attention, which was perhaps fortunate. Father came on as the colorful bullfighter, the idol of the arena now suddenly ill at ease and himself a gauche taurus in the china shop of high society, the gentlemen snubbing him, the ladies gathering about him in shocked fascination. I spoke three lines to him, the most dramatic of which was "The bull can't help being a bull, can he?" after which I shook hands with Doña Sol in a willowy manner, called a languid "Are you coming, Don Pablo?" to I forget whom, and exited left. And that was my part.

We opened in Buffalo and toured for a few weeks before coming into New York. My salary was sixty dollars a week. Father charged me five dollars a day and indulgently paid all hotel bills including most meals. However, in the theatre he showed me no favoritism and he saw to it that as the star's daughter I rated no special privileges and that in regard to dressing rooms, rehearsal calls, and Pullman accommodations I was to receive the same treatment as anyone in a similarly humble position in the company. He offered little comment upon my performance. There was scarcely enough of that to comment upon. Albeit on the matter of my make-up he offered plenty. In my zeal I had purchased a variegated assortment of greasepaint, eye-shadow, rouge, and sundry cosmetics, enough for an army. Dabbling about with it for at least two hours prior to every show, I tried out all possible color combinations and a few impossible ones, piling on greasepaint as thick as marsh-mallow icing, slathering my eyelids with blue, purple, brown, and even green shadowing, beading lashes until they drooped beneath the load, calcimining my neck and arms with liquid white, and even outlining the veins of my hands to indicate the blue blood of my aristocratic characterization. Father stood it for about ten days and then he sent his valet with a summons for me to report to him in his dressing room immediately. I clattered down the flights of iron stairs leading from the chorus room which I shared with the other ladies of the second-act party. Father stood waiting for me with a towel in one hand and a jar of Albolene in the other.

"Sit down," he ordered peremptorily, indicating the chair in front of his make-up mirror. Then in a loud, practical tone he remarked, "You look like hell," and with several vigorous swipes of towel and Albolene, cleaned off my lurid layers. Then, using his own grease sticks and liners, he showed me a make-up which he said looked more like a human being and less like a face on a totem pole. I was subdued and, after a time, grateful.

We opened on Broadway at the Empire, that beloved gilt-proscenium-and-red-plush theatre which really *is* a theatre. It was a lovely and exciting temple in which to dedicate my novitiate. *Blood and Sand* was looked forward to as being an important event in the theatrical season. Ibáñez' current popularity, Father's loyal following, the Empire tradition, and the smart audience that has always been the Gilbert Miller specialty, made for the opening night's coming under the "brilliant premier" heading. I was dazzled, terrified, and elated. Mother went through her customary first-night agony out front. She sat alone in a back-row seat on the aisle, doubtless for purposes of possible escape in case she couldn't stand it. I think she was certain that Father would forget all his lines and that I would trip and fall flat on my face. The latter unhappy certainty I shared with her. Father took it all with an impressive calm which quite belied his inner nervousness except at a few odd moments when he did a few odd things, one of which was to rummage about frantically looking for a certain prop which he was all the while clutching in his own hand.

The show went over without any hitches. Father remembered all his lines and I neither tripped nor fell flat on my face. At the finish, the house was rewardingly enthusiastic. I took a bow with the general ensemble, then scuttled off to the wings where I stood to watch the rest of the curtain calls—the featured players, Father and Catherine Calvert, Father and Tom Cushing the author, Father and Gilbert Miller, and then Father alone, time after cheering time. During one of his calls he caught sight of me standing off at the side, came over to me, snatched up my hand, and to my panic and delight led me onto the set and down to the footlights, where he made a gesture which indicated that he was therewith introducing his daughter to the public and we both bowed, first to the house, then to each other. The curtain came down. Father squeezed my hand, dropped it, smiled, and said, "Well, Miss, you've made your New York début. From now on—" he waved me off the stage—"you're on your own," and he strode back for another solo call.

THE END